Berryman's Understanding

Berryman's Understanding

REFLECTIONS ON THE POETRY
OF JOHN BERRYMAN

EDITED BY
HARRY THOMAS

Northeastern University Press   *Boston*

Northeastern University Press

Library of Congress Cataloging in Publication Data

Berryman's understanding : reflections on the poetry of John
  Berryman / edited by Harry Thomas
   p. cm.
  Bibliography: p.
  Includes index.
  ISBN 1-55553-027-3 (alk. paper)
  1. Berryman, John, 1914–1972. 2. Berryman, John, 1914–1972—
Interviews. 3. Poets, American—20th century—Biography.
4. Poets, American—20th century—Interviews. I. Thomas,
Harry, 1952–
PS3503.E744Z565   1988   87-32919
811'.54—dc19   CIP

Designed by Daniel Earl Thaxton.

Composed in Fairfield by The Composing Room of Michigan.
Printed and bound by Hamilton Printing Company, Rensselaer, New York.
The paper is Sebago Antique, an acid-free sheet.

MANUFACTURED IN THE UNITED STATES OF AMERICA
92 91 90 89 88   5 4 3 2 1

Acknowledgments

I gratefully acknowledge the following:

The *Centennial Review* and Mrs. Rose Wasserstrom, for permission to reprint "Cagey John: Berryman as Medicine Man," by William Wasserstrom. Copyright © 1968 by the *Centennial Review.*

Denis Donoghue, for permission to reprint "Berryman's Long Dream." Copyright © 1969 by Denis Donoghue.

Encounter, for permission to reprint "Berryman's Songs," by Philip Toynbee, copyright © 1965 by *Ecounter,* and "Gaiety & Lamentation: The Defeat of John Berryman," by Douglas Dunn, copyright © 1974 by *Encounter.*

Farrar, Straus & Giroux, for permission to reprint Saul Bellow's Foreword to Berryman's *Recovery,* copyright © 1973 by Saul Bellow, and "For John Berryman," from *The Collected Prose of Robert Lowell,* copyright © 1972 by the estate of Robert Lowell.

The *Harvard Advocate,* for permission to reprint "An Interview with John Berryman," "A Bright Surviving Actual Scene: *Berryman's Sonnets,*" by William Meredith, and "Living with Henry," by Adrienne Rich. Copyright © 1969 by the *Harvard Advocate.*

Michael Heffernan, for permission to reprint "John Berryman: The Poetics of Martyrdom." Copyright © 1984 by Michael Heffernan.

Greg Kuzma, editor of *A Book of Rereadings in Recent American Poetry,* and Paul Mariani, for permission to reprint " 'Lost Souls in Ill-Attended Wards': Berryman's 'Eleven Addresses to the Lord,' " by Paul Mariani. Copyright © 1979 by Greg Kuzma.

William Meredith, for permission to reprint "In Loving Memory of the Late Author of *The Dream Songs.*" Copyright © 1969 by William Meredith.

The *Nation,* for permission to reprint Hayden Carruth, "Love, Art, and Money," The *Nation* magazine/The Nation Company, Inc. Copyright 1970.

The *Paris Review* and Viking/Penguin, for permission to reprint "The Art of Poetry: An Interview with John Berryman," by Peter Stitt, from *Writers at Work Vol. 4*. Copyright © 1972 *Paris Review*.

Poetry magazine and its editor, for permission to reprint "No Middle Flight: Berryman's *Homage to Mistress Bradstreêt*," by Stanley Kunitz. Copyright © 1957 by *Poetry* magazine.

Prairie Schooner, for "Screwing Up the Theorbo: Homage in Measure to Mr. Berryman," by John Frederick Nims; reprinted from *Prairie Schooner*, by permission of University of Nebraska Press. Copyright 1958 University of Nebraska Press. Also reprinted by permission of John Frederick Nims.

Princeton University Press, for permission to reprint "Berryman," by Robert Pinsky. Copyright © 1976 by Robert Pinsky.

Salmagundi, for permission to reprint "John Berryman: A Question of Imperial Sway," by John Bayley. Also reprinted by permission of John Bayley. Copyright © 1973 by *Salmagundi*.

Eileen Simpson, for permission to reprint "Jobless in New York," from *Poets in Their Youth*. Copyright © 1982 by Eileen Simpson.

The University of Minnesota Press, for permission to reprint "Secret Terror in the Heart," by Joseph Warren Beach, copyright © 1960 University of Minnesota Press.

Contents

Acknowledgments   *v*

Chronology   *xi*

Introduction   *Harry Thomas*   *xv*

Part I: Interviews with Berryman

An Interview with John Berryman   3
HARVARD ADVOCATE

*The Art of Poetry: An Interview with John
Berryman*   *18*
PETER STITT, PARIS REVIEW

Part II: Memoirs

Jobless in New York   47
EILEEN SIMPSON

For John Berryman   67
ROBERT LOWELL

John Berryman   74
SAUL BELLOW

In Loving Memory of the Late Author of The Dream
Songs   *80*
WILLIAM MEREDITH

Part III: Berryman's Poetry

Secret Terror in the Heart   91
JOSEPH WARREN BEACH

A Bright Surviving Actual Scene: Berryman's
Sonnets   97
WILLIAM MEREDITH

No Middle Flight: Berryman's Homage to Mistress
Bradstreet   *110*
STANLEY KUNITZ

*Screwing Up the Theorbo: Homage in Measure to
Mr. Berryman*   *117*
JOHN FREDERICK NIMS

Living with Henry   *127*
ADRIENNE RICH

Berryman's Songs   *133*
PHILIP TOYNBEE

*Gaiety & Lamentation: The Defeat of John
Berryman*   *139*
DOUGLAS DUNN

Berryman's Long Dream   *152*
DENIS DONOGHUE

Cagey John: Berryman as Medicine Man   *167*
WILLIAM WASSERSTROM

Berryman   *186*
ROBERT PINSKY

*John Berryman: A Question of Imperial
Sway*   *192*
JOHN BAYLEY

Love, Art, and Money   *213*
HAYDEN CARRUTH

*"Lost Souls in Ill-Attended Wards": Berryman's "Eleven
Addresses to the Lord"*   *219*
PAUL MARIANI

John Berryman: The Poetics of Martyrdom   232
MICHAEL HEFFERNAN

Bibliography   249

Index   253

Chronology

1914   Born John Allyn Smith, 25 October, the elder son of John Allyn Smith, a banker, and Martha (Little) Smith, a schoolteacher, in McAlester, Oklahoma.

1926   Family moves to Tampa, Florida, where, on 26 June, John Allyn Smith Sr. commits suicide by shooting himself in the chest. On 8 September Martha Smith marries John Angus Berryman, 48, their landlord. The family moves to New York City. The future poet now called Berryman.

1928   John Berryman attends private school in Connecticut.

1932   Enters Columbia College; studies under Mark Van Doren; publishes first poems and reviews in the *Columbia Review.*

1936   Goes to England to study for two years at Clare College, Cambridge, on Kellett Scholarship.

1937   Meets Beryl Eaman, with whom he falls in love. Is first American to win Oldham Shakespeare Scholarship.

1938   Returns to New York: meets Bhain Campbell, poet and scholar, whom he will later eulogize as his "Lycidas." Is named poetry editor of the *Nation.*

1939   Meets Delmore Schwartz; moves to Detroit to teach at Wayne State University; lives with Bhain Campbell and his wife; is diagnosed as suffering from *petit mal.*

1940   Named Instructor in English at Harvard; twenty poems appear in *Five Young American Poets.*

1942   First book, *Poems,* published; marries Eileen Mulligan.

1943   Bitter year of unemployment, self-doubts. Through R. P. Blackmur is appointed to teach English at Princeton.

1944   Awarded Rockefeller Foundation research fellowship to prepare edition of *King Lear.*

1945   Contracts to write book on Stephen Crane; writes "The Imaginary Jew."

1946   Named Associate in Creative Writing at Princeton.

1947   In April reaches nadir of unhappiness, believing he has squandered his poetic gift; in May meets and falls in love with "Lise," with whom he has affair recorded in *Berryman's Sonnets;* in December notes in his journal, "1947 has made me a poet again."

1948   Writes first lines of "Homage to Mistress Bradstreet"; publishes *The Dispossessed;* meets Saul Bellow.

1949   Several successes: Guarantors Prize (*Poetry*), Shelley Memorial Award (Society of America), Alfred Hodder Fellowship (Princeton).

1950   Publishes *Stephen Crane.*

1952   Awarded Guggenheim Fellowship.

1953   "Homage to Mistress Bradstreet" published in *Partisan Review;* separates from Eileen; moves to New York.

1954   Teaches in Writers Workshop at Iowa, but is dismissed; moves to Minneapolis, his father's hometown.

1955   Writes first "Dream Song"; begins teaching at University of Minnesota.

1956   Divorced from Eileen; marries Elizabeth Ann Levine, known as Ann.

1957   Son, Paul, is born.

1958   Publishes chapbook of poems, *His Thought Made Pockets & The Plane Buckt.*

1959   Divorced from Ann.

1961   Marries Kathleen (Kate) Donahue.

1962   Daughter, Martha, is born.

1964   Publishes 77 *Dream Songs.*

1965   Wins Pulitzer Prize for 77 *Dream Songs.*

1966   Lives with family in Dublin, on Guggenheim Fellowship.

1967   Publishes *Berryman's Sonnets* and *Short Poems.*

1968   Publishes *His Toy, His Dream, His Rest,* for which he wins the National Book Award the following year; publishes *The Dream Songs.*

1969   Receives treatment for alcoholism.

1970   Publishes *Love & Fame.*

1971   Daughter, Sarah Rebecca, is born.

1972   Jumps from Washington Bridge, Minneapolis, 7 January.

Introduction

In the photographs I have seen of John Berryman when he
was in his mid-twenties, he is usually looking away, as though
absorbed in a book or face just out of the camera's frame. Two
features stand out: the long, equine oval of the head (he was
fond of saying he had the constitution, if not the head, of a
horse), and the eyelids, not puffy but low-hanging, the whites
of the eyes blocked out from above. In one outdoor photograph
that shows him leaning back against a brick parapet, he gazes
directly at the camera, his face squinched in a half-smile
against the sun, his arms wrapped awkwardly across his stomach. The posture is self-conscious, aloof; but more than anything the photograph shows a young man of high character,
serious, exacting, self-possessed. At Cambridge University,
where he had recently been a fellow, he was remembered for
his "lordly urbanity." In an essay he wrote at this time, he
quoted with approval a remark by John Dewey, "To maintain
the integrity of the self is in the end the whole battle of life."

In a series of *Life* magazine photographs from the mid-six-
ties, his hair is longer and uncombed, and has receded above
the scored forehead. The head's shape seems even more
equine than in his youth. The massive, untrimmed beard
makes an impression of goatishness. He stares ravenously,
theatrically into the camera, his eyes and mouth animated
with the consciousness that he has become that most anoma-
lous of characters in this country, the celebrity poet. In an interview a few years later, thinking of Genet, he will roar, "I
am not a homosexual crook, I am a heterosexual maniac!"

Now, nearly twenty years after his death, John Berryman's
life and work read like a parable of one kind of poet's progress
in this century. The sentence might be more accurate without
the qualifying *one kind of poet's.* For the parable has little to do
with specific data of his curriculum vitae, its disciplines and
excesses, very little to do with his defeat, as Douglas Dunn

has called it. The parable has little to do with the Romantic poet's feeling of being in conflict with his environment, though perhaps only the very comfortable would deny the reality of this conflict or the enormous reserves of will that Berryman had to possess to resolve the conflict in his favor, when he could. The parable has somewhat more to do with the course of Berryman's career, his gradual desertion of New Critical strictures for the freedom of Whitman and prose. Stated briefly, the parable is of a man who longed, and learned how, to be himself. After passing through periods of adolescent amnesia, adoption, scholarly selflessness, Eliotic impersonality, and various personae, Berryman gradually came to discover who he was. Being witness to this discovery is our reward as his readers. I have entitled this anthology *Berryman's Understanding,* rather than perhaps the opposite phrase, to underscore my interest in the kind of criticism, exemplified I think by the essays and reviews that make up Part III, that subordinates theory to elucidatory perception, that inquires steadily into the poet's art, that ends by offering us one writer's largest understanding of another's understanding of his life.

This is not to slight the two interviews and four memoirs that appear in Parts I and II, pieces which I have included not so as to play into the hands of tabloid mythmakers who would engross us in the exploits of the poet or give us gossipy foreshortenings of his work, but out of respect for the kind of inquiry that is interested in the relations between art and life and in the significant process that transforms the discrete details of personality and event into formal patterns. Berryman shared this interest deeply; in fact, in the opening paragraph of *The Freedom of the Poet,* he announced it as the leitmotif of his criticism:

> Shakespeare and Ben Jonson apart, only of Christopher Marlowe among the playwrights of the first Elizabeth is enough known personally to make feasible an exploration of those connexions, now illuminating, now mysterious, between the artist's life and his work, which interest an increasing number of readers in this century, and the existence of which is denied only by very young persons or writers whose work perhaps really does bear no relation to their lives, *tant pis pour eux.*

Written in 1952, this sentence declares Berryman's opposition, after years of advocacy, to Eliot's notion of the impersonality of poetry. Behind it lies Berryman's mature conviction
that all poetry is fundamentally the issue and the expression
of personality. Beginning as early as 1947, the year in which
he wrote *Berryman's Sonnets* (not published until 1967),
Berryman came to regard his poems, and not just his, as com-
posite records consisting, on the one hand, of observation of
the world as it is and must be accepted, and, on the other, of
the individual self's struggle for definition. Both as a poet who
made art and as a scholar who sought to illuminate the art of
others, Berryman believed in the usefulness of biographical
facts. Their usefulness, as well as their brilliance, is the reason I have chosen to include the interviews—one the justifia-
bly famous interview conducted by Peter Stitt for the *Paris
Review* just a year-and-a-half before Berryman's death—and
the memoirs. The latter are not only vivid reminiscences of
the man, they illustrate how biography can inform criticism.

Berryman wrote of Hardy, his "reputation has always been
furiously unstable." So was Berryman's during his life, so has
it been since his death. Strong claims have been registered for
and against him. Indeed, the spectrum of opinion is breath-
taking, from Adrienne Rich, "For many, he is *the* master," to
Hayden Carruth, "Berryman's poetry is usually interesting
and sometimes witty but almost never moving." The reader
whose responses I have liked most as indicating the fluctuat-
ing and fractious nature of Berryman's reputation is James
Dickey, who in 1964, in a review of *77 Dream Songs*, wrote,
"Berryman . . . is sometimes very nearly a great poet," but
who seven years later, in *Sorties*, stripped the laurel from the
head he had crowned by calling Berryman's poetry "phony
and ersatz." I side with Rich and others who see Berryman as
a master but have thought it important to include in this collection the two harshly dissenting reviews by Carruth and
Philip Toynbee.

There is somewhat more agreement about the relative merits of Berryman's books. Though both *Homage to Mistress
Bradstreet* and *Love & Fame* have their advocates—indeed, the
latter has had, and may well continue to have, a profound effect on the writing of several young American and British
poets, Lawrence Joseph and Michael Hofman to name just

two—most readers seem to agree that *The Dream Songs* is Berryman's greatest achievement, that the first three sections, 77 *Dream Songs*, operate at a high level more consistently than the last four, *His Toy, His Dream, His Rest,* and that the impression made by reading several songs individually—I think first of Songs 4, 14, 29, 45, 47, 50, 51, 75, 282, 384, 385—is greater than that made by reading the work from end to end. In choosing the pieces that appear in this book I have more or less held to this judgment of Berryman's work. Only a few good pieces have been written about Berryman's work before *Homage*, the most valuable being Joseph Warren Beach's brief meditation on the theme of fear in *The Dispossessed* and William Meredith's brilliant elucidation of *Berryman's Sonnets*, its language and position in Berryman's development. Both are included in this volume. I have also reprinted the reviews of *Homage* by John Frederick Nims and Stanley Kunitz. It is hard to think of a more judicious review of a book of poems than Kunitz's, or of a more exhaustively responsible one than Nims's. The issues they raise have not been superseded by later criticism. The reviews are models of critical appraisal.

Up to now criticism of *The Dream Songs* has covered a few matters—language, plot, the relation between *The Dream Songs* and Berryman's other books, the relation between Berryman and Henry—repeatedly and rather well. Surprisingly, several large features of the work—its comedy, its place in the tradition of personal epics, the triangular relation between Henry, Berryman, and Berryman's real father—have been pretty much ignored or treated perfunctorily. The pieces on *The Dream Songs* in Part III are, to my mind, the best studies we have of the first set of subjects. The essays by John Bayley, Denis Donoghue, and William Wasserstrom explore wonderfully and well the issues of persona and Berryman's development. Robert Pinsky's short piece, which is taken from his book *The Situation of Poetry,* is an excellent discussion of Berryman's language and suggestive about the connections between style and persona.

One subject has teased the minds of nearly all those who have written of *The Dream Songs:* the relation between Berryman and Henry. The problem is basically to what extent Henry is a fictional character, autonomous, with his own past, and to what extent he is a depository for the attitudes, emotions, and experiences of John Berryman. If Henry is largely the latter, one wonders why Berryman took the trouble to invent him, why he didn't speak, as he did later in *Love & Fame,* in his own I-voice. Every critic of Berryman has labored, it seems, to find the just-right epithet for Henry's identity and function. John Bayley calls him "The Berrymanness of Berryman." Robert Lowell said, "Henry is Berryman seen as himself, as *poète maudit,* child and puppet." The problem so perplexed some reviewers of 77 *Dream Songs,* and Berryman was so perplexed by their perplexity, that six years later, when *His Toy, His Dream, His Rest* appeared, Berryman provided a gloss on Henry in a "Note." The gloss was an attempt to dispel the notion that the poet and his character were identical. Of course it didn't dispel it. Henry is not, literally, Berryman, but this is a simpleminded and conventional point (Macbeth is not Shakespeare, etc.). The truth seems to be that Henry is a patterning, a clarifying, of Berryman's mental life, and one that out of anti-dualist necessity draws on the details of Berryman's real experience.

In his essay William Wasserstrom makes much, rightly, of the name Henry. He locates its sources in other Henrys of American literature, chiefly the several in Crane's stories, and Hemingway's hero in *A Farewell to Arms.* In *The Dream Songs* it is Berryman's name for a bad man, who is and is not the adult John Berryman. One of Berryman's chief concerns in all his endeavors was what he described, in writing of *Macbeth,* as "the exploration, in a very gifted and ambiguous and active man, of man's possibilities downward." Henry is such an exploration, undertaken as art and self-analysis. The source of the impulses that led the gifted man downward is felt to be the suicide of Berryman's father, in 1926.

Both Berryman and his commentators have speculated that the "departure" mentioned in Song 1 refers not only to his father's suicide, but to the "great loss," as Berryman called it, of birth, the fall from the warm security of the womb. It is my contention that both Berryman and Henry suffered the two losses, suicide and birth, but that they suffered the second loss at different times. Berryman was born on October 25, 1914, in McAlester, Oklahoma; Henry was born eleven years later, at dawn on June 12, 1926. His place of birth: Clear-

water Isle, Florida, the site of John Smith Sr.'s suicide. For
Henry, the two great losses were not merely analogous, as
they were for Berryman, they were one and the same event.
The moment his father shot himself, Henry fell into being.
As Berryman sometimes complained, some part of him died
with his father. That part was replaced by Henry, who grew.

This relation between Berryman and Henry, victim and
survivor, is the subject of forty-five or fifty of the Dream
Songs. Perhaps Song 145 explores it most richly:

> Also I love him: me he's done no wrong
> for going on forty years—forgiveness time—
> I touch now his despair,
> he felt as bad as Whitman on his tower
> but he did not swim out with me or my brother
> as he threatened—
>
> a powerful swimmer, to   take one of us along
> as company in the defeat sublime,
> freezing my helpless mother:
> he only, very early in the morning,
> rose with his gun and went outdoors by my window
> and did what was needed.
>
> I cannot read that wretched mind, so strong
> & so undone. I've always tried. I–I'm
> trying to forgive
> whose frantic passage, when he could not live
> an instant longer, in the summer dawn
> left Henry to live on.

The poem hinges on the relative pronoun "whose" in line 16.
The word ought, in the logic of the context, to refer to the
father, the one whose suicide and "mind" the poet is trying to
understand and forgive. But by omitting the implied "him" at
the end of line 15, Berryman makes the grammatical subject
of "whose" not the father but the "I" of line 14. The burden
of the final lines is, then, the revelation that it was the son
who departed life "in the summer dawn," leaving behind
Henry. Two persons, John Smith Sr. and John Smith Jr.
(Berryman's given name), were, in the world of *The Dream
Songs,* shot at dawn on June 12, 1926. Henry is *their* legacy.
In short, Henry is the embodiment of Berryman's loss (his fa-

ther's suicide), an embodiment that survived what Berryman himself could not, in some sense, survive, and an embodiment that survives *in* the surviving Berryman. Moreover, Henry remembers the loss that he embodies.

For me this book satisfies several desires, the first being the desire to arrange a sort of choral homage to a body of poetry I admire and find instructive, the second being to help others to come to a better understanding of the poetry. From conversations and letters I know that others, especially some who teach modern poetry, have felt the need for such a book; I have felt the need in my own teaching. Books like this one have already been devoted to the best of Berryman's peers—Bishop, Jarrell, Lowell—so it seems right that the most perceptive criticism of Berryman, whose poetry at its best is the equal of theirs, be made equally available. My hope is that others will find what they need in this book, and that out of readings of it will come new essays as patient, insightful, and rich as those included here.

I

Interviews with Berryman

↲

An Interview with
John Berryman

HARVARD ADVOCATE

The publication of His Toy, His Dream, His Rest *was celebrated in
New York on October 25, 1968; the following day, Mr. Berryman arrived
in Boston to speak with the* Advocate *and to read at Brandeis University.
On Sunday, the twenty-seventh, David McClelland, John Plotz, Robert
B. Shaw, and Thomas Stewart visited Mr. Berryman in the guest suite of
Quincy House at Harvard, armed with tape recorder and phonograph.
After listening to Bob Dylan and Robert Johnson for several minutes, we
got down to cases.*

INTERVIEWER: *Could you talk about where you were born and
where you came from and how you started writing poetry?*

Yes, I can do that very quickly. I was born in Oklahoma; my
father was a banker and my mother was a schoolteacher; they
were the only people who could read and write for hundreds
of miles around and they were living in the same boarding
house, so they got married; so I arrived. Son number one.
Then we moved to Florida, and my father killed himself.

INTERVIEWER: *How old were you then?*

I was twelve. Then we moved to Gloucester, Massachusetts,
and then New York and I was in school for some years on
Long Island, in Jackson Heights, P.S. 69, that was the

John Plotz et al., "An Interview with John Berryman," *Harvard Advocate* 103,
no. 1 (spring 1969): 4–9.

number of the school. Then I went to a Connecticut prep
school—South Kent; I was there for four years, but got very
bored in South Kent, so they gave me college boards a year
early, so I skipped 6th Form. I went from the 5th straight into
Columbia. Then I was at Columbia for four years—or rather
three and a half years since I got thrown out.

INTERVIEWER: *What was that about?*

Well, I wasn't going to class and things like that, you know,
and I flunked a course, lost my scholarship. Then I went back
in. By this time the administration knew me very well. I used
to get notes from the Dean saying, "Dean Hawkes would like
you to call on him at your earliest convenience." I used to say
to myself, "That's damn white of the Dean. I must drop in on
him." Until, Plotz, one day a message arrived, saying, "If you
are not in the Dean's office by eleven o'clock you are suspended."

INTERVIEWER: *And you went?*

I went—and he suspended me.

INTERVIEWER: *How did you get from there to Cambridge?*

Well, during my last couple of years, I was a good boy. I toed
the line and was a decent character. So they gave me everything—even made me Phi Beta Kappa. And they gave me
their main travelling fellowship; and then I was two years at
Cambridge, and then I came back to New York and lived in
New York for a year. Then I taught at Harvard for three
years, then I taught at Princeton off and on for ten years, and
now I'm at Minnesota, where I'm not very often, but I sometimes go there: I bought a house.

INTERVIEWER: *When did you first start writing?*

I was very late in developing—very late in developing. I was
about nineteen when I wrote four sonnets for my mother's
birthday—and they were about the worst sonnets that the
world has ever seen, but I thought they were quite good, and

my mother thought they were terrific. I have always had a very close relation with my mother—that's very bad for me, I'm told.

INTERVIEWER: *Did studying under Mark Van Doren at Columbia have an influence?*

Oh, yes. I always wanted to be a writer—I wrote a science fiction novel when I was twelve; the chief character was called E-Coro-'aka. But a poet? I never imagined that. All I knew about poetry then was, "Abou Ben Adhem, may his tribe increase,/ Awoke one night from a deep dream of peace" and "Breathes there the man with soul so dead/ Who never to himself has said,/ This is my own, my native land"—junk like that. Who wants to write that? So I never imagined being a poet, until I reviewed Mark Van Doren's book, A *Winter Diary,* which appeared after about seven years of silence, because he was having trouble getting a publisher. I became friends with him and I called him "Sir"—a habit I had picked up at prep school, when we had to call not only the masters, but the 6th Formers "Sir." So I called Mark "Sir"; so he said, "If you call me 'sir' once more I'll kick you in the ass." I was very touched by this, so I didn't call him "sir" anymore.

INTERVIEWER: *What other poets did you especially enjoy and feel influenced by?*

Yeats. Yeats was my master. I went through a long period of hating Yeats, but now I regard him as extremely good. And Auden. I had to get free of both Yeats and Auden.

INTERVIEWER: *Why do you call* The Dream Songs *one poem rather than a group of poems in the same form?*

Ah—it's personality—it's Henry. He thought up all these things over all the years. The reason I call it one poem is the result of my strong disagreement with Eliot's line—the impersonality of poetry, an idea which he got partly from Keats (a letter) and partly from Goethe (again a letter). I'm very much against that; it seems to me on the contrary that poetry comes out of personality. For example, Keats—I'm thinking of

"La Belle Dame Sans Merci," I'm thinking of that; and I'm thinking of Hopkins—any one of the sonnets. So I don't buy this business about the eighteenth century being impersonal, either. Now Johnson's best poem in my opinion is about a factor in his household—I forget the name of it—and it's a beautiful poem, and it's extremely personal.

INTERVIEWER: *What is the relationship between* 77 Dream Songs *and* His Toy, His Dream, His Rest?

Well, 77 *Dream Songs* is just the first three books.

INTERVIEWER: *Do you see a gap between the two volumes?*

No, I don't see a gap; it's a continuous relationship. Except, there's this: at the end of the first volume, 77 *Dream Songs,* Henry goes into orbit. He was "making ready to move on." Well, I was already well ahead of him.

INTERVIEWER: *I noticed that Henry's state of death, Book IV, corresponded to the epic convention of placing a descent into the underworld in the center of the narrative; was there any consideration of that in structuring the poem?*

I don't think so. *Opus Posthumous* is just a recovery from the end of Book Three in the first volume of *Dream Songs.* The placement of the poems in *The Dream Songs* is purely personal.

INTERVIEWER: *Is there any ulterior structure to* The Dream Songs?

Ah—you mean, somebody can get to be an associate professor or an assistant professor by finding it out? Mr. Plotz, there is none. *Il n'y en a pas!* There's not a trace of it. Some of the Songs are in alphabetical order; but, mostly, they just belong to areas of hope and fear that Henry is going through at a given time. That's how I worked them out.

INTERVIEWER: *In the last volume you said the poem's ultimate structure is according to Henry's nature.*

Now, that's right.

INTERVIEWER: *So, in fact, the book has no plot?*

Those are fighting words. It has a plot. Its plot is the personality of Henry as he moves on in the world. Henry gains ten years. At one time his age is given as forty-one, "Free, black, and forty-one," and at a later point he's fifty-one. So the poem spans a large area, you see that.

INTERVIEWER: *You admire Stephen Crane, we know, and many of his characters are named "Henry"; is this the origin of the name?*

Oh, no—that's all just accident and junk. I'll tell you how the name Henry came into being. One time my second wife and I were walking down an avenue in Minneapolis and we decided on the worst names that you could think of for men and women. We decided on Mabel for women, and Henry for men. So from then on, in the most cozy and adorable way, she was Mabel and I was Henry; and that's how Henry came into being.

INTERVIEWER: *What is the relationship between you and Henry?*

I think I'll leave that one to the critics. Henry does resemble me, and I resemble Henry; but on the other hand I am not Henry. You know, I pay income tax; Henry pays no income tax. And bats come over and they stall in my hair—and fuck them, I'm not Henry; Henry doesn't have any bats.

INTERVIEWER: *Would you talk about Henry in terms of heroism, as the hero of a poem?*

Well, he's very brave, Henry, in that he keeps on living after other people have dropped dead. But he's a hopeless coward with regard to his actual death. That never comes out in the poem, but he is afraid of death. I tried to make it clear in the epigraphs from Sir Francis Chichester and Gordon.

INTERVIEWER: *Why is Henry called "Mr. Bones"?*

There's a minstrel show thing of Mr. Bones and the interlocutor. There's a wonderful remark, which I meant to use as an epigraph, but I never got around to it. "We were all end-men," Plotz—that's what it says—"We were all end-men."

INTERVIEWER: *Who said that?*

One of the great minstrels. Isn't that adorable? "We were all end-men, and interlocutors." I wanted someone for Henry to talk to, so I took up another minstrel, the interlocutor, and made him a friend of my friend Henry. He is never named; I know his name, but the critics haven't caught on yet. Sooner or later some assistant professor will become an associate professor by learning the name of Henry's friend.

INTERVIEWER: *What about the influence of blues and minstrel shows on* The Dream Songs?

Heavy. I have been interested in the language of the blues and Negro dialects all my life, always been. Especially Bessie. I picked all of it up from records, although while I was at Columbia the Apollo on 125th Street used to have blues singers. It was a completely coony house, and I used to go there sometimes; but mostly from records. For example, I never heard Bessie herself—she died.

INTERVIEWER: *You listened primarily to Bessie Smith. Who else?*

Victoria Spivey and Teddy Grace. [*Sings.*]

> He went away and never said goodbye.
> I could read his letters but I sure can't read his mind.
> I thought he's lovin me but he was leavin all the time.
> Now I know that my true love was blind.

I found out that wasn't Victoria Spivey; it was Teddy Grace. As for others, oh, I could go down the line.

INTERVIEWER: *Why did you choose to employ the Negro dialect in* The Dream Songs?

Well, that's a tough question. I'll tell you. I wrote a story once called "The Imaginary Jew." I was in Union Square in New York, waiting to see my girl, and I was taken for a Jew (I had a beard at the time). There was a tough Irishman who wanted to beat me up, and I got into the conversation, and I couldn't convince them that I wasn't a Jew. Well, the Negro business—the blackface—is related to that. That is, I feel extremely lucky to be white, let me put it that way, so that I don't have that problem. Friends of mine—Ralph Ellison, for example, in my opinion one of the best writers in the country—he has the problem. He's black, and he and Fanny, wherever they go, they are black.

INTERVIEWER: *I'm taking Chaucer from Whiting now—*

Is he still teaching? How splendid!

INTERVIEWER: *He was talking about Chaucer's use of dialect. Trying to give an example in modern English to show how drastic the mixture of dialects was in Chaucer, he said it was as if a poet writing today would have a line ending in the word "wile," slightly archaic, and rhyme it with "honey-chile." I thought—wait, I know someone who would do that.*

Well, it does attract me.

INTERVIEWER: *When you were going through all the dream songs you'd written, how many did you discard?*

I killed about fifty in Greece. I wrote about a hundred in Dublin, and I killed about fifty in Greece. I killed a lot of songs in Ireland, too.

INTERVIEWER: *About your other long poems—did you revise the sonnets extensively between the time when they were written and when they were first published?*

No. I didn't. All I did was fix up identifiable symbols—namely, I didn't want *her* to be identified, so I changed the name of the place, and street names, and I changed her name. I'd used her name a lot, and it was very difficult, because sometimes there were rhymes. So I had to change her name into a name that would rhyme. That's about all I did.

INTERVIEWER: *A question about the sources of* Mistress Bradstreet. *Your interest in American history seems relatively unusual for a contemporary American poet. Have you always been pre-occupied with early American figures?*

Well, yes—because my people have been here a long time. I have a great-great grandmother who's Canadian, but otherwise all my people have been here since the Revolution— that's a long time. About the Bradstreet poem: I don't like her work, but I loved her—I sort of fell in love with her; and wrote about her, putting myself in it. It took me two years to get over the Bradstreet poem (it took me five years to write it, and two to get over it) and I don't think I incorporated any of it into *The Dream Songs*—I don't think so.

INTERVIEWER: *Had you ever thought that you would write a poem that long before you got into it?*

No, as a matter of fact, I didn't know, because I was very wrong about the Bradstreet poem—I thought I could do it in fifty lines, but when it worked out it came to 450.

INTERVIEWER: *Do you feel that narrative is becoming increasingly the province of poets?*

No, actually I don't—history teaches me that most of my colleagues, my friends, poets, can't write narrative poems. They just can't do it—and some of them have tried. Lowell tried it in *Mills of the Kavanaughs*—and that's a bad failure. And other people have tried; and I remember one afternoon with William Carlos Williams—my wife was waiting and the taxi was waiting—with Flossie, his wife, at the table, and Bill took me upstairs and said he was descended from Emily Dickinson, and I said that was wonderful, William, I didn't know that. And then he said he was also descended from Shelley, and he opened a trunk and took out the documents to show me. Now, writing poems is scary and very few people will be found who can do it.

INTERVIEWER: *Do you find that, since you've been writing long poems for such a long time, you don't feel like writing short ones?*

I don't write short ones—no, I don't. You're right.

INTERVIEWER: *Except when an occasion comes up, like the Kennedy assassination.*

Ah, that's a very special kind of poem. When Kennedy died I was living at the Chelsea in New York, at the hotel; I'm not much of a TV fan at all, but I got a set in immediately and they brought it in and for four days, like everybody else in the United States, I was watching TV, about all the murders and so forth, and I did write one poem about his death—it's called "Formal Elegy"—and one reviewer in the *Times Literary Supplement* said, "Mr. Berryman, whose recent poems are all an attack on organized poetry, has a new poem now, the title of which is deeply ironic. It is called 'Formal Elegy.' " The title isn't wrong, it's right.

INTERVIEWER: *What do you see as the present relationship between politics and poetry in terms of your own work?*

Oh, I don't think I can answer that question, but I'll try. Robert Bly makes a living out of the war, and I'm against this. He uses my name in different cities; and he finally rang me up once and asked me to read in a given city at a given time, and I told him to go fuck himself. And he said, "Do you mean you're not willing to read against the war?" And I said, "No." And he said, "Well, I'm appalled." And I said, "Well, be appalled!" and hung up. I'm completely against the war—I hate everything about it. But I don't believe in works of art being used as examples. I would like to write political poems, but aside from "Formal Elegy," I've never been moved to do so, because my favorites in the current campaign were McCarthy and Rockefeller; I would love to have had a chance to vote between either one of them, but they both got bombed and the shit was poured on them. The current candidates—the existing candidates—don't seem to me interesting; they seem to me extremely boring and troublesome and I wish they weren't there. I agree with you—I feel like laughing when I think of these candidates. Humphrey—my God—Humphrey who's repudiated every position that he ever took, you know. And Nixon, who has never held any position, is going to win, and be our next president; we're going to have to say "President Nixon."

INTERVIEWER: *Please!*

I'm sorry, John, that's what we're going to have to say now.

INTERVIEWER: *A formal question about the unit in* The Dream Songs *of three stanzas—did you have any idea of this particular length from earlier poems, specifically* The Nervous Songs, *which have a similar structure?*

Yes, well, the stanza is complicated. It goes 5-5-3-5-5-3, 5-5-3-5-5-3, 5-5-3-5-5 3—that's the business—and it's variously rhymed, and often it has no rhyme at all, but it sounds as if it rhymed. That I got from Yeats—three six-line stanzas. His songs don't really resemble mine, but I did get that from him. It's rather like an extended, three-part sonnet. You know, the Italians have it much better than we—when I was writing sonnets, years ago, I was troubled by the fact that their sonnets were much better than ours because they could get more into it. They had eleven syllables per line, instead of ten. But you add it up, you see, and it comes to more. I made up the Bradstreet stanza in 1948—it's a splendid stanza, it breaks in 3-5, not 4-4—and my new poem has a completely different stanza; it's a seven-line stanza and it's about Mo-tzu—and I invented it in 1948 also—and since then I've been reading Chinese philosophy and art and history and so on. Let me see if I can remember the stanza—it goes like this:

> Sozzled, Mo-tzu, after a silence, vouchsafed
> a word alarming. "We must love them all."
> Affronted, the fathers jumped—
> "Yes," he went madly on, and waved in quest

of his own dreadful subject. "O the fathers,"
he cried, "must not be all."
Whereat, upon consent we broke up for the day.

Isn't that beautiful? It's a poem about Heaven. It's called
"Scholars at the Orchid Pavilion," a single poem—which I
still feel I can do in about fifty lines, but it may work out to be
a whole book.

INTERVIEWER: *Is this "Scholars at the Orchid Pavilion" mainly
what you're working on now?*

No, I'm translating Sophocles, with a back-up by a classical
scholar at the University of Cincinnati. I do the translation,
and then I show it to him. It's in verse. But to mount on one of
those sentences—it's scary, because you can see the period
way down at the end of the third line, or the sixth line. You
have to get up on top of that sentence and ride it down.

INTERVIEWER: *Which do you find harder, Chinese or Greek?*

Chinese—much harder. Greek has an alphabet. Chinese
doesn't have any alphabet—it's every goddamn *word*—you
have to learn each individual word. It's scary.

INTERVIEWER: *Could you talk about how—physically—you
write your poems? Do you do several drafts, start with a line, a
page, or several drafts, just write them out? What is the process?*

Well, you feel uneasy, and you get going with a pencil or a
pen, and rhymes emerge, sentences emerge.

> Henry Hankovitch, con guítar,
> did a short Zen pray,
> on his tatami in a relaxed lotos
> fixin his mind on nuffin, rose-blue breasts,
> and gave his parnel one French kiss.

You know what a parnel is? It's the mistress of a priest.

> enslaving himself he withdrew from his blue
> Florentine leather case an Egyptian black
> & flickt a zippo.

Henry and Phoebe happy as cockroaches
in the world-kitchen woofed, with all away.
The international flame, like despair, rose
or like the foolish Paks or Sudanese

Henry Hankovitch, con guítar,
did a praying mantis pray
who even more obviously than the increasingly fanatical
     Americans
cannot govern themselves. Swedes don't exist,
Scandinavians in general do not exist,
take it from there.

Now what happened? Something began to boil around in my
mind.

INTERVIEWER: *When you say you start out with an uneasiness
in beginning to write—do you ever worry about the uneasiness
that instigates the sitting down to write going away? Is this something that you can turn on when you want to?*

No, you can't, no, it depends on accidents. I took my new
wife to see Scollay Square several years ago . . . and Scollay
Square was not Scollay Square—everything was removed—
all the nightclubs, everything was gone—it was a goddam
government project. But I took my wife there to see Scollay
Square and later I was moved to write about it but I didn't feel
friendly to the idea, so I did not write about it, so I have never
written about it.

INTERVIEWER: *You have two poems, I think—at least two—
about Charles Whitman on the Texas tower. Why is it that that
appeals to you so much?*

Well, the guy had a complete armory with him, do you know
that? It's unbelievable. And even *Time* magazine (which I
hate and which I read every week, cover to cover; every Tuesday afternoon I have a big war with *Time* magazine) they did a
cover story on him called "The Madman on the Tower," and
that was very moving to me. Anyway, the word Whitman is
very ambiguous in our time.

INTERVIEWER: *Do you revise your work at all?*

Oh, heavily, very heavy. Mostly they're unrecognizable by the time I'm finished with them. Although many of them I don't revise at all.

INTERVIEWER: *How do you see your role as a teacher in relation to your poetry?*

There's no connection. Teaching keeps my relations with my bank going. Otherwise they would be very stuffy with me. I teach my kids, heavy. I'm giving two courses. The University of Minnesota loves me dearly, so I only teach two courses, each one for an hour and a half. One course is in the American character, seen mostly from abroad. I use De Tocqueville, and D. H. Lawrence, and various other foreign characters, and then I zero in on *The Scarlet Letter* and *Moby-Dick* and so on. The other course is about the meaning of life, and I use the high religions—Christianity and Buddhism—and then I use other books.

INTERVIEWER: *Which poets living and writing now do you particularly admire?*

Well, I'm very keen on Auden, and very keen on Robert Lowell, and I'm very keen on Ezra Pound. I would think they were the three best poets working in our language. I couldn't choose between them or among them.

INTERVIEWER: *How did you view generally the state of American poetry today? Are you encouraged by the quality of work being printed?*

Oh, I don't know. It's all a matter of what any individual is doing.

INTERVIEWER: *What do you think of the Beats, Ginsberg especially?*

Ginsberg I like very much—I love him. He doesn't shake your hand, he comes and kisses you—and that's extreme. But

I like him very good. I don't like his work very much, but in general he's an excellent operator.

INTERVIEWER: *What about women poets?*

Well, among the women poets Miss Moore is obviously the best. But very close to her is Miss Bishop—very close.

INTERVIEWER: *What about Louise Bogan?*

Oh, no—Louise Bogan I read out; she blows through a different realm of existence.

INTERVIEWER: *How do you feel British poetry compares with that of America?*

Well, Edwin Muir is dead, and Auden is still alive. I regard him as a British, not an American poet. . . . I'll tell you a story about Auden. He came over here and pretended to be an American for some years, and he was elected to the National Institute of Arts and Letters, which I'm a member of, too. They were having a fantastic conversation about uniforms— about whether or not they should have uniforms. And Auden got up and said, "We in England feel . . . ," but then he suddenly remembered that it was the *American* Institute of Arts and Letters!

INTERVIEWER: *What do you think of Basil Bunting's verse?*

My God—Basil Bunting? The only connection I can make here is from Yvor Winters. Yvor Winters once published a letter in *Hound and Horn,* saying, "Mr Bunting seems to offer me some kind of challenge. I will be happy to meet him at his own weapons—prose or verse; Marquess of Queensberry rules; my weight is 180." That's all I know about Basil Bunting. And I don't think he took up the challenge, either.

INTERVIEWER: *You said yesterday that to be a poet you had to sacrifice everything. Can you amplify on that, and tell why and how you first decided to make the sacrifice and be a poet?*

Well, being a poet is a funny kind of jazz. It doesn't get you anything. It doesn't get you any money, or not much, and it doesn't get you any prestige, or not much. It's just something you *do*.

INTERVIEWER: *Why?*

That's a tough question. I'll tell you a real answer. I'm taking your question seriously. This comes from Hamann, quoted by Kierkegaard. There are two voices, and the first voice says, "Write!" and the second voice says, "For whom?" I think that's marvellous; he doesn't question the imperative, you see that. And the first voice says, "For the dead whom thou didst love"; again the second voice doesn't question it; instead it says, "Will they read me?" And the first voice says, "Aye, for they return as posterity." Isn't that good?

The Art of Poetry

AN INTERVIEW WITH
JOHN BERRYMAN

PETER STITT, PARIS REVIEW

On a Sunday afternoon in late July 1970, John Berryman gave a reading of his poems in a small "people's park" in Minneapolis near the west bank campus of the University of Minnesota. Following the reading, I intro-duced myself—we hadn't seen each other since I was his student, eight years earlier—and we spent the afternoon in conversation at his house. He had had a very bad winter, he explained, and had spent much of the spring in the extended-care ward at St. Mary's Hospital. I asked him about doing an interview. He agreed, and we set up an appointment for late October.

Berryman spent a week in Mexico at the end of the summer—and had "a marvelous time." A trip to upstate New York for a reading followed, and by early October he was back at St. Mary's. It was there that the in-terview was conducted, during visiting hours on the 27th and 29th of October.

He looked much better than he had during the summer, was heavier and more steady on his feet. He again smoked, and drank coffee almost continually. The room was spacious and Berryman was quite at home in it. In addition to the single bed, it contained a tray-table that extended over the bed, a chair, and two nightstands, one of which held a large AM-FM radio and the usual hospital accoutrements. Books and papers covered the other nightstand, the table, and the broad window sill.

Berryman was usually slow to get going on an answer, as he made false starts looking for just the right words. Once he started talking, he would continue until he had exhausted the subject—thus some of his answers are very long. This method left unasked questions, and the most important of these were mailed to him later for written answers. In contrast to the taped

---

Peter Stitt, "The Art of Poetry," *Paris Review* 53 (winter 1972): 177–207.

answers, the written answers turned out to be brief, flat, and even dull.
(These have been discarded.) By way of apology, he explained that he was
again devoting his energies almost entirely to writing poetry.

An edited typescript of the interview was sent him in January 1971. He
returned it in March, having made very few changes. He did supply some
annotations, and these have been left as he put them.

INTERVIEWER: *Mr. Berryman, recognition came to you late, in*
comparison with writers like Robert Lowell and Delmore
Schwartz. What effect do you think fame has on a poet? Can this
sort of success ruin a writer?

I don't think there are any generalizations at all. If a writer
gets hot early, then his work ought to become known early. If
it doesn't, he is in danger of feeling neglected. We take it that
all young writers overestimate their work. It's impossible not
to—I mean if you recognized what shit you were writing, you
wouldn't write it. You have to believe in your stuff—every day
has to be the new day on which the new poem may be *it*. Well,
fame supports that feeling. It gives self-confidence, it gives a
sense of an actual, contemporary audience, and so on. On the
other hand, unless it is sustained, it can cause trouble—and
it is very seldom sustained. If your first book is a smash, your
second book gets kicked in the face, and your third book, and
lots of people, like Delmore, can't survive that disappoint-
ment. From that point of view, early fame is very dangerous
indeed, and my situation, which was so painful to me for
many years, was really in a way beneficial.

I overestimated myself, as it turned out, and felt bitter, bit-
terly neglected; but I had certain admirers, certain high judges on my side from the beginning, so that I had a certain
amount of support. Moreover, I had a kind of indifference on
my side—much as Joseph Conrad did. A reporter asked him
once about reviews, and he said, "I don't read my reviews. I
measure them." Now, until I was about thirty-five years old, I
not only didn't read my reviews, I didn't measure them, I never even looked at them. That is so peculiar that close friends
of mine wouldn't believe me when I told them. I thought that

was indifference, but now I'm convinced that it was just that I had no skin on—you know, I was afraid of being killed by some remark. Oversensitivity. But there was an *element* of indifference in it, and so the public indifference to my work was countered with a certain amount of genuine indifference on my part, which has been very helpful since I became a celebrity. Auden once said that the best situation for a poet is to be taken up early and held for a considerable time and then dropped after he has reached the level of indifference.

Something else is in my head; a remark of Father Hopkins to Bridges. Two completely unknown poets in their thirties—fully mature—Hopkins one of the great poets of the century, and Bridges awfully good. Hopkins with no audience and Bridges with thirty readers. He says, "Fame in itself is nothing. The only thing that matters is virtue. Jesus Christ is the only true literary critic. But," he said, "from any lesser level or standard than that, we must recognize that fame is the true and appointed setting of men of genius." That seems to me appropriate. This business about geniuses in neglected garrets is for the birds. The idea that a man is somehow no good just because he becomes very popular, like Frost, is nonsense also. There are exceptions, Chatterton, Hopkins of course, Rimbaud, you can think of various cases, but on the whole, men of genius were judged by their contemporaries very much as posterity judges them. So if I were talking to a young writer, I would recommend the cultivation of extreme indifference to both praise and blame, because praise will lead you to vanity and blame will lead you to self-pity, and both are bad for writers.

INTERVIEWER: *What is your reaction to such comments as: "If Berryman is not America's finest living poet, then he is surely running a close second to Lowell"?*

Well, I don't know. I don't get any *frisson* of excitement back here, and my bank account remains the same, and my view of my work remains the same, and in general I can say that everything is much the same after that is over.

INTERVIEWER: *It seems that you, along with Frost and several other American writers, were appreciated earlier in England than in America.*

That's true. More in Frost's case. Stephen Crane is another.

INTERVIEWER: *Why do you think this is true?*

I wonder. The literary cultures are still very different. Right this minute, for example, the two best reviewers of poetry in English, and perhaps the only two to whom I have paid the slightest attention, are both Englishmen—Kermode and Alvarez. Of course, that's just a special case—ten years ago it was different, but our people have died or stopped practicing criticism. We couldn't put out a thing like the *Times Literary Supplement*. We just don't have it. Education at the elite level is better in England, humanistic education—never mind technical education, where we are superior or at least equal—but Cambridge, Oxford, London, and now the redbrick universities provide a much higher percentage of intelligent readers in the population—the kind of people who listen to the Third Programme and read the *Times Literary Supplement*. They are rather compact and form a body of opinion from which the reviewers both good and mediocre don't have to stand out very far. In our culture, we also, of course, have good readers, but not as high a percentage—and they are incredibly dispersed geographically. It makes a big difference.

INTERVIEWER: *You, along with Lowell, Sylvia Plath, and several others, have been called a confessional poet. How do you react to that label?*

With rage and contempt! Next question.

INTERVIEWER: *Are the sonnets "confessional"?*

Well, they're about her and me. I don't know. The word doesn't mean anything. I understand the confessional to be a place where you go and talk with a priest. I personally haven't been to confession since I was twelve years old.

INTERVIEWER: *You once said: "I masquerade as a writer. Actually I am a scholar." At another time you pointed out that your passport gives your occupation as "Author" and not "Teacher." How do your roles as teacher and scholar affect your role as poet?*

Very, very hard question. Housman is one of my heroes and always has been. He was a detestable and miserable man. Arrogant, unspeakably lonely, cruel, and so on, but an absolutely marvelous minor poet, I think, and a great scholar. And I'm about *equally* interested in those two activities. In him they are perfectly distinct. You are dealing with an absolute schizophrenic. In me they seem closer together, but I just don't know. Schwartz once asked me why it was that all my Shakespearian study had never showed up anywhere in my poetry, and I couldn't answer the question. It was a piercing question because his early poems are really very much influenced by Shakespeare's early plays. I seem to have been sort of untouched by Shakespeare, although I have had him in my mind since I was twenty years old.

INTERVIEWER: *I don't agree with that. One of* The Dream Songs, *one of those written to the memory of Delmore Schwartz—let me see if I can find it. Here, number 147. These lines:*

> Henry's mind grew blacker the more he thought.
> He looked onto the world like the act of an aged whore.
> Delmore Delmore.
> He flung to pieces and they hit the floor.

That sounds very Shakespearian to me.

That sounds like *Troilus and Cressida,* doesn't it? One of my very favorite plays. I would call that Shakespearian. Not to praise it, though, only in description. I was half-hysterical writing that song. It just burst onto the page. It took only as long to compose as it takes to write it down.

INTERVIEWER: *Well, that covers scholarship. How about teaching? Does teaching only get in the way of your work as a poet?*

It depends on the kind of teaching you do. If you teach creative writing, you get absolutely nothing out of it. Or English—what are you teaching? People you read twenty years ago. Maybe you pick up a little if you keep on preparing, but very few people keep on preparing. Everybody is lazy, and poets, in addition to being lazy, have another activity which is very demanding, so they tend to slight their teaching. But I give courses in the history of civilization, and when I first began teaching here I nearly went crazy. I was teaching Christian origins and the Middle Ages, and I had certain weak spots. I was okay with the *Divine Comedy* and certain other things, but I had an awful time of it. I worked it out once, and it took me nine hours to prepare a fifty-minute lecture. I have learned much more from giving these lecture courses than I ever learned at Columbia or Cambridge. It has forced me out into areas where I wouldn't otherwise have been, and, since I am a scholar, these things are connected. I make myself acquainted with the scholarship. Suppose I'm lecturing on Augustine. My Latin is very rusty, but I'll pay a certain amount of attention to the Latin text in the Loeb edition, with the English across the page. Then I'll visit the library and consult five or six old and recent works on St. Augustine, who is a particular interest of mine anyway. Now all that becomes part of your equipment for poetry, even for lyric poetry. The Bradstreet poem is a very learned poem. There is a lot of theology in it, there is a lot of theology in *The Dream Songs*. Anything is useful to a poet. Take observation of nature, of which I have absolutely none. It makes possible a world of moral observation for Frost, or Hopkins. So scholarship and teaching are directly useful to my activity as a writer.

INTERVIEWER: *But not the teaching of creative writing. You don't think there is any value in that for you as a poet.*

I enjoy it. Sometimes your kids prove awfully good. Snodgrass is well known now, and Bill Merwin—my students—and others, and it's delightful to be of service to somebody. But most of them have very little talent, and you can't over-encourage them; that's impossible. Many of my friends teach creative writing. I'm not putting it down, and it certainly is an honest way of earning a living, but I wouldn't recommend it to a poet. It is better to teach history or classics or philosophy or the kind of work I do here in humanities.

INTERVIEWER: *You have given Yeats and Auden as early influences on your poetry. What did you learn from them?*

Practically everything I could then manipulate. On the other hand, they didn't take me very far, because by the time I was writing really well, in 1948—that's the beginning of the Bradstreet poem and the last poems in the collection called *The Dispossessed*—there was no Yeats around and no Auden. Some influence from Rilke, some influence from a poet whom I now consider very bad, Louis Aragon, in a book called *Crèvecoeur*—he conned me. He took all his best stuff from Apollinaire, whom I hadn't then read, and swept me off my feet. I wrote a poem called "Narcissus Moving," which is as much like Aragon as possible, and maybe it's just as bad. I don't know. Then the Bradstreet poem—it is not easy to see the literary ancestry of that poem. Who has been named? Hopkins. I don't see that. Of course there are certain verbal practices, but on the whole, not. The stanza has been supposed to be derived from the stanza of "The Wreck of the Deutschland." I don't see that. I have never read "The Wreck of the Deutschland," to tell you the truth, except the first stanza. Wonderful first stanza. But I really just couldn't get onto it. It's a set piece, and I don't like set pieces. I'll bet it's no good—well, you know, not comparable with the great short poems. Then Lowell has been named. I see the influence of *Lord Weary's Castle* in some of the later poems in *The Dispossessed.* There's no doubt about it. In the Bradstreet poem, as I seized inspiration from *Augie March*, I sort of seized inspiration, I think, from Lowell, rather than imitated him. I can't think, offhand—I haven't read it in many years—of a single passage in the Bradstreet poem which distinctly sounds like Lowell. However, I may be quite wrong about this, since people have named him. Other people? I don't think so.

INTERVIEWER: *How about Eliot? You must have had to reckon with Eliot in one way or another, positively or negatively.*

My relationship with Eliot was highly ambiguous. In the first place, I refused to meet him on three occasions in England, and I think I mentioned this in one of the poems I wrote last spring. I had to fight shy of Eliot. There was a certain amount of hostility in it, too. I only began to appreciate Eliot much later, after I was secure in my own style. I now rate him very high. I think he is one of the greatest poets who ever lived. Only sporadically good. What he would do—he would collect himself and write a masterpiece, then relax for several years writing prose, earning a living, and so forth; then he'd collect himself and write another masterpiece, very different from the first, and so on. He did this about five times, and after the *Four Quartets* he lived on for twenty years. Wrote absolutely nothing. It's a very strange career. Very—a pure system of spasms. My career is like that. It is horribly like that. But I feel deep sympathy, admiration, and even love for Eliot over all the recent decades.

INTERVIEWER: *You knew Dylan Thomas pretty well, didn't you?*

Pretty well, pretty well. We weren't close friends.

INTERVIEWER: *Any influence there?*

No. And that's surprising, very surprising, because we used to knock around in Cambridge and London. We didn't discuss our poetry much. He was far ahead of me. Occasionally he'd show me a poem or I'd show him a poem. He was very fond of making suggestions. He didn't like a line in a poem of mine, later published by Robert Penn Warren in the *Southern Review,* called "Night and the City"—a very bad poem modeled on a poem by John Peale Bishop called "The Return." Well, Dylan didn't like one line, and so he proposed this line: "A bare octagonal ballet for penance." Now, my poem was rather incoherent, but couldn't contain—you know, in the military sense—it couldn't contain that! I was very fond of him. I loved him, and I thought he was a master. I was wrong about that. He was not a master; he became a master only much later on. What he was then is a great rhetorician. Terrific. But the really great poems only came towards the end of World War II, I think. There was no influence.

INTERVIEWER: *Do you think he had an impulse towards self-destruction?*

Oh, absolutely. He was doomed already when I first knew him. Everybody warned him for many years.

INTERVIEWER: *Can one generalize on that? So many of the poets of your generation have encountered at least personal tragedy—flirting with suicide, and so on.*

I don't know. The record is very bad. Vachel Lindsay killed himself. Hart Crane killed himself, more important. Sara Teasdale—quite a good poet at the end, killed herself. Then Miss Plath recently. Randall—it's not admitted, but apparently he did kill himself—and Roethke and Delmore might just as well have died of alcoholism. They died of heart attacks, but that's one of the main ways to die from alcoholism. And Dylan died in an alcoholic coma. Well, the actual cause of death was bronchitis. But he went into shock in the Chelsea, where I was staying also, and they got him to the hospital in an ambulance, where he was wrongly treated. They gave him morphine, which is contraindicated in cases of alcoholic shock. He wouldn't have lived anyway, but they killed him. He lay in a coma for five days.

INTERVIEWER: *You were there, weren't you?*

I was in the corridor, ten feet away.

INTERVIEWER: *What was it like to take high tea with William Butler Yeats?*

All I can say is that my mouth was dry and my heart was in my mouth. Thomas had very nearly succeeded in getting me drunk earlier in the day. He was full of scorn for Yeats, as he was for Eliot, Pound, Auden. He thought my admiration for Yeats was the funniest thing in that part of London. It wasn't until about three o'clock that I realized that he and I were drinking more than usual. I didn't drink much at that time; Thomas drank much more than I did. I had the sense to leave. I went back to my chambers, Cartwright Gardens, took a cold bath, and just made it for the appointment. I remember the taxi ride over. The taxi was left over from the First World

War, and when we arrived in Pall Mall—we could see the
Atheneum—the driver said he didn't feel he could get in. Finally I decided to abandon ship and take off on my own. So I
went in and asked for Mr. Yeats. Very much like asking, "Is
Mr. Ben Jonson here?" And he came down. He was much tall-
er than I expected, and haggard. Big though, big head, rather
wonderful looking in a sort of a blunt, patrician kind of way,
but there was something shrunken also. He told me he was
just recovering from an illness. He was very courteous, and
we went in to tea. At a certain point, I had a cigarette, and I
asked him if he would like one. To my great surprise he said
yes. So I gave him a Craven-A and then lit it for him, and I
thought, "Immortality is mine! From now on it's just a question of reaping the fruits of my effort." He did most of the
talking. I asked him a few questions. He did not ask me any
questions about myself, although he was extremely courteous
and very kind. At one point he said, "I have reached the age
when my daughter can beat me at croquet," and I thought,
"Hurrah, he's human!" I made notes on the interview after-
wards, which I have probably lost. One comment in particular I remember. He said, "I never revise now"—you know
how much he revised his stuff—"but in the interests of a
more passionate syntax." Now that struck me as a very good
remark. I have no idea what it meant, and still don't know,
but the longer I think about it, the better I like it. He recom-
mended various books to me, by his friend, the liar, Gogarty,
and I forget who else. The main thing was just the presence
and existence of my hero.

INTERVIEWER: *William Faulkner once ventured to rate himself
among contemporary novelists. He rated Thomas Wolfe first, himself second, Dos Passos third, Hemingway fourth, and Steinbeck
fifth.*

Oh, no! Really? That's deluded! The list is abominable. I
think what must have happened is this. There are two ways to
rank writers: in terms of gift and in terms of achievement. He
was ranking Wolfe in terms of gift. Wolfe had a colossal gift.
His achievement, though—to rank him first and Hemingway
fourth is openly grotesque.

INTERVIEWER: *Would you be interested in doing this, in ranking yourself among contemporary American poets?*

I don't think I could do it. I'll tell you why. First, most of these characters are personal friends of mine, and you just don't sit around ranking your friends. After I published *The Dispossessed* in '48, I quit reviewing poetry. By that time I knew most of the people writing verse, and how can you deliver a fair judgment of the man you had dinner with the night before? Preposterous! It's supposed to be easy, but actually it's impossible. My love of such poets as Schwartz, *In Dreams Begin Responsibilities,* Roethke, and Lowell, *Lord Weary's Castle,* is very great. I would love to be in their company, and I feel convinced that I am, but I don't want to do any ranking. It's just not a sweat.

INTERVIEWER: *In* The Dream Songs *there is a passage about assistant professors becoming associate professors by working on your poems. How do you feel about being cannon fodder for aspiring young critics and graduate students?*

As for the graduate students, some of the work they do is damned interesting. A woman somewhere in the South did an eighty-page thesis investigating the three little epigraphs to the 77 *Dream Songs* and their bearing on the first three books of the poem. I must say that her study was exhaustive—very little left to be found out on that subject! But it's good, careful work. I take a pleased interest in these things, though there is ineptness and naïveté, and they get all kinds of things wrong and impute to me amazing motives. Another woman thought I was influenced by Hebrew elegiac meter. Now, my Hebrew is primitive, and I don't even know what Hebrew elegiac meter is—and, moreover, neither does she. It's a harmless industry. It gets people degrees. I don't feel against it and I don't feel for it. I sympathize with the students.

The professional critics, those who know what the literary, historical, philosophical, and theological score is, have not really gone to work yet, and may not do so for a long time yet. I did have a letter once from a guy who said: "Dear Mr. Berryman, Frankly I hope to be promoted from assistant professor to associate professor by writing a book about you. Are you willing to join me in this unworthy endeavor?" So I joined him. I answered all his questions. I practically flew out to pour out his drinks while he typed.

INTERVIEWER: *I would like to change the subject now and talk about your work. Let's start with* The Dream Songs. *As you know, there is some controversy over the structure of the work— why it was first published in two volumes, why it consists of seven sections of varying lengths, and so on. What structural notion did you have in mind in writing it?*

Several people have written books about *The Dream Songs*, not published, and one of them, a woman, sees it as a series of three odysseys, psychological and moral, on the part of Henry, corresponding vaguely to Freud's differentiation of the personality into superego or conscience, ego or façade or self, and id or unconscious. Each has a starting point and a terminus and so forth. I don't know whether she is right or not, but if so, I did not begin with that full-fledged conception when I wrote the first dream song.

I don't know what I had in mind. In *Homage to Mistress Bradstreet* my model was *The Waste Land*, and *Homage to Mistress Bradstreet* is as unlike *The Waste Land* as it is possible for me to be. I think the model in *The Dream Songs* was the other greatest American poem—I am very ambitious— "Song of Myself"—a very long poem, about sixty pages. It also has a hero, a personality, himself. Henry is accused of being me and I am accused of being Henry and I deny it and nobody believes me. Various other things entered into it, but that is where I started.

The narrative such as it is developed as I went along, partly out of my gropings into and around Henry and his environment and associates, partly out of my readings in theology and that sort of thing, taking place during thirteen years—awful long time—and third, out of certain partly preconceived and partly developing as I went along, sometimes rigid and sometimes plastic, structural notions. That is why the work is divided into seven books, each book of which is rather well unified, as a matter of fact. Finally, I left the poem open to the circumstances of my personal life. For example, obviously if I hadn't got a Guggenheim and decided to spend it in Dublin, most of book VII wouldn't exist. I have a personality and a plan, a metrical plan—which is original, as in *Homage to Mistress Bradstreet*. I don't use other people as metrical models. I don't put down people who do—I just don't feel satisfied with them.

I had a personality and a plan and all kinds of philosophical and theological notions. This woman thinks the basic philosophical notion is Hegelian, and it's true that at one time I was deeply interested in Hegel. She also thinks, and so do some other people, that the work is influenced by the later work of Freud, especially *Civilization and Its Discontents*, and that is very likely. For years I lectured on the book every year here at Minnesota, so I am very, very familiar with it—almost know it word by word. But at the same time I was what you might call open-ended. That is to say, Henry to some extent was in the situation that we are all in in actual life—namely, he didn't know and I didn't know what the bloody fucking hell was going to happen next. Whatever it was he had to confront it and get through. For example, he dies in book IV and is dead throughout the book, but at the end of the poem he is still alive, and in fairly good condition, after having died himself *again*.

The poem does not go as far as "Song of Myself." What I mean by that is this: Whitman denies that "Song of Myself" is a long poem. He has a passage saying that he had long thought that there was no such thing as a long poem and that when he read Poe he found that Poe summed up the problem for him. But here it is, sixty pages. What's the notion? He doesn't regard it as a literary work at all, in my opinion—he doesn't quite say so. It proposes a new religion—it is what is called in Old Testament criticism a wisdom work, a work on the meaning of life and how to conduct it. Now, I don't go that far—*The Dream Songs* is a literary composition, it's a long poem—but I buy a little of it. I think Whitman is right with regard to "Song of Myself." I'm prepared to submit to his opinion. He was crazy, and I don't contradict madmen. When William Blake says something, I say thank you, even though he has uttered the most hopeless fallacy that you can imagine. I'm willing to be their loving audience. I'm just hoping to hear something marvelous from time to time, marvelous and true. Of course *The Dream Songs* does not propose a new system;

that is not the point. In that way it is unlike "Song of Myself."
It remains a literary work.

INTERVIEWER: *Christopher Ricks has called* The Dream
Songs *a theodicy. Did you have any such intention in writing the
poem?*

It is a tough question. The idea of a theodicy has been in my
mind at least since 1938. There is a passage in Delmore's first
book, *In Dreams Begin Responsibilities,* which goes: "The theodicy I wrote in my high school days / Restored all life from
infancy." Beautiful! He is the most underrated poet of the
twentieth century. His later work is *absolutely* no good, but his
first book is a masterpiece. It will come back—no problem. So
that notion's always been with me. I can't answer the question. I simply don't know. I put my stuff, in as good condition
as I can make it, on the table, and if people want to form opinions, good, I'm interested in the opinions. I don't set up as a
critic of my own work. And I'm not kidding about that.

INTERVIEWER: *You once said that, among other things, a long
poem demands "the construction of a world rather than the reliance upon one already existent." Does the world of* The Dream
Songs *differ from the existent world?*

This is connected with your previous question. I said that
The Dream Songs in my opinion—only in my opinion—does
not propose a new system, like Whitman. But as to the creation of a world: it's a hard question to answer. Suppose I take
this business of the relation of Henry to me, which has interested so many people, and which is categorically denied by
me in one of the forewords. Henry both is and is not me, obviously. We touch at certain points. But I am an actual human
being; he is nothing but a series of conceptions—my conceptions. I brush my teeth; unless I say so somewhere in the
poem—I forget whether I do or not—he doesn't brush his
teeth. He only does what I make him do. If I have succeeded
in making him believable, he performs all kinds of other actions besides those named in the poem, but the reader has to
make them up. That's the world. But it's not a religious or
philosophical system.

INTERVIEWER: *Where did you get the name "Henry"?*

Ah, big sweat about that too. Did I get it from *The Red Badge of Courage* or *A Farewell to Arms* or what? O.K., I'll tell you where it came from. My second wife, Ann, and I were walking down Hennepin Avenue one momentous night. Everything seemed quite as usual, but it was going to puzzle literary critics on two continents many years later. Anyway, we were joking on our way to a bar to have a beer, and I decided that I hated the name Mabel more than any other female name, though I could mention half a dozen others that I didn't like either. We had passed from names we liked to names we disliked, and she decided that Henry was the name that she found completely unbearable. So from then on, for a long time, in the most cozy and affectionate lover kind of talk—we hadn't been married very long at this time—she was Mabel and I was Henry in our scene. So I started the poem. The poem began with a song that I killed. I've never printed it. It set the prosodic pattern, but for various reasons I killed it. It had not only a hero but a heroine. It was mostly about Henry, but it also had Mabel in it. It began:

> The jolly old man is a silly old dumb
> with a mean face, humped, who kills dead.
> There is a tall who loves only him.
> She has sworn "Blue to you forever,
> grey to the little rat, go to bed."
> I fink it's bads all over.

It winds up:

> Henry and Mabel ought to but can't.
> Childness let's have us honey—

Then, for reasons which I don't remember, I wiped Mabel out and never printed that song. For a long time after that, every now and then Ann would complain that Mabel didn't seem to be taking any part in the poem, but I couldn't find myself able to put her back in the poem, so it has no heroine. There are groups of heroines, but no individual heroine. By the way, that first song sounds quite good. Maybe I ought to pull it out.

INTERVIEWER: *You once said in speaking of* Homage to Mistress Bradstreet *that you started out thinking you would write a fifty-line poem and ended up with fifty-seven stanzas. When you started* The Dream Songs, *did you know how long it was going to be or how far you were going to go?*

No, I didn't. But I was aware that I was embarked on an epic. In the case of the Bradstreet poem, I didn't know. The situation with that poem was this. I invented the stanza in '48 and wrote the first stanza and the first three lines of the second stanza, and then I stuck. I had in mind a poem roughly the same length as another of mine, "The Statue"—about seven or eight stanzas of eight lines each. Then I stuck. I read and read and read and thought and collected notes and sketched for five years, until, although I was still in the second stanza, I had a mountain of notes and draftings—no whole stanzas, but passages as long as five lines. The whole poem was written in about two months, after which I was a ruin for two years. When I finally got going, I had this incredible mass of stuff and a very good idea of the shape of the poem, with the exception of one crucial point, which was this. I'll tell you in a minute why and how I got going. The great exception was this; it did not occur to me to have a dialogue between them— to insert bodily Henry into the poem . . . *Me,* to insert me, in my own person, John Berryman, *I,* into the poem . . .

INTERVIEWER: *Was that a Freudian slip?*

I don't know. Probably. Nothing is accidental, except physics. Modern physics is entirely accidental. I did not have the idea of putting him in as a demon lover. How he emerged was this. The idea was not to take Anne Bradstreet as a poetess—I was not interested in that. I was interested in her as a pioneer heroine, a sort of mother to the artists and intellectuals who would follow her and play a large role in the development of the nation. People like Jefferson, Poe, and me.* Well, her life was very hard in many, many ways. The idea was to make it even harder than it had been in history. There is a lot of histo-

---

* Get the delusion (J. B., March 1971).

ry in the poem. It is a historical poem, but a lot of it is invented too. I decided to tempt her. She was unbelievably
devoted to her husband. Her few really touching passages,
both in verse and in prose, are about her love for her husband, who was indeed a remarkable man—and she was a remarkable woman, and she loved him, with a passion that can
hardly be described, through their whole life together, from
the age of sixteen on. I decided to tempt her. I could only do
this in a fantasy; the problem was to make the fantasy believable, and some people think I have completely failed with
that. It is not for me to judge. I am deeply satisfied. I only do
the best I can—I think I succeeded and some other people
do too.

So, with the exception of the dialogue in the middle—that's
the middle third of the poem—all the rest was one whole
plan, but it took a series of shocks to get it going. What happened? My wife and I were living in Princeton, had been for a
year. She was in the hospital in New York for an operation,
what they call a woman's operation, a kind of parody of childbirth. Both she and I were feeling very bitter about this since
we very much wanted a child and had not had one. So I had
very, very strong emotions and solitude. Second, at this point
Saul Bellow had almost finished *Augie March,* his first important novel and one of the great American novels, I think. His
later novels are far more important still, but *Augie March* is a
landmark. He had almost finished that and wanted me to see
it. We didn't know each other very well—since then he has
become perhaps my best friend—but he was living just a few
blocks away. I remember sitting in my chair, drinking as usual, reading the typescript. It was very long, about 900 pages. I
was amazed. The word "breakthrough" has become kind of a
cliché. Every two minutes somebody in *Life, Time,* or *Fortune* has a breakthrough. But the term does describe something that actually happens. A renaissance. Suddenly, where
there was pure stasis, the place is exploding. For example, the
twelfth century—suddenly Europe was blazing with intelligence and power and insight, fresh authority, all the things
that had been missing for centuries. I recognized in *Augie
March* a breakthrough—namely, the wiping out of the negative personality that had created and inhabited his earlier
work. Some critics like those novels, but in my opinion they're

shit. They're well written, and if you look closely you can see a genius coming, but the genius is absolutely not there—he is in a straightjacket. In *Augie* he's there.

My plans for the Bradstreet poem had got very ambitious by that time. I no longer had any idea of a fifty-line poem. That was five years before. My idea was now very ambitious. The Bradstreet poem is just as ambitious as *The Dream Songs*. Saul once said to me that it is the equivalent of a 500-page psychological novel. That is exactly my opinion, also—in spite of the fact that it is short, the poem is highly concentrated. So I was exhilarated. One of my pals had made a major attempt. You know, these things don't happen very often. Most even very fine artists don't try to put up the Parthenon, you know, and most of those who do turn out to be imposters. Merely grandiose, like Benjamin Haydon, Keats's friend. A very good, very minor painter who thought he was Michelangelo, then killed himself. It's hard to take the risk of joining that terrible, frightful company. Contemptible, pathetic, they move your heart but they draw you to scorn. Saul had decided to make a big attempt, so my idea of my poem improved.

And the third thing was that I had recently reread, for the first time in many years, *Anna Karenina,* which I think is the best portrait of a woman in world literature. You just can't mention any other attempt at a woman, except perhaps *Madame Bovary.* I recently reread it for a seminar I am giving, and I have a very high regard for it. It's a beauty. It deserves its reputation, which is saying a lot. But *Anna Karenina* is even greater. The only woman in American literature is Hester Prynne, and she is very good. I have great respect for her and the book, but *Mistress Bradstreet* is much more ambitious. It is very unlikely that it is better, but it attempts more. * So again my notion of my poem expanded. The fourth thing that got me going was this. I had been in group therapy. The analyst who had been treating me individually for several years set up a group. There were two lawyers, a chemist, an alcoholic housewife, a psychiatric social worker, and me. I tried to run the group, of course, and they all killed me. I would leave, and come back, and so on, but it was a shattering business—I mean emotionally shattering—much more so

---

* Delusion (J. B., March 1971).

than individual therapy had been. That had been kind of cozy. Well, I got fed up and left the group forever, and this left me blazing with hostility and feelings of gigantism, defeated gigantism. So these four things—the deep wound of Eileen's tragic operation, Saul's wonderful daring, Tolstoy's commanding achievement, and the emotional shock of my experience with the group—swung me into action, and suddenly I was on fire every second.

INTERVIEWER: *What was your method of composition on that poem? You must have worked very hard to finish it in two months.*

I started out writing three stanzas a day, but that was too much, so I developed a more orderly method. I got one of those things that have a piece of glassine over a piece of paper, and you can put something in between and see it but not touch it. I would draft my stanza and put it in there. Then I would sit and study it. I would make notes, but I wouldn't touch the manuscript until I thought I was in business—usually not for hours. Then I'd take it out, make the corrections, put it back in, and study it some more. When I was finally satisfied, I'd take it out and type it. At that point I was done— I never touched any stanza afterward. I limited myself to one a day. If I finished at eleven in the morning, I still did not look at the next stanza until the next morning. I had a terrible time filling the hours—whiskey was helpful, but it was hard.

INTERVIEWER: *Do you consider your latest book,* Love & Fame, *a long poem?*

Love & Fame is very shapely and thematically unified, and in that it resembles a long poem. But it is absolutely and utterly not a long poem at all; it's a collection of lyrics. The last eleven all happen to be prayers, but even there each poem is on its own. This is even more true in the earlier sections. It is unified through style and because most of the poems are autobiographical, based on the historical personality of the poet. By historical I mean existing in time and space, occupying quanta.

INTERVIEWER: *How does the composition of* Love & Fame *compare with that of your earlier work? Did you write these poems more quickly than the long poems?*

The composition was like that of the Bradstreet poem, and to some extent like that of *The Dream Songs,* many of which were also written in volcanic bursts. Not all. I worked daily over a period of years, but sometimes I would write fifty in a burst and then not write any for months. The Bradstreet poem, as I say, took two months. *Love & Fame* took about three months.

INTERVIEWER: *What made you turn back to the short form after having written two long poems?*

When I finished *The Dream Songs,* two years ago, I was very tired. I didn't know whether I would ever write any more poems. As I told you, it took me two years to get over the Bradstreet poem before I started *The Dream Songs.* Your idea of yourself and your relation to your art has a great deal to do with what actually happens. What happened in this case was something that contradicted my ideas, as follows. I saw myself only as an epic poet. The idea of writing any more short poems hadn't been in my mind for many years. The question after *The Dream Songs* was whether I would ever again attempt a long poem, and I thought it improbable, so I didn't expect to write any more verse.

But suddenly one day last winter I wrote down a line: "I fell in love with a girl." I looked at it, and I couldn't find anything wrong with it. I thought, "God damn it, that is a *fact.*" I felt, as a friend of mine says: "I feel comfortable with that." And I looked at it until I thought of a second line, and then a third line, and then a fourth line, and that was a stanza. Unrhymed. And the more I looked at it, the better I liked it, so I wrote a second stanza. And then I wrote some more stanzas, and you know what? I had a lyric poem, and a very good one. I didn't know I had it in me! Well, the next day I knocked out a stanza, changed various lines, this and that, but pretty soon it looked classical. As classical as one of the *Rubáiyát* poems—without the necessities of rhyme and meter, but with its own necessities. I thought it was as good as any of my early poems, and some of them are quite good; most of them are not, but some are. Moreover, it didn't resemble any verse I had ever written in my entire life, and moreover the subject was entirely new, solely and simply myself. Nothing else. A subject on which I am an expert. Nobody can contradict me.* I believe strongly in the authority of learning. The reason Milton is the greatest English poet except for Shakespeare is because of the authority of his learning. I am a scholar in certain fields, but the subject on which I am a real authority is me, so I wiped out all the disguises and went to work. In about five or six weeks I had what was obviously a book called *Love & Fame*.

I had forty-two poems and was ready to print them, but they were so weird, so unlike all my previous work, that I was a little worried. I had encouragement from one or two friends, but still I didn't know what to do. I had previously sent the first poem to Arthur Crook at the *Times Literary Supplement*. He was delighted with it and sent me proof. I in turn was delighted that he liked the poem, so I corrected the proof and sent him five more—I didn't want the poem to appear alone. So he printed the six, which made up a whole page—very nice typographically—and this was further encouragement. But I still wasn't sure. Meanwhile, I was in hospital. I was a nervous wreck. I had lost nineteen pounds in five weeks and had been drinking heavily—a quart a day. So I had my publisher in New York, Giroux, Xerox a dozen copies, which I sent out to friends of mine around the country for opinions. It is a weird thing to do—I've never heard of anybody else doing it—but I did it, looking for reassurance, confirmation, wanting criticism and so on, and I got some very good criticism. Dick Wilbur took "Shirley & Auden," one of the most important lyrics in Part I—some of the poems are quite slight and others are very ambitious—and gave it hell. And I agreed—I adopted almost every suggestion.

I also got some confirmation and reassurance, but there were other opinions as well. Edmund Wilson, for whose opinion I have a high regard, found the book hopeless. He said

---

* Delusion (J. B., March 1971).

there were some fine lines and striking passages. How do you like that? It is like saying to a beautiful woman, "I like your left small toenail; that's very nice indeed," while she's standing there stark naked looking like Venus. I was deeply hurt by that letter. And then other responses were very strange. Mark Van Doren, my teacher, an old, old friend and a wonderful judge of poetry, also wrote. I forget exactly what he said, but he was very heavy on it. He said things like "original," and "will be influential," and "will be popular," and so on, but "will also be feared and hated." What a surprising letter! It took me days to get used to it, and it took me days even to see what he meant. But now I see what he means. Some of the poems are threatening, very threatening to some readers, no doubt about it. Just as some people find me threatening—to be in a room with me drives them crazy. And then there is a good deal of obscenity in the poems, too. And there is a grave piety in the last poems, which is going to trouble a lot of people. You know, the country is full of atheists, and they really are going to find themselves threatened by those poems. The *Saturday Review* printed five of them, and I had a lot of mail about them—again expressing a wide variety of opinion. Some people were just purely grateful for my having told them how to put what they'd felt for years. Then there are others who detest them—they don't call them insincere, but they just can't believe it.

INTERVIEWER: *There has always been a religious element in your poems, but why did you turn so directly to religious subject matter in these poems?*

They are the result of a religious conversion which took place on my second Tuesday in treatment here last spring. I lost my faith several years ago, but I came back—by force, by necessity, because of a rescue action—into the notion of a God who, at certain moments, definitely and personally intervenes in individual lives, one of which is mine. The poems grow out of that sense, which not all Christians share.

INTERVIEWER: *Could you say something more about this rescue action? Just what happened?*

Yes. This happened during the strike which hit campus last
May, after the Cambodian invasion and the events at Kent
State. I was teaching a large class—seventy-five students—
Tuesday and Thursday afternoons, commuting from the hospital, and I was supposed to lecture on the Fourth Gospel. My
kids were in a state of crisis—only twenty-five had shown up
the previous Thursday, campus was in chaos, there were no
guidelines from the administration—and besides lecturing, I
felt I had to calm them, tell them what to do. The whole thing
would have taken no more than two hours—taxi over, lecture, taxi back. I had been given permission to go by my psychiatrist. But at the beginning of group therapy that morning
at ten, my counselor, who is an Episcopalian priest, told me
that he had talked with my psychiatrist, and that the permission to leave had been rescinded. Well, I was shocked and
defiant.

I said, "You and Dr. So and So have no authority over me. I
will call a cab and go over and teach my class. My students
need me."

He made various remarks, such as "You're shaking."

I replied, "I don't shake when I lecture."

He said, "Well, you can't walk and we are afraid you will
fall down."

I said, "I can walk," and I could. You see I had had physical
permission from my physician the day before.

Then the whole group hit me, including a high official of
the university, who was also in treatment here. I appealed to
him, and even he advised me to submit. Well, it went on for
almost two hours, and at last I submitted—at around eleven-
thirty. Then I was in real despair. I couldn't just ring up the
secretary and have her dismiss my class—it would be grotesque. Here it was, eleven-thirty, and class met at one-fif-
teen. I didn't even know if I could get my chairman on the
phone to find somebody to meet them. And even if I could,
who could he have found that would have been qualified? We
have no divinity school here. Well, all kinds of consolations
and suggestions came from the group, and suddenly my counselor said, "Well, I'm trained in divinity. I'll give your lecture
for you."

And I said, "You're kidding!" He and I had had some very

sharp exchanges. I had called him sarcastic, arrogant, tyran-
nical, incompetent, theatrical, judgmental, and so on.

He said, "Yes, I'll teach it if I have to teach it in Greek!"

I said, "I can't believe it. Are you serious?"

He said, "Yes, I'm serious."

And I said, "I could kiss you."

He said, "Do." There was only one man between us, so I
leaned over and we embraced. Then I briefed him and gave
him my notes, and he went over and gave the lecture. Well,
when I thought it over in the afternoon, I suddenly recalled
what has been for many years one of my favorite conceptions.
I got it from Augustine and Pascal. It's found in many other
people too, but especially in those heroes of mine. Namely,
the idea of a God of rescue. He saves men from their situa-
tions, off and on during life's pilgrimage, and in the end. I
completely bought it, and that's been my position since.

INTERVIEWER: *What about the role of religion in your earlier
works? I remember that when the* Sonnets *came out, one critic,
writing in the* New York Review of Books, *spoke of "the absence
of thematic substance" in your poems generally. Another critic,
writing in the* Minnesota Review, *picked this up and disagreed
with it, pointing out what he felt was a firm religious basis in the
sonnets — the question of guilt and atonement, etc. What would
you say about the role of religion generally in your poetry?*

It's awfully hard for me to judge. I had a strict Catholic training. I went to a Catholic school and I adored my priest, Father
Boniface. I began serving Mass under him at the age of five,
and I used to serve six days a week. Often there would be nobody in the church except him and me. Then all that went to
pieces at my father's death, when I was twelve. Later, I went
to a High Church Episcopalian school in Connecticut, called
South Kent, and I was very fond of the Chaplain there. His
name was Father Kemmis, and, although I didn't feel about
him as I had about Father Boniface as a child, I still felt very
keen, and was a rapt Episcopalian for several years. Then,
when I went to Columbia, all that sort of dropped out. I never
lost the sense of God in the two roles of creator and sus-
tainer—of the mind of man and all its operations, as a source

of inspiration to great scientists, great artists, saints, great
statesmen. But my experience last spring gave me a third
sense, a sense of a God of rescue, and I've been operating with
that since. Now the point is, I have been interested not only
in religion but in theology all my life. I don't know how much
these personal beliefs, together with the interest in theology
and the history of the church, enter into particular works up
to those addresses to the Lord in *Love & Fame*. I really think it
is up to others—critics, scholars—to answer your question.

By the way, those addresses to the Lord are not Christian
poems. I am deeply interested in Christ, but I never pray to
him.* I don't know whether he was in any special sense the
son of God, and I think it is quite impossible to know.† He
certainly was the most remarkable *man* who ever lived. But I
don't consider myself a Christian. I do consider myself a
Catholic, but I'd just as soon go to an Episcopalian church as
a Catholic church. I do go to Mass every Sunday.

INTERVIEWER: *Let's turn to new directions. What has happened
to the poem about heaven set in China, titled "Scholars at the Orchid Pavilion," which you were working on a couple of years ago?
Are you still working on that?*

I intended that to be rather a long poem. As with the Bradstreet poem, I invented the stanza—it's a very beautiful, sort
of hovering, seven-line stanza, unrhymed—and wrote the
first stanza and stuck. I then accumulated notes on Chinese
art history in most of the major forms. Chinese art is much
more complicated than ours—they have many forms. I have a
whole library on Chinese art and early Chinese philosophy,
Chinese history, Chinese folk tales, ghost stories, all kinds of
Chinese stuff. I even tried to learn classical Chinese one
time, but I decided after a few days that it was not for me.

Anyway, I finally decided that I was nowhere, that all this
accumulation of knowledge was fascinating and valuable to
me, but that I was personally not destined to write a Chinese
epic. So at that point I felt fine, and I wrote a second stanza,

---

* Situation altered; see "Ecce Homo," poem to be published in the *New Yorker* (J. B., March 1971).

† Delusion (J. B., March 1971).

and a third stanza, and a fourth stanza. They're not as good as the first stanza, but they are all pretty good. And then I put some asterisks and that's what I'll publish sooner or later. I may say, "Scholars at the Orchid Pavilion: A Fragment."

INTERVIEWER: *Where do you go from here?*

I have written another book of poetry, called *Delusions*. It won't be out for some time yet, however. We're doing a volume of my prose, probably spring or fall of '72. After that—I am very much interested in the question, or will be when I get my breath back from the composition of the last nine months. I've written over a hundred poems in the last six months. I'm a complete wreck. I'm hopelessly underweight, and the despair of about four competent doctors. When I get my breath back—it may be next spring—maybe I'll begin to think. I don't know whether I'll ever write any more verse at all. The main question is whether I will ever again undertake a long poem, and I just can form no idea.

There are certain subjects that have interested me for a long time, but nothing commanding and obsessive, as both the Bradstreet poem and *Dream Songs* were. What is involved in the composition of a long poem, at least by my experience, is five to ten years. I don't know how long I'll live. Probably I wouldn't be able to begin it for—well it took me two years to get over the Bradstreet poem. I finished *The Dream Songs* only two years ago, and I've written two more books since, besides a lot of other literary work. I've been working on a play, an anthology, and revising the volume of my criticism. I probably wouldn't get to it for at least three to five years. That makes me getting on to sixty. Taking on a new long poem at the age of sixty is really something. I have no idea whether I would still have the vigor and ambition, need, that sort of thing, to do it.

I have a tiny little secret hope that, after a decent period of silence and prose, I will find myself in some almost impossible life situation and will respond to this with outcries of rage, rage and love, such as the world has never heard before. Like Yeats's great outburst at the end of his life. This comes out of a feeling that endowment is a very small part of achievement. I would rate it about fifteen or twenty percent. Then you have historical luck, personal luck, health, things like that, then you have hard work, sweat. And you have ambition. The incredible difference between the achievement of A and the achievement of B is that B *wanted* it, so he made all kinds of sacrifices. A could have had it, but he didn't give a damn. The idea that everybody wants to be president of the United States or have a million dollars is simply not the case. Most people want to go down to the corner and have a glass of beer. They're very happy. In *Henderson the Rain King,* the hero keeps on saying, "I want. I want." Well, I'm that kind of character. I don't know whether that is exhausted in me or not, I can't tell.

But what I was going on to say is that I do strongly feel that among the greatest pieces of luck for high achievement is ordeal. Certain great artists can make out without it, Titian and others, but mostly you need ordeal. My idea is this: the artist is extremely lucky who is presented with the worst possible ordeal which will not actually kill him. At that point, he's in business. Beethoven's deafness, Goya's deafness, Milton's blindness, that kind of thing. And I think that what happens in my poetic work in the future will probably largely depend not on my sitting calmly on my ass as I think," "Hmm, hmm, a long poem again? Hmm," but on being knocked in the face, and thrown flat, and given cancer, and all kinds of other things short of senile dementia. At that point, I'm out, but short of that, I don't know. I hope to be nearly crucified.

INTERVIEWER: *You're not knocking on wood.*

I'm scared, but I'm willing. I'm sure this is a preposterous attitude, but I'm not ashamed of it. *

---

* Delusion (J. B., March 1971).

II

Memoirs

Jobless in New York

EILEEN SIMPSON

Despair, rather than happiness, was the subject of our conversations as we walked by the East River during the months
we lived in New York and John looked for a job. The optimism
he had felt as he'd drawn up a list of government agencies and
colleges gave way to uneasiness as one possibility after another came to nothing. Washington did not need a man of his
talents. Ivy League colleges couldn't make new appointments,
chairmen of English departments wrote, until they knew how
many students the Army and Navy would send them. Princeton, the strongest possibility, was reluctant to ask him to hold
out until fall, when they would know their needs, because the
chances were so slim. That left smaller colleges and pre-
paratory schools. John sent out fifty letters of application and
waited. New York publishing houses might need an editor,
magazines a writer. He sent out more letters and waited.
Twice a day he waited for the mail. All day he waited for the
phone to ring. James Agee, whom Delmore knew and thought
would be helpful at *Time,* would return John's call at any moment, so the secretary said. John waited. While waiting, he
read the want ads and typed more letters of application to tu-
toring schools, night schools, teachers' agencies, libraries—
any place where he thought he could do the job. Through
June, July and August he waited.

Often as I was leaving the office at Rockefeller Plaza where
I had taken a temporary job as a typist, I found John at the
door. His expression told me there was nothing but bad news.
Agee hadn't called. Or the mail had contained news of near
misses: The college had just hired an English instructor, the

Excerpted from Eileen Simpson, *Poets in Their Youth* (Random House, 1982),
pp. 51–70.

47

magazine a writer, the night school a teacher. As he pointed out, the wartime economy was thriving, people were earning more money than they had in years and he couldn't find work no matter how much he lowered his sights. He forced himself to tolerate the painful intrusion on his privacy that applications and interviews demanded. "Every day I'm made to peel off my skin—to no purpose." He wasn't sleeping, he wasn't eating, he was plagued by a host of physical ailments.

In little better shape myself, I tried to fight off panic. Agee was probably working toward a deadline on the Ingrid Bergman article and would call as soon as he'd handed it in. Tomorrow's mail was bound to bring an offer. What about going to a movie?

Movies were now less an entertainment than a drug. Four or five hours at a double feature brought the next day, with its possible phone calls, its possible offers, that much closer. At the Apollo on Forty-second Street, our opium den, we saw *La Kermesse Héroique, Un Carnet de Bal, Hôtel du Nord, Doctor Knock, Topaze, Drôle de Drame, Bizarre Bizarre.* Or we went to another cheap movie house nearby and saw *Mr. Lucky, Top Hat, Mission to Moscow.* We saw all these and more, some for the second and third time, while we waited. Movie houses were cheaper than the book and record shops we had haunted our first summer together. In any case we were too restless to listen to music, or even to read very much, and besides we were camping out in my sister's apartment, or my aunt's, without a phonograph or a library.

Once, on the palest promise of good news, we forsook Forty-second Street and crossed the Hudson to the Palisades Amusement Park. The rides, which hurled us up, threw us down, jerked us around in a trope of our daily existence, were hardly amusing but worth the price of admission. Briefly and violently they wrenched us out of an intolerable reality.

It was just before my semimonthly pay envelope arrived, when we didn't have the price of admission to a movie house no matter how cheap, that we walked by the East River. Although I thought that day-to-day I was hearing all the indignities John was exposed to, it was on these drugless walks that those he had tried to conceal came out, often in response to an unguarded question of mine. Was the pain he had complained of any better? It was so bad, and so like the pain Bhain Campbell had suffered before his illness was diagnosed, that John was certain he had cancer. The image of his friend in the agony of his terminal illness, glittering eyes in a skeletal face, haunted John's dreams.

Or I'd ask about developments at *Time*. Agee, who had finally returned his call, had arranged for an interview with Whittaker Chambers, a senior editor. Chambers asked John to write a book review, shredded it, asked him to write another, shredded that, then dismissed him with the question, "Have you ever blown up a bridge?" "The pretentious bastard!" John shook with rage reporting it. "As if one had to have the daring of a revolutionary to write Timese, for Christ's sake." To be in a position where he could be patronized by "a hack writer" like Chambers *and,* instead of being able to tell him what to do with his "back of the book," go away with a hook in the throat that there were "frequently" openings, and that Chambers would keep him in mind, was degrading. What did Chambers care that John was desperate enough to read meaning into his thoughtlessly used "frequently"?

On one of our walks, John showed me a letter from the headmaster of a prep school where he had been considered and where, we both thought, an appointment was certain. Early one Saturday we had taken the train from Grand Central to northern Connecticut, a ride that carried John back to his adolescence, as we traveled the route and heard the mournful whistle so familiar from his return trips to South Kent. The stirring up of old memories, and the recognition of the passage of time (what had he to show for the years since his schooldays?) absorbed him so thoroughly that he seemed not to be taking in what the headmaster was saying about the duties that would be expected of him: teacher of English, supervisor of a dormitory, hockey coach. John was the very model of a good applicant, making all the right responses, displaying interest in the hockey field, the kitchen, the assembly hall, even engaging in small talk with the headmaster's wife.

The jaunty headmaster looked positively boyish in a tweed jacket and brown-and-white saddle shoes. An expression of low-grade anxiety never left his wife's face, making her look old enough to be his mother. This is what happens to women at a boys' school, I thought as she showed me around. Our spacious quarters had a kitchen, but we'd find we didn't need it, she said, for we'd take all our meals with the boys, John at the head of one table, I at the head of another. The school was so isolated, and there was "so much doing," that I'd find I was kept very busy. For diversion, once a week a group of faculty members "piled into a car and drove to the nearest town to the pictures." I'd find it was like being part of a large family.

John living in a large family? Taking all his meals with the boys? Coaching hockey? So great was his eagerness to be employed again that he told himself, and tried to convince me, that he could manage it. Just think: with room and board provided, we could save most of his salary, on which we could live abroad after a couple of years. Until then there would be the long summer vacation, during which he could write. And as for the isolation, with New York only four hours away by train, it wouldn't be as though we were in the Maine woods.

Yes, it would, I thought, remembering John's stories of the interminable snowbound winters at South Kent. John wouldn't last more than a month in such a place, and while I could, I'd hate it. I needn't have worried. The headmaster's letter said they had decided that what they needed was a coach who could teach English rather than an English master who could coach hockey.

How much John had counted on the appointment I realized when he admitted (I had noticed the date on the letter and asked about it) that he had had this bit of bad news for more than a week. The day he received it, he had answered a want ad and had been hired as an encyclopedia salesman because he couldn't bear going another day without earning some money. Without my knowing it, he had been ringing doorbells in Harlem, the district to which he had been assigned, trying to sell to occupants of tenements who couldn't afford the daily paper a set of reference books they'd have to go into debt to buy and would never read. When he saw their circumstances, he went through the prepared sales pitch he'd been taught with so little conviction that he left relieved in conscience at not having made a sale, while at the same time being crushed that he had walked the burning pavement for nothing.

The cycle of supplication and rejection which had been his daily round for three months was so speeded up in his attempts to make himself into a salesman that he felt like an animal. "I am no longer a man, but a dog, *a begging dog*." He,

whose ruling passion was the love of poetry and the desire to
make it, had not written a word in months. His mind had
been so little free that images didn't occur to him. Was it possible that only a few months ago he had lived the life so natural to him, spending his days reading, thinking and writing?
Was it possible that he had put together a book of poems and
had even hoped to find a publisher? How, in so short a time,
had he been reduced to the person he was now—a man on the
run, pleading for one job after another for which he was un-
suited by training and temperament. In his wildest nightmares he had never imagined himself trying to sell encyclope-
dias to keep afloat financially—and *not* selling them, so that
he had to continue imposing on my family's hospitality as we
limped along on my salary.

What kind of man was it who, with his intelligence and education—honors from Columbia, the Kellett Fellowship to
Cambridge, the Charles Oldham Shakespeare Scholarship
while at Clare, poetry editorship of the *Nation,* four years of
teaching experience at Wayne and Harvard—couldn't support a wife? The fault must be his. He was in some way responsible. The burden of guilt, never light, that he carried
around, had become so crushing that he could hardly drag
himself out of bed in the morning. He honestly believed he
was making every effort to find work. But *was* he? He tortured
himself with uncertainty. Once before I had not believed
him. Why should I now? How could I believe in him when he
no longer believed in himself?

All this he shouted into the night, walking by the river at
such a furious pace that I had to run to keep up with him.
Rushing to the railing that bordered the esplanade, he cried
in anguish that there was no way out but suicide. That he was
capable of leaping onto the railing, I knew. That he was un-
hinged enough to jump was terrifyingly possible.

John balancing on a ledge. Below, danger. I had seen it once
before. At the time it had been as exotic as a bit of pantomime
from a Nō play, and had been followed by so much real drama
that the scene had remained in my mind as a one-of-a-kind
still that couldn't be fitted into a context.

A prenuptial party had been given for us by a group of Russian émigrés my aunt had come to know when I was about

fourteen. On our holidays, we entertained them. On theirs, they entertained us. In between they found frequent excuses to have people in for evenings of singing Russian songs, dancing Russian dances, eating Russian dishes, the only respite they allowed themselves from their otherwise ceaseless struggle to become Americans and make their way in their professions as engineers and doctors in a puzzling and highly competitive city. Throughout my high school days their parties had been a counterpoint to dates and dances. The urbanity of the men in the group, their hand-kissing, their "Kreutzer Sonata"–like conversations studded with French expressions, their grace as partners in a mazurka, had made the young men I was going out with seem callow.

The Solkonikoffs, the couple to whom I had been closest, had given the party. John, in excellent spirits, was a success with the Russians, they with him. His mother and my aunt pretended cordiality. Home on leave, Bob Giroux (who still thought he could be John's best man) looked handsome in his Navy uniform. He charmed the women and warmed the hearts of the men in the group, all of whom had been doing their service in the Imperial Navy at the time of the revolution. We danced the dances and sang the songs I loved. It being an especially festive occasion, Vladimir, the host, poured more than the usual amount of vodka for the men and wine for the women, as I realized when someone proposed that a toast be drunk out of Bob's officer's cap (which my aunt rescued in the nick of time).

The dashing Vladimir—black hair parted in the middle and slicked down, lynx-eyed, dressed in a chalk-striped suit nipped in at the waist—had taken a great interest in what he called my *formation* during my high school and college days, inviting me to the ballet, to the opera, to hear the Don Cossacks and to supper afterward at the Russian Tea Room. When not looking after his guests, he leaned against the wall, one hand in his trouser pocket, the other holding a cigarette, and trained his gaze on my fiancé. He could not claim, as he had done about the college boys I'd brought to their parties, that John was too young for me. Or that he was insufficiently worldly. But was he a . . . ?

The climax of the evening was a series of toasts to our future, during which a drinking song was sung. Then came

John's turn to propose a toast. Vladimir passed him a tumbler of vodka. After John had had a swallow, he made as if to pass the tumbler back. No, to prove he was "a real man," John must drink "*Piei do dna*—to the bottom." It was John's first taste of vodka. He didn't like it. Even less did he like having his manliness questioned. While the others sang the refrain, "*Piei do dna, piei do dna*" faster and faster, John drained the glass.

Soon afterward the party broke up. John and I were staying with his mother so that we could all get an early start the next morning to drive to Westchester for lunch with my great-uncle and aunt, who had not yet met the groom-to-be. On the way back to the apartment John sang "*Piei do dna*" in full voice and slightly off key. He was, as he said, high as a kite. Never having seen him either high or boisterous before, I was amused. The singing was less amusing when it continued in his mother's kitchen. The vodka had done its work; he was not merely high, he was drunk. I had just taken this in when there was an exchange between mother and son to which John reacted with a flare-up of anger such as I'd come to expect whenever they were together for too long. I entered the kitchen at the moment when he turned from her, threw open the door to the terrace and with the skill of a gymnast leaped onto the ledge of the shoulder-high wall that enclosed it. The ledge was wider than his foot, but not much. Below was the cement sidewalk. As Mrs. Berryman shrieked, John started walking, slowly putting one foot in front of the other: the drunk giving himself the test he always fails. It was this scene, and the moment of paralysis I felt before going to him, that remained framed in my memory.

At my great-uncle's luncheon table the next day, a very subdued John toyed with his food, had an obligatory sip of champagne and impressed my relatives with his seriousness. On the way back to the city, he wondered aloud why drinkers drank if the following day they felt the way he had been feeling. About the incident on the terrace, he and his mother said not a word. They behaved as if it hadn't occurred (was it possible that John didn't remember it?). I so wished it hadn't occurred that, after a sleeples night, I told myself I was exaggerating its seriousness. John, who drank very little—a bottle of ale, a glass or two of sherry, "a little Scotch with a lot of water"—had been made drunk by *my* friend, and in an explosion of anger that had been building up toward his mother since he had been down from Boston, had tried to frighten her.

Terrorize her, was the way Mrs. Berryman put it to me later. It had been his way as a boy, and it always worked. As a child he had had an "angelic" disposition, was all a mother could want in a son—intellectually precocious, affectionate, obedient, and when not obedient, which was rare, *so* winning. (Once when she'd sat him down on his little chair to reprimand him for a minor infraction of the rules—for not putting his toys in their box?—he had looked up at her as she talked with what she thought was touching earnestness. When she had finished and asked, "Do you understand?" he had said, so pleased with his observation he couldn't bear not to share it with her, "I can see myself in your eyeglasses.")

He had been wonderful company during those years when Allyn (John's father), had often been away from home on his job as a bank examiner. In the small Southwestern towns in Oklahoma where they lived, first McAlester, then Anadarko, where Mrs. Berryman had imagined herself as Carol Kennicott in *Main Street,* her son had been more rewarding company than her contemporaries. They shared the same magazines, through which she had introduced him to Faulkner and Hemingway, the same library books. It was later, when he was ten and eleven and was allowed to go about independently, that he and the other boys began to climb oil derricks. As her perceptive son quickly discovered, his mother had a horror of two things, snakes and heights. He was sure-footed and agile. The derricks were an attractive jungle gym for boys to climb. Only after he saw her reaction did his play become a weapon.

It was a weapon he used infrequently in those days. If his conscience, which told him that disobedience was a sin, hadn't been sufficient reason for renouncing an activity other boys were permitted to engage in, his lack of tolerance for his mother's show of displeasure would have been. Despite the birth of his younger brother Bob, five years his junior, he was still her favorite. Nevertheless, he had become vaguely aware that he was no longer the sole object of her love at the moment when tension developed between his parents that he was almost old enough to understand.

His mother had fallen "madly and irrevocably" in love with another man, as she told me when she talked about this period in her life. In refusing to leave her husband and sons for Bob Kerr, she had thrown away her only chance for happiness. Kerr, who was on his way to becoming a Senator when she knew him, later served as governor of Oklahoma. How different a life with him would have been! For as Bob Kerr's star was rising, Allyn's was sinking. As the result of a disagreement with a colleague at the bank, Allyn felt he had to resign. Although he found another job quickly enough, he decided to move his family to Florida. It was the mid-twenties. The land boom was on. The family, including John's grandmother, who owned property in Tampa, half of which she had given her daughter and son-in-law as a wedding present, moved to what was thought to be the land of opportunity. They arrived in 1925. By the following year the boom was over. So, too, it turned out, was Allyn's life.

The circumstances of his death I heard recounted so often, and so variously, that to this day they remain a puzzle. John tried to tell me what he thought happened shortly before he returned to Harvard at the end of our first summer together. Previously he had said only that his father was a Minnesotan, from a Roman Catholic family, who had become a small-town banker in Oklahoma. There he met Martha Little, a local schoolteacher, and when she was eighteen and he twenty-seven they married. For unexplained reasons, the family moved to Florida where Allyn died when John was twelve. There were no photographs of Allyn around, nor were there any of his artifacts, except the gold watch John wore. There was also John's habit of arranging dollar bills so that they faced the same way before he put them in his wallet, which I suspected mimicked a mannerism of his father's. (It was the only way in which John's handling of money resembled a banker's.)

On the occasion when he said there was something he had been trying to tell me about his father, must tell me before he returned to Boston, the cigarette in his hand trembled. I wished I could admit that I already knew what he had been nerving himself up to say, but couldn't do so without betraying that what he thought was a dark family secret his mother had revealed to many people, among them Jean Webster, from whom I had heard it. So as we sat opposite each other at a table in a coffee shop I watched the color drain from his face as he struggled to begin.

"The move to Tampa had been a disastrous mistake. How my sensible grandmother—or I *think* she was sensible—could have been so misguided as to join the speculators rushing to Florida is difficult for me to understand. They put my brother and me in a convent school (for how long I'm not sure; long enough to teach me what it must feel like to be an orphan), and went off on a reconnaissance trip. Sounds sensible, doesn't it? They returned from the trip convinced that it would be a good move. They collected us from the convent and back we went. Daddy opened a real estate office in Tampa, and with their pooled capital they bought land, which he then tried to resell. There were no buyers. How soon he began to panic I don't know. The newspapers reported that other speculators were committing suicide every day . . . "
John broke off. Gripping his head in his hands, he sat, trembling. After a while he said, "This will have to wait. I'll try to tell you another time."

Since I knew it would never get any easier, I urged him to continue, reassuring him that no matter what it was, it would make no difference to our relationship.

"They began to quarrel. At night I'd hear them in the next room. Or, braced for the angry voices to begin, I couldn't fall asleep."

Was this the beginning of his insomnia? I wondered.

"One day, Daddy, agitated and depressed, took me on his back and swam far out in the Gulf at Clearwater, threatening to drown us both. Or so Mother claimed. Another time he took Bob. Early one morning he got out his gun and put a bullet through his head."

John sank back in the booth, exhausted by the effort he had made. Throughout the narration he had behaved, as I told him, as if he were confessing a crime *he* had committed, as if he had been responsible for his father's death. Shame and culpability were what he clearly felt. Why? At first he was startled by my reaction and said he wasn't sure why he felt this way. Perhaps it was the sense of having somehow been responsible that everyone close to a suicide feels. As for shame—yes, there was that. Soon after the tragedy, his mother remarried. His stepfather wanted to adopt him and Bob. With his mother's consent that, too, was quickly arranged. Should he not, young as he was, have protested out of loyalty to his dead father? He did not, and his name became John Berryman. "A good name for a poet, isn't it? Well it's a damn lie. My real name is ludicrously unpoetic. It is Smith. John Smith."*

The reaction I had been unable to simulate about his father's suicide I showed at the revelation about his name. I had not heard it before. Nor, I suspect, had Jean, Mark Van Doren or any of the other friends of John's his mother had talked to. (I say "I suspect" because John asked me never to talk about this outside the family, so I wasn't able to check.)

John Allyn McAlpin Berryman was the way he had signed his earliest published poems, John went on to say. Discarding one of his father's names, and one of his stepfather's, he adopted the shortened form when the long form began to strike him as pretentious. "What I should have done, what I cannot forgive myself for not having done, was to take the name John Smith. This act of disloyalty I will never, never be able to repair. To 'make a name' for myself, . . . Can you see how ambivalent my feelings are about this ambition?"

John's mother's version of the events of June, 1926, I heard after John had returned to Boston at the end of our first summer together. She invited me to dinner so we could get to know each other better. Striding into the restaurant dressed in the bright colors and bold jewelry she favored, she commanded a different table from the one the headwaiter had

---

* There was an instability about the names in this family that was often confusing to outsiders. Martha Little took the nickname Peggy after her marriage to John Allyn Smith. He was known as Allyn or John Allyn. Their first son was named for him at baptism, but was called Billy as a baby, then John when he reached school age. Robert Jefferson, his brother, was Bob in the family, but he called himself Jeff, and was Jeff to his wife and friends.

When John's mother remarried she changed her first name from Martha to Jill, or Jill Angel. Her second husband, John Angus McAlpin Berryman, was called John Angus by everyone except his stepsons. To them he was Uncle Jack. Bob's wives and I called our mother-in-law Mir, a name which, like Jill Angel, she had invented.

seated me at and issued a series of commands in a voice that
echoed of the Southwest, the twang only partly hidden by acquired Northern inflections. She was not beautiful (as John
thought she was), but she was attractive and, to my eyes,
glamorous because of her youthful appearance, her élan and
vitality. Mother and son looked alike and they didn't. What
resemblance there was heightened because each wore eyeglasses. Although Mrs. Berryman frequently pointed to one
physical characteristic they shared, the shape of the thumb, I
suspected that the rest of John's hand, as well as a good deal of
his angularity, his hollow cheeks and broad shoulders, he had
inherited from his father's people, whom she described, with
amusement at her exaggeration, as "Grant Wood types."

My future mother-in-law was as eager to talk about Allyn
as her son had been reluctant to do so. During the first dinner
together, and others we had that fall and winter, John Allyn
Smith's biography was often her subject. The defects in his
personality undoubtedly were caused by his mother, she said.
Mrs. Smith was a formidable, even a cold woman, which explained why Allyn, though not intentionally cruel, was un-
feeling and egocentric, never aware of any desires but his
own.

The only child of a domineering widowed mother, Martha,
as she was then called, had been living away from home only a
short time when she had met Allyn. Encouraged by her mother, she married this man nine years her senior. "What does a
girl of eighteen know about life? Especially a girl raised as I
was. In those days it was Mother and Allyn who made the de-
cisions. The move to Florida was their idea. Allyn didn't have
the temperament to be a speculator. When things began to go
badly, he became frantic, depressed; he couldn't sleep, and
walked the beach at night. At dawn one day he was cleaning
his gun; it went off and killed him."

After a moment of astonishment, I took it that Mrs. Berryman, not realizing that John had already told me about the
suicide, was giving me the version she had invented to tell
outsiders. Or, rather, some outsiders, some of the time, for
Jean, Mark and undoubtedly others had heard about the suicide. At another dinner she approached the truth more closely. During that terrible period before the end, "Allyn
threatened suicide more than once. But when I saw the gun, I

knew he had been cleaning it. You see, Allyn was a weak
man. He wouldn't have had the courage to kill himself."

In the years to come, I realized that the circumstances of
her first husband's death were part of an ever-changing myth
she periodically reworked, usually in response to her older
son's longing to be convinced that she was not responsible for
driving his father to suicide. For extended periods the subject
did not come up between them (though it was never far from
their minds). At a time of crisis, either following a violent
quarrel or when John was re-examining his life, he would
turn to her and ask her to go over the ground anew. She would
oblige, sometimes in person, sometimes in three- and four-
page single-spaced typewritten letters, with fresh inventions
and interpretations, which he accepted or (privately)
ridiculed, depending on his need at the moment.

The first summer we knew each other, John had given me
an expurgated version of what he believed had happened.
After we married, when he began to talk somewhat more can-
didly about his mother, he said that the quarrels between his
parents had not only been over money. They had been over another man. His mother wanted a divorce. The simultaneous
failure of his father's business and his marriage, which
brought with it the possibility of losing his sons, drove him to
despair and to suicide. With "unseemly haste" his mother
married the much older and more successful Berryman. She
accepted his wish to adopt her sons and change their name
(if, indeed, she hadn't herself suggested it, in part to protect
them from scandal that might grow out of the newspaper reports and legal proceedings that followed Allyn's death). She
also made a rapid shift from Catholicism, to which she had
been converted on her marriage to Allyn, to the Episcopal
church, changing her children's religion at the same time.

The accidental-death ending John never for a moment accepted, at least not as an adult. What he did waver over was
the degree to which he believed in his mother's responsibility.
The Smiths and John Angus Berryman lived in the same
building. Did his mother drive his father to despair by flirting
under his nose with the courtly older man? By insisting on a
divorce when her husband was frantic with worry, had she
not pushed him to that last, desperate act?

If, in one of the confrontations between mother and son,

Mrs. Berryman was able to convince John that his father had been a failure not only as a breadwinner but also as a lover and that, having given up her chance of happiness with Bob Kerr she had a right to insist on it with Berryman, John was won over and became sympathetic with her point of view. The price he paid for this sympathy was a damaging view of his father's manliness and, by extension, his own. If, however, her behavior convinced him that her flirtatiousness with Berryman and her insensitivity to what his father was suffering drove him to suicide, he believed her responsible. *

In the difficult months following John's return from England he blamed his mother for his father's suicide. Throughout his two years abroad he had been writing long and intimate letters ("nauseatingly intimate" was the way he characterized them when he reread them years later) to the mother who, once again, had made him the center of her life. As her second husband became elderly, it was to her older son she had turned for interest and excitement, closely following

---

* The evolving myth, which not only I but my sisters-in-law and my sister heard throughout the years, was the subject of countless hours of speculation among us. What had really happened? We had always to remain tentative about our conclusions because all our information came from one eyewitness reporter. John's maternal grandmother, who might have given another view, was seldom in New York, and when she was I never saw her alone.

Was Allyn less intelligent than his wife? Was he "weak"? Certainly he had been successful in his career up to the moment when he resigned from the bank, a gesture motivated by a scruple which made it impossible for him to continue working alongside of a colleague with whom he had had a serious disagreement. If John's strong conscience, even scrupulosity, in his youth and the early years of our marriage came from either parent, it was from his father.

While the Bob Kerr "affair" did not have the ring of authenticity, and may have been little more than the crush of a restless young wife, Allyn was probably unable to ignore Martha's flirtations with other men in their bridge-playing circle. Whether this influenced his decision to move to Florida is not clear.

It was in Tampa that Allyn's instability seems to have shown up for the first time. His profound depression was probably caused in equal part by financial failure and the breakup of his marriage. (That he was unfaithful, and had previously asked for a divorce, a variant which entered the myth late, none of us credited, except perhaps John, upon occasion.)

If the incident of swimming out in the Gulf at Clearwater occurred early in the family's stay in Florida, as is possible, it may have been no more of a suicide attempt than John's first effort to climb a derrick had been. Allyn, a strong swimmer, took Bob for the kind of ride in the water a small boy would have loved. His mother, who was more timid in the water, would have been

his intellectual development in college, reading the books he read, encouraging him in his ambition to become a writer, entertaining his friends. His letters from Cambridge told her in detail about his study of Shakespeare, about B., about the London theater, about travel to Heidelberg and Paris and, most importantly, about his writing plans.

Reading the letters from New York she sent him in return, John had not taken in how greatly her life was changing in his absence. After the failure of Mr. Berryman's business she had taken a job in advertising, where, with her intelligence, energy and gift for language, she made a success. The account executive she became had adopted speech mannerisms and a style of dressing that reflected her new milieu, and that John felt had coarsened her. The most shocking concession she had made to the business world, one she felt necessary for a woman entering it over the age of forty, was to present an appearance so youthful as to rule out having grown sons, especially one who, in his efforts to look older than he was,

---

frightened, not the small boy. I say Bob rather than John because that's the way we all heard it. I think that when John was told the story his mother said he was the one who was on his father's back. Later, this hardened into the official version. John was permanently substituted for Bob at the time when John questioned his mother as to whether Allyn had favored either son, suspecting, with reason, that Allyn might have felt a closer kinship with Bob. Both were excluded from the "passionate devotion" Martha felt for her firstborn.

After weeks of begging Martha not to leave him, of threatening to commit suicide, Allyn chose:

A bullet on a concrete stoop
close by a smothering southern sea
spreadeagled on an island, by my knee.

There is little likelihood that John saw his father dead. Martha found Allyn. While she and Berryman were making arrangements, John's grandmother, who also lived in the house, looked after the boys.

Soon after the "departure," Martha and Berryman married, the family moved north, the boys were adopted and their names changed. Mr. Berryman, a kindly and sensible man from all reports, adopted an avuncular attitude toward the boys. John's style of dress when I first met him derived from his stepfather, as did many of his notions about how things should be done in the house. (No matter what the temperature, John never appeared at the table without a jacket and tie. Nor would he permit any deviation from Uncle Jack's recipes—he was something of a gourmet—for preparing certain dishes.) How much this man had displaced him in his mother's affection John seemed not to have taken in until he was sent away to school.

had raised a beard. John and Bob were her younger brothers, she told her colleagues. It was as a brother that, on his return from England, she introduced John to her new friends.

The deception about her sons being her brothers she was sorry for, Mrs. Berryman said. But why had John taken it so hard? "Poor lamb! When he came home from England, did he expect to find me sitting by the fire in a rocker, like Whistler's mother?" Her laughter filled the restaurant.

John had taken it so hard because he needed to believe in her as a reliable reporter. If she was capable of saying he was her brother, what was she not capable of saying about other relationships? About his father above all, but also about Uncle Jack. Had he really retired to Maryland, as she'd written in one of her letters to England? Or had he been rusticated there after his mother fell in love with a colleague and found it inconvenient to have an elderly husband in the house? Had his mother been unfaithful with the new man under Uncle Jack's eyes, driving him away?

As for his mother's insensitivity, wasn't her complete lack of understanding of what he, John, was going through during the painful transition after he returned from England, when he felt estranged from America, couldn't find a job and was ill, indicative of how she must have behaved with his father during the weeks when he was contemplating suicide?

In their outbursts, which occurred whenever they were together for too long, each feared to say unforgettable and unforgivable things that would cause an irreparable break. Mrs. Berryman, denying this in the beginning, said, "You mustn't make too much of our scenes (I see you're very sensitive to them). John and I love each other dearly. But in a close relationship between two people with strong personalities there are bound to be occasions when the strong bully the strong." From her laugh as she said this, one got the feeling that she recuperated quickly.

Not so John. He so little felt that the contest was between equals that he resorted to the use of two weapons, each more damaging to himself than to her: the threat of suicide, and episodes of fainting. She was not so convinced Allyn's death was accidental that she didn't tremble when John said, in effect: I will do what my father did. The fainting spells frightened her almost as much. They turned her from an adversary into the mother John had known as a small boy.

To determine the cause of these episodes John underwent a neurological examination while he was teaching at Wayne. During part of the time when he was living with Bhain Campbell and his wife (before Bhain's illness), John's behavior had been so bizarre, withdrawn, suspicious, irritable, explosive and depressed, that Bhain had called in a psychiatrist. Schizophrenia and a brain tumor, both of which had been considered, were ruled out. The electroencephalogram showed a pattern of irregular brain waves. On the basis of the readings (which in those days were often crude), a diagnosis of petit mal epilepsy was made and Dilantin, a specific for epilepsy, prescribed.

The first of these episodes I witnessed was brought on, as the initial one had been, by a quarrel with his mother. At a moment when I was afraid he might strike out at her in rage and frustration, a gesture which would have been shockingly foreign to him, he fell to the ground instead. As if by the throw of a switch, Mrs. Berryman's hysteria dropped away and she became a ministering angel. She removed John's tie, opened his collar, asked me to help her lift his seemingly lifeless body to the couch, put a cold compress on his brow, covered him with a blanket and, tiptoeing out of the room, closed the door, saying we must let him rest. From past experience she knew he would remain in a semicomatose state for hours.

Had John been taking care of himself? she asked. Her son had no idea of the most elementary rules of health, as I would discover. He didn't know what it was to live by a routine, with regular meals, daily exercise and sufficient sleep. He behaved as if these rules didn't apply to him, when he actually needed them more than most people. Had he been up all night working?

He had. So, too, had she. One reason for the ferocity of the quarrel was that they were both irritable from lack of sleep. Mother, like son, often worked through the night and went for long periods without eating. Mother, like son, seemed incapable of predicting that action a (staying up all night) frequently resulted in consequence b (fatigue and irritability the following day). In John's style of living, as in much else, he followed his mother's example rather than her sage counsel. A stronger nervous system and better recuperative powers permitted her to get away with what for him was dangerous.

During this, the first of countless scenes that I was to witness between them, I had been a helpless observer; exasperated with both at first for not seeing that it was obviously fatigue that was making them hypersensitive to the slights of which each accused the other, becoming sympathetic with John as his mother goaded him, then fearful for both as, at the climax, the very air became electrified. The so-called seizure that followed I watched not with horror—as I had supposed I would when John confessed his medical history and I, in ignorance of the disease, imagined a grand mal episode with thrashing arms and legs and foaming at the mouth—but with disbelief. It looked to me as though an impulse John had had to attack his mother physically when he could no longer reach her with words had been subverted, striking him down instead. He had prevented himself from doing the unforgivable and simultaneously transformed his enemy into a devoted nurse.

I knew nothing of neurology, but I felt certain that a misdiagnosis had been made. Nor did anything I read in the public library change my view. Perhaps he had had a real seizure while living with the Campbells in Detroit. What I had seen was not one. At the time John and I had our first serious disagreement (over my unwillingness to go to live with him in Boston until his relationship with B. was resolved), and he again seemed to be on the verge of fainting, I told him I didn't believe he had epilepsy. The episode was aborted, but John asked angrily, "What right have you to question the word of experts?"

No right. Still, I felt they were wrong and refused to back down.

John, to whom this indication of the limits of my docility came as a surprise, was startled by my firmness. "How do you explain the attacks, then?"

Not having the proper vocabulary, realizing I was on shaky ground, I said awkwardly that what I had seen mimicked a seizure; it was not the real thing. I could understand why they happened when he was with his mother (though I didn't say what I thought his thwarted impulse toward her had been). If he were to react similarly whenever we had a disagreement, a relationship between us would be impossible.

John had no further attacks. Though for some time thereafter he continued to worry about the return of his "illness" whenever he was under great pressure, petit mal was never again mentioned by him or anyone else in the family. Only the draft board, which classified him as 4F, continued to follow the Detroit diagnosis. The price of the so-called cure—for we all thought it was that when, even during the terrible summer of job-hunting, he had no seizures—was that I had left John with the feeling I thought he had been play-acting, the very thing he accused himself of in periods of soul-searching and self-doubt.

On the summer night that he ran along by the East River shouting that he couldn't go on, that no one believed in him, not even I, this is what he meant. Had I not accused him of faking the seizures?

"Faking" was his word, I said, not mine.

If he could fake seizures, could he not also fake the search for a job? He thought he was looking for one. But *was* he? After B. came to visit from England, he had said he was looking for work so they could get married. A lie. He hadn't been looking. Believing that what a writer should do was write, he had not at all accepted that he would have to earn a living some other way. Had he *still* not accepted it? Was that what was wrong? Torturing himself over this question was pushing him to the brink of madness. He would rather be dead than go on as he was.

After I dragged him away from the railing and got him to sit with me on a bench, I tried to convince him that I was certain he was doing all he could to find a job. The reason he wasn't having any success was that the kind of work he was qualified for was not available. What he had mostly been doing had been applying for jobs that didn't exist. Black as the situation was at the moment, I was sure he'd receive an offer before long. When it came, he would be able to get back to writing, would find a publisher and would become a first-rate poet. I was so sure that he would one day be famous (if not that he would soon be offered a job), that after hours of talking I was able to convince him.

If we were to survive this period, however, we would have to take precautions. He must quit the encyclopedia company and take a week's vacation from the ordeal, and from the city heat, at my aunt's summer cottage on Long Island. These suggestions he was only too happy to accept. Seeing how shaken I had been by his impulse to vault over the railing, he also promised never again to threaten suicide.

It was during this terrible night that, for the first time, I began to see the seriousness of John's psychological instability. If I had not done so before, it was not his fault. He had told me about his breakdown after he returned from England, he had told me about his "craziness" in Detroit, he had even told me he'd had an hallucination one day at Harvard. He had told me his history and I had only half listened, believing that with love and care and a reasonably orderly life he would be well. Now I saw that no amount of love and care could protect him from external circumstances, and that these could bring him to the edge of madness. What had been the cause of the symptom of fainting was still there, and could at any time manifest itself in another form.

Before our marriage, I had worried about our relationship being threatened by his "unspeakably powerful possessive adoring MOTHER." After the night on the esplanade I became aware of the presence of a tall mute shadowy figure whose features I could not make out, a figure whose power over John was as strong as his mother's. It was the specter of John Allyn Smith.

For John Berryman

ROBERT LOWELL

I sit looking out a window at 3:30 this February afternoon. I see a pasture, green out of season and sunlit; in an hour more or less, it will be black. John Berryman walks brightly out of my memory. We met at Princeton through Caroline Gordon, in 1944, the wane of the war. The moment was troubled; my wife, Jean Stafford, and I were introduced to the Berrymans for youth and diversion. I remember expected, probably false, images, the hospital-white tablecloth, the clear martinis, the green antiquing of an Ivy League college faculty club. What college? Not Princeton, but the less spruce Cambridge, England, John carried with him in his speech rhythms and dress. He had a casual intensity, the almost intimate mumble of a don. For life, he was to be a student, scholar, and teacher. I think he was almost *the* student-friend I've had, the one who was the student in essence. An indignant spirit was born in him; his life was a cruel fight to set it free. Is the word for him courage or generosity or loyalty? He had these. And he was always a performer, a prima donna; at first to those he scorned, later to everyone, except perhaps students, his family, and Saul Bellow.

From the first, John was humorous, learned, thrustingly vehement in liking . . . more adolescent than boyish. He and I preferred critics who were writers to critics who were not writers. We hated literary discussions animated by jealousy and pushed by caution. John's own criticism, mostly spoken, had a poetry. Hyper-enthusiasms made him a hot friend, and could also make him wearing to friends—one of his dearest, Delmore Schwartz, used to say no one had John's loyalty, but

Robert Lowell, "For John Berryman," *New York Review of Books* 18 (April 6, 1972): 3–4.

67

you liked him to live in another city. John had fire then, but not the fire of Byron or Yevtushenko. He clung so keenly to Hopkins, Yeats, and Auden that their shadows paled him.

Later, the Berrymans (the first Berrymans, the first Lowells) stayed with us in Damariscotta Mills, Maine. Too many guests had accepted. We were inept and uncouth at getting the most out of the country; we didn't own or drive a car. This gloomed and needled the guests. John was ease and light. We gossiped on the rocks of the millpond, baked things in shells on the sand, and drank, as was the appetite of our age, much less than now. John could quote with vibrance to all lengths, even prose, even late Shakespeare, to show me what could be done with disrupted and mended syntax. This was the start of his real style. At first he wrote with great brio bristles of clauses, all breaks and with little style to break off from. Someone said this style was like Emily Dickinson's mad-dash punctuation without the words. I copied, and arrived at a manner that made even the verses I wrote for my cousins' *bouts rimés* (with "floor," "door," "whore," and "more" for the fixed rhymes) leaden and unintelligible. Nets so grandly knotted could only catch logs—our first harsh, inarticulate cry of truth.

My pilgrimage to Princeton with Randall Jarrell to have dinner with the Berrymans was not happy. Compared with other poets, John was a prodigy; compared with Randall, a slow starter. Perpetrators of such misencounters usually confess their bewilderment that two talents with so much in common failed to jell. So much in common—both were slightly heretical disciples of Bernard Haggin, the music and record critic. But John jarred the evening by playing his own favorite recordings on an immense machine constructed and formerly used by Haggin. This didn't animate things; they tried ballet. One liked Covent Garden, the other Danilova, Markova, and the latest New York Balanchine. Berryman unfolded leather photograph books of enlarged British ballerinas he had almost dated. Jarrell made cool, odd evaluations drawn from his forty, recent, consecutive nights of New York ballet. He hinted that the English dancers he had never seen were on a level with the Danes. I suffered more than the fighters, and lost authority by trying not to take sides.

Both poet-critics had just written definitive essay-reviews

of my first book, *Lord Weary's Castle*. To a myopic eye, they seemed to harmonize. So much the worse. Truth is in minute particulars; here, in the minutiae, nothing meshed. Earlier in the night, Berryman made the tactical mistake of complimenting Jarrell on his essay. This was accepted with a hurt, glib croak, "Oh, thanks." The flattery was not returned, not a muscle smiled. I realized that if the essays were to be written again. . . . On the horrible New Jersey midnight local to Pennsylvania Station, Randall analyzed John's high, intense voice with surprise and coldness. "Why hasn't anyone told him?" Randall had the same high, keyed-up voice he criticized. Soon he developed chills and fevers, ever more violent, and I took my suit coat and covered him. He might have been a child. John, the host, the insulted one, recovered sooner. His admiration for Randall remained unsoured, but the dinner was never repeated.

Our trip a year later to Ezra Pound at St. Elizabeths Hospital near Washington was softer, so soft I remember nothing except a surely misplaced image of John sitting on the floor hugging his knees, and asking with shining cheeks for Pound to sing an aria from his opera *Villon*. He saw nothing nutty about Pound, or maybe it was the opposite. Anyway, his instincts were true—serene, ungrudging, buoyant. Few people, even modern poets, felt carefree and happy with Pound then. . . . When we came back to my room, I made the mistake of thinking that John was less interested in his new poems than in mine. . . . Another opera. Much later, in the ragged days of John's first divorce, we went to the Met Opera Club, and had to borrow Robert Giroux's dinner jacket and tails. I lost the toss and wore the tails. I see John dancing in the street shouting, "I don't know you, Elizabeth wouldn't know you, only your mother would."

Pound, Jarrell, and Berryman had the same marvelous and maddening characteristic: they were self-centered and unselfish. This gave that breathless, commanding rush to their amusements and controversies—to Jarrell's cool and glowing critical appreciations, to Berryman's quotations and gossip. His taste for what he despised was infallible; but he could outrageously hero-worship living and dead, most of all writers his own age. Few have died without his defiant, heroic dirge. I

think he sees them rise from their graves like soldiers to answer him.

Jarrell's death was the sadder. If it hadn't happened, it
wouldn't have happened. He would be with me now, in full
power, as far as one may at fifty. This might-have-been (it's a
frequent thought) stings my eyes. John, with pain and joy like
his friend Dylan Thomas, almost won what he gambled for.
He was more eccentric than Thomas, less the natural poet of
natural force, yet had less need to be first actor. He grew
older, drier, more toughly twisted into the varieties of experience.

I must say something of death and the *extremist poets*, as we
are named in often pre-funerary tributes. Except for Weldon
Kees and Sylvia Plath, they lived as long as Shakespeare, outlived Wyatt, Baudelaire, and Hopkins, and long outlived the
forever Romantics, those who really died young. John himself
lived to the age of Beethoven, whom he celebrates in the most
ambitious and perhaps finest of his late poems, a monument
to his long love, unhampered expression, and subtle criticism.
John died with fewer infirmities than Beethoven. The consolation somehow doesn't wash. I feel the jagged gash with
which my contemporaries died, with which we were to die.
Were they killed, as standard radicals say, by our corrupted
society? Was their success an aspect of their destruction?
Were we uncomfortable epigoni of Frost, Pound, Eliot, Marianne Moore, etc.? This bitter possibility came to us at the
moment of our *arrival*. Death comes sooner or later, these
made it sooner.

I somehow smile, though a bit crookedly, when I think of
John's whole life, and even of the icy leap from the bridge to
the hard ground. He was springy to the end, and on his feet.
The cost of his career is shown by an anecdote he tells in one
of the earlier *Dream Songs*—as a boy the sliding seat in his
shell slipped as he was rowing a race, and he had to push back
and forth, bleeding his bottom on the runners, till the race
was finished. The bravery is ignominious and screams. John
kept rowing; maybe at the dock no one noticed the blood on
his shorts—his injury wasn't maiming. Going to one of his
later Minnesota classes, he stumbled down the corridor, un-
helped, though steadying himself step by step on the wall,
then taught his allotted hour, and walked to the ambulance he

had ordered, certain he would die of a stroke while teaching. He was sick a few weeks, then returned to his old courses— as good as before.

The brighter side is in his hilarious, mocking stories, times with wives, children, and friends, and surely in some of the sprinted affairs he fabled. As he became more inspired and famous and drunk, more and more John Berryman, he became less good company and more a happening—slashing eloquence in undertones, amber tumblers of bourbon, a stony pyramid talking down a rugful of admirers. His almost inhuman generosity sweetened this, but as the heart grew larger, the hide grew thicker. Is his work worth it to us? Of course; though the life of the ant is more to the ant than the health of his anthill. He never stopped fighting and moving all his life; at first, expert and derivative, later the full output, more juice, more pages, more strange words on the page, more simplicity, more obscurity. I am afraid I mistook it for forcing, when he came into his own. No voice now or persona sticks in my ear as his. It is poignant, abrasive, anguished, humorous. A voice on the page, identified as my friend's on the telephone, though lost now to mimicry. We should hear him read aloud. It is we who are labored and private, when he is smiling.

I met John last a year or so ago at Christmas in New York. He had been phoning poems and invitations to people at three in the morning, and I felt a weariness about seeing him. Since he had let me sleep uncalled, I guessed he felt numbness to me. We met one noon during the taxi strike at the Chelsea Hotel, dusty with donated, avant-garde constructs, and dismal with personal recollections, Bohemia, and the death of Thomas. There was no cheerful restaurant within walking distance, and the seven best bad ones were closed. We settled for the huge, varnished unwelcome of an empty cafeteria-bar. John addressed me with an awareness of his dignity, as if he were Ezra Pound at St. Elizabeths, emphatic without pertinence, then brownly inaudible.

His remarks seemed guarded, then softened into sounds that only he could understand or hear. At first John was ascetically hung over, at the end we were high without assurance, and speechless. I said, "When will I see you again?"

meaning, in the next few days before I flew to England. John said, "Cal, I was thinking through lunch that I'll never see you again." I wondered how in the murk of our conversation I had hurt him, but he explained that his doctor had told him one more drunken binge would kill him. Choice? It is blighting to know that this fear was the beginning of eleven months of abstinence . . . half a year of prolific rebirth, then suicide.

I have written on most of Berryman's earlier books. 77 *Dream Songs* are harder than most hard modern poetry, the succeeding poems in *His Toy* are as direct as a prose journal, as readable as poetry can be. This is a fulfillment, yet the 77 *Songs* may speak clearest, almost John's whole truth. I misjudged them, and was rattled by their mannerisms. His last two books, *Love & Fame* and *Delusions, Etc.,* move. They may be slighter than the chronicle of dream songs, but they fill out the frame, alter their speech with age, and prepare for his death—they almost bury John's love-child and ventriloquist's doll, Henry. *Love & Fame* is profane and often in bad taste, the license of John's old college dates recollected at fifty. The subjects may have been too inspiring and less a breaking of new ground than he knew; some wear his gayest cloth. *Love & Fame* ends with an intense long prayer sequence. *Delusions* is mostly sacred and begins with a prayer sequence.

Was riot or prayer delusion? Both were tried friends. The prayers are a Roman Catholic unbeliever's, seesawing from sin to piety, from blasphemous affirmation to devoted anguish. Their trouble is not the dark Hopkins discovered in himself and invented. This is a traditionally Catholic situation, the *Sagesse,* the wisdom of the sinner, Verlaine in jail. Berryman became one of the few religious poets, yet it isn't my favorite side, and I will end with two personal quotations. The first is humorous, a shadow portrait:

> My marvelous black new brim-
>   rolled felt is both stuffy and raffish.
> I hit my summit with it, in firelight.
> Maybe I only got a Yuletide tie
>   (increasing sixty) & some writing paper

but ha(haha) I've bought myself a hat!
Plus strokes from position zero!

The second is soberly prophetic and goes back twenty-six
years to when John was visiting Richard Blackmur, a few days
before or after he visited me:

HENRY'S UNDERSTANDING
He was reading late, at Richard's, down in Maine,
aged 32? Richard and Helen long in bed,
my good wife long in bed.
All I had to do was strip & get into my bed,
putting the marker in the book, & sleep,
& wake to a hot breakfast.

Off the coast was an island, P'tit Manan,
the bluff from Richard's lawn was almost sheer.
A chill at four o'clock.
It only takes a few minutes to make a man.
A concentration upon now and here.
Suddenly, unlike Bach,

& horribly, unlike Bach, it occurred to me
that *one* night instead of warm pajamas,
I'd take off all my clothes
& cross the damp cold dawn & totter down the bluff
into the terrible water & walk forever
under it out toward the island.

John Berryman

Saul Bellow

He wrote in one of his last letters to me, "Let's join forces,
large and small, as in the winter beginning of 1953 in Princeton, with the Bradstreet blazing and Augie fleecing away.
We're promising!"

The Bradstreet was indeed blazing then; Augie was not
nearly so good. Augie was naïve, undisciplined, unpruned.
What John liked was the exuberance of its language and its
devotion to the Chicago streets. I had, earlier, published two
small and correct books. He did not care for them. In Augie
there was a Whitmanesque "coming from under" which he
found liberating. I admired the Bradstreet. What he said was
true; we joined forces in 1953, and sustained each other.

The Princeton John was tallish, slender, nervous, and gave
many signs that he was inhibiting erratic impulses. He wore a
blue blazer, a button-down shirt, flannel trousers, cordovan
shoes. He spoke in a Princeton mutter, often incomprehensible to me. His longish face with its high color and blue eyes I
took to be of Irish origin. I have known blue-eyed poets apparently fresh from heaven who gazed at you like Little Lord
Fauntleroy while thinking how you would look in your coffin.
John was not one of these blue-eyed serpents. Had you, in a
word-association test, said "Devil" to him, he would have answered "John Webster." He thought of nothing wicked. What
he mainly thought about was literature. When he saw me
coming, he often said, "Ah!" meaning that a literary discussion was about to begin. It might be The Tempest that he had
on his mind that day, or Don Quixote; it might be Graham
Greene or John O'Hara; or Goguel on Jesus, or Freud on

Excerpted from John Berryman, Recovery (Farrar, Straus & Giroux, 1973),
pp. ix–xiv.

dreams. There was little personal conversation. We never discussed money, or wives, and we seldom talked politics. Once
as we were discussing Rilke I interrupted to ask him whether
he had, the other night, somewhere in the Village, pushed a
lady down a flight of stairs.

"Whom?"

"Beautiful Catherine, the big girl I introduced you to."

"Did I do that? I wonder why?"

"Because she wouldn't let you into the apartment."

He took a polite interest in this information. He said,
"That I was in the City at all is news to me."

We went back to Rilke. There was only one important topic. We had no small-talk.

In Minneapolis one afternoon Ralph Ross and I had to
force the window of a house near Seven Corners to find out
what had happened to John. No one had seen him in several
days. We arrived in Ross's Jaguar, rang the bell, kicked at the
door, tried to peer through the panes and then crawled in over
a windowsill. We found ourselves standing on a bare gritty
floor between steel bookstacks. The green steel shelves from
Montgomery Ward's, meant for garages or workshops, for
canned peaches in farmers' cellars, were filled with the elegant editions of Nashe and Marlowe and Beaumont and
Fletcher which John was forever importing from Blackwell's.
These were read, annotated, for John worked hard. We found
him in the bedroom. Face down, rigid, he lay diagonally
across the double bed. From this position he did not stir. But
he spoke distinctly.

"These efforts are wasted. We are unregenerate."

At the University of Minnesota John and I shared an office in
a temporary wooden structure to the north of the School of
Mines. From the window we saw a gully, a parking lot, and
many disheartening cars. Scorched theology books from a fire
sale lined one of the walls. These Barths and Brunners looked
as if they had gone through hell. We had no particular interest in them but they helped to furnish forth a mental life in
the city of Minneapolis. Minneapolis was the home of Honeywell, of heart surgery, of Pillsbury, of the Multi Phasic test,
but it was not celebrated as the home of poems and novels.
John and I strolled sometimes, about a pond, through a park

and then up Lake Street, "where the used cars live!" What on earth were we doing here! An interesting question. We talked about Yeats. The forces were still joined. We wrote things.

> Drop here, with honor due, my trunk and brain
> among the passioning of my countrymen
> unable to read, rich, proud of their tags
> and proud of me. Assemble all my bags!
> Bury me in a hole, and give a cheer,
> near Cedar on Lake street, where the used cars live.

He was proud of the living of these cars. That, he said, was "Delicious!" a favorite expression. My offering to him at that time was a story called "Leaving the Yellow House." This, too, he declared delicious, though he found it faulty, inconclusive. (We told each other exactly what we thought.)

Tense, he stood at his desk as I entered the office. He was greatly excited. He said, "Pal, I have written some new verses. They are *delicious!*"

When he broke a leg and Dr. Thomes was called in the middle of the night, John said, as the splint was being applied, "You must hear this new Dream Song!" He recited it as they carried him to the ambulance.

I would visit John at an institution (not the one in this novel) called, I believe, The Golden Valley. He was not there because he had broken his leg. The setting of The Golden Valley was indeed golden. It was early autumn, and the blond stubble fields shone. John's room was furnished simply. On the floor was the straw *tatami* mat on which he performed his Yoga exercises. At a collapsible bridge table he wrote Dream Songs. He said, "As you can see, they keep me in a baby crib. They raise the sides at night to keep me from falling out. It is Humiliating! Listen, pal, I have written something new. It is," he assured me, raising hands that shook, "Absolutely a knockout!"

He put a finger to the bridge of his glasses, for nothing was steady here. Things shook and dropped. Inside and outside they wavered and flew. The straw of Golden Valley swirled on the hills.

John had waited a long time for this poet's happiness. He had suffered agonies of delay. Now came the poems. They were killing him.

Nitid. They are shooting me full of sings.
I give no rules. Write as short as you can, in order,
of what matters.

Inspiration contained a death threat. He would, as he wrote
the things he had waited and prayed for, fall apart. Drink was
a stabilizer. It somewhat reduced the fatal intensity. Perhaps
it replaced the public sanction which poets in the Twin Cities
(or in Chicago, in Washington or New York) had to do without. This sanction was not wickedly withheld. It simply did
not exist. No one minded if you bred poodles. No one objected
if you wrote Dream Songs. Some men of genius were fortunate. They could somehow come to terms with their respec-
tive countries. Others had women, the bottle, the hospital.
Even in France, far from the Twin Cities, a Verlaine had
counted heavily on hospitals and prisons.

John drank, of course, and he took refuge in hospitals, but
he also studied and taught. The teaching was important. His
lectures were conscientiously, even pedantically prepared. He
gave them everything he had. He came in from Golden Valley
by cab to address his Humanities class.

He walked up the stone stairs of the university building
looking very bad. He wore a huge Western sort of hat. Under
the flare of the brim his pale face was long and thin. With
tremulous composure, shoulders high, he stalked into the
classroom. While the taxi waited, he gave his lecture. His
first words were shaky, inaudible, but very soon other instruc-
tors had to shut their doors against his penetrating voice. He
sweated heavily, his shaky fingers turned the numbered cards
of his full and careful lecture outline, but he was extremely
proud of his dependability and his power to perform. "Henry"
was indeed one of the steadiest men on the block, as faithful
to his schedule as Kant, as precise and reliable as a Honeywell
product. His talk ended. Then, peanut-faced under the enormous hat and soaked in sweat, he entered the cab and was returned to The Golden Valley, to the *tatami* mat and the bridge
table, to the penitential barrenness of the cure. No wonder
after these solitary horrors that he was later grateful for group
therapy, submitting democratically and eagerly to the crit-
icisms of wacky truckers, graceful under the correction of
drinking plumbers and mentally disturbed housewives. In

hospitals he found his society. University colleagues were
often more philistine, less tolerant of poets than alcoholics or
suicidal girls. About *these* passioning countrymen he did not
need to be ironical. Here his heart was open.

But everything went into his poems. His poems said everything. He himself said remarkably little. His songs were his
love offerings. These offerings were not always accepted. Laid
on the altar of, say, an Edmund Wilson, they sometimes were
refused. Wilson, greatly respected by John, had written him a
harsh letter about his later poems, and John was wounded by
this the last time I saw him. I read Wilson's letter. John sat at
my table, meteor-bearded like John Brown, coughing softly
and muttering that he couldn't understand—these were some
of his best things. Then he snatched up the copy of *Love &
Fame* which he had brought me and struck out certain
poems,* scribbling in the margins, "Crap!" "Disgusting!" But
of one poem, "Surprise Me," he wrote shakily, "This is certainly one of the truest things I've been gifted with."

I read it again now and see what he meant. I am moved by
the life of a man I loved. He prays to be surprised by the
"blessing gratuitous" "on some ordinary day." It would have to
be an ordinary day, of course, an ordinary American day. The
ordinariness of the days was what it was all about.

He had arrived during a sub-zero wave to give a reading in
Chicago. High-shouldered in his thin coat and big Homburg,
bearded, he coughed up phlegm. He looked decayed. He had
been drinking and the reading was a disaster. His Princeton
mutter, once an affectation, had become a vice. People
strained to hear a word. Except when, following some arbitrary system of dynamics, he shouted loudly, we could hear
nothing. We left a disappointed, bewildered, angry audience.
Dignified, he entered a waiting car, sat down, and vomited.
He passed out in his room at the Quadrangle Club and slept
through the faculty party given in his honor. But in the morning he was full of innocent cheer. He was chirping. It had
been a great evening. He recalled an immense success. His
cab came, we hugged each other, and he was off for the air-
port under a frozen sun.

He was a full professor now, and a celebrity. *Life* inter-

---

* From the second (1972) edition Berryman deleted six poems.

viewed him. The *Life* photographer took ten thousand shots of him in Dublin. But John's human setting was oddly thin. He had, instead of a society, the ruined drunken poet's God to whom he prayed over his shoulder. Out of affection and good-will he made gestures of normalcy. He was a husband, a citizen, a father, a householder, he went on the wagon, he fell off, he joined AA. He knocked himself out to be like every-body else—he liked, he loved, he cared, but he was aware that there was something peculiarly comical in all this. And at last it must have seemed that he had used up all his resources. Faith against despair, love versus nihilism, had been the themes of his struggles and his poems. What he needed for his art had been supplied by his own person, by his mind, his wit. He drew it out of his vital organs, out of his very skin. At last there was no more. Reinforcements failed to arrive. Forces were not joined. The cycle of resolution, reform and relapse had become a bad joke which could not continue.

Towards the last he wrote

> It seems to be *dark* all the time.
> I have difficulty walking.
> I can remember what to say to my seminar
> but I don't know that I want to.
>
> I said in a Song once: I am unusually tired.
> I repeat that & increase it.
> I'm vomiting.
> I broke down today in the slow movement of K.365.
>
> I certainly don't think I'll last much longer.

In Loving Memory
of the Late Author
of The Dream Songs

WILLIAM MEREDITH

In their late eighties, Severn and Trelawny were laid to rest in the *Cimitero Accatolica* in Rome beside the young men whose genius had been the chief events of their lives, Keats dead at 25, Shelley at 29. What a crowd of us there would be, by that criterion, in John Berryman's graveyard—men and women who survive him knowing that their encounters with him constitute an identity, whatever other identities we achieve before the grave.

A man does not want to jostle or seem proprietary in speaking of such a friendship. Dozens of us appear by our right names in his poems—the only disclaimer is the mystifying one for Henry himself "(not the poet, not me)"—but nobody sues. Probably the impulse to bear witness should take as its tone the agonized modesty of one of his last poems:

> Happy to be here
> and to have been here, with such lovely ones
> so infinitely better.

I knew him first after WW II when I was teaching and doing some rather casual graduate work at Princeton. The appointment as R. P. Blackmur's assistant in the creative writing courses at the university was an annual one; that is, one person couldn't hold it for more than one year consecutively, and for several years Berryman and I held it alternately. But we were not friends then. He was formidable in his learning

---

Excerpted from Richard J. Kelly, *John Berryman: A Checklist* (Scarecrow Press, 1972), pp. xi–xx.

and in his pride of learning; I was even less read then than now. We had many friends in common, but we kept at the opposite ends of parties—or perhaps only I did. If we liked anything about one another it was the jokes we made.

The friendship that came about suddenly and remains a chief event in my life started in Vermont in the summer of 1962 at the Bread Loaf School of English. We lived under the same roof there for six weeks, with most of the other faculty, in a big summer "cottage" in the mountains. The fact that he and I drank gin at noon, which had to be elaborately overlooked and was, when that was possible, may have thrown us together at first. But the lucid fact of Kate Berryman, during that summer as during the whole last decade of his life, translated what was difficult about John into terms that less extraordinary people could understand. From the start, my friendship was always with both Kate and John, and I will never know how much I owe it to her translations of him and me, especially at the start.

Berryman came to know Robert Frost that summer, visiting him (and the close friends of his later years, the Theodore Morrisons) at the Homer Noble Farm, a mile down the road from the Bread Loaf campus. There were not many visits, but he came close to Frost. (Besides the "Three around the Old Gentleman," there are two other references to these visits in *The Dream Songs* and one in *Delusions, Etc.*) If I had to guess what Frost liked best about him, I would say either his edgy wit or his knowledge of American history or his wife. The meetings were notable because Frost did not generally take to younger poets with egos the size of his own, and accomplishments to support them, but he took to Berryman.

At the beginning of the summer John gave a reading at the school. He started off with a recitation from memory of Frost's "The Oven Bird," an early poem I had long felt was a key to Frost's diction, the colloquial language that once astonished readers, in two lines especially:

> The bird would cease and be as other birds
> But that he knows in singing not to sing.

This was before John's first visit to the cabin. In other words, he was not one of Bread Loaf's summer converts but a

man who lived with Frost's work, as I did. I think that was
one of our first expressed affinities.

That evening was the first time I had heard *Dream Songs*
read, though I was to hear them at all hours for the next several weeks. Once he came to my room at 4 A.M. for what was
supposed to be a private reading of a song just finished. The
acoustics of the big wooden house made it an unpopular public event. When John read aloud, the etymology of the word
aloud was brought forcibly home.

We spent many hours of those days and nights together.
Kate was pregnant, but to be sociable she sometimes drank
some of the gallon jug of Gallo or Italian Swiss Colony sherry
with which, extraordinarily (a habit from the war-time
drouth?), our martinis were always made. The Berrymans had
many friends, students and faculty. *The Dream Songs* were
new to all of us then, and John would read the new ones that
were birthing week by week as another man might tell anec-
dotes. The anecdotal quality of them emerged in his readings:
it was the character of Henry who dangled from strings and
told you his droll, outrageous life.

It was not until the end of that summer of '62 that Berryman made a serious attempt to find the structure of what I
think had been, up to then, an improvisational work. He and
Kate lingered a few weeks after the summer session, in a cabin further up the valley belonging to a remarkable lady who
has befriended many writers, including this one, Mrs. Frank
A. Scott. There John set in order for the first time the con-
tents of a small brown suitcase that contained, in profuse disorder, a literary event of 1964. Dream Song 62 records a brief
philosophical exchange he had at this time with a rabbit, outside the cabin. He worked there until it was time for him to go
to Providence in September, where that year he taught Edward Honig's courses at Brown University.

I move now to the last visit I had with him. In May of 1971
he was invited, with a number of other poets, to a kind of poetry festival at Goddard College in northern Vermont. I drove
from New London to pick him up in Hartford, and we
planned to go on to my house at Bread Loaf. But the aging
Mercedes that I affect lost a carburetor on the way, and we
stayed at Woodstock that night. His talk was rangy, but returned to religion ("the idiot temptation to try to live the

Christian life" is a phrase I remember) and to the disease of
alcoholism, of which he felt he had at last been cured. He
who would never wear decorations was wearing a rosette: the
badge of three months' abstinence, from Alcoholics Anonymous. Walking late in a cold mist, he stopped once on a sedate
19th-century street of that handsome town and spoke, in a
voice that made windows go up in the quiet night, the legend
he had decided on for his tombstone. It was to say simply:
John Berryman, 1914–19— ("There's no particular hurry
about that last date"), and then, very loud: "FantASTic! FantASTic! Thank Thee, Dear Lord!" We shared a room that
night at the Woodstock Inn. I had forgotten the terrible intensity of his cigarette cough.

After lunch the next day, two Goddard students came to
drive us the last 60 or 75 miles to Plainfield. At one point in
the drive, and I can't remember how he came to the remark,
he said, "You and I are the last of the unreconstructed snobs,
Meredith." Partly it was said to shock the pleasantly recon-
structed students, a young man and a young woman. (She
drove like a liberated woman. They were both bright.) But remembering the remark makes me aware now of another affinity between Berryman and myself, a yearning for decorum,
even for old-fashioned manners. I'm not speaking about our
social behavior, which is dubious in both cases, but about a
social ideal. At heart, Berryman was a courtly man, though
usually (like most of us) he could act out only a parody of that.
The forms of behavior that attracted him were as traditional
as the forms of prosody.

He took a long, deliberate time to master prosody. The *terza
rima* of "Canto Amor" (1946) is virtuoso, self-conscious still.
Some of the Petrarchan *Sonnets,* which date from the same
decade, are slightly contrived. Even in *The Dream Songs* are
occasional lines that seem to have rhymed themselves wilfully
into existence:

> At Harvard & Yale must Pussy-cat be heard
> in the dead of winter when we must be sad
> and feel by the weather had.
>
> (108)

But what makes the prosody consistently astonishing, from
beginning to end (see, in the last book, the form of "Scholars

of the Orchid Pavilion" and "He Resigns") is the sense of individual selection of the form for each poem. Even in the ones where you feel an excess of formality, like the "Canto Amor," or in a particular sonnet where the tradition seems to go sterile, or in a Dream Song where there is an effect of doggerel, the flaw is appropriate to the feeling of the poem, is not really a flaw but a felt, if not a calculated, effect.

Throughout his work there seems to have been an absolute and passive attention to the poem's identity, which produced this accuracy of form. It is an accuracy that dims noticeably in certain poems in the last two books—poems which could be described on the one hand as willful or unmannerly, on the other hand as deeply troubled. They represent a wrestling with new beginnings, I think, an agony of genius renewing itself. One does not patronize them by saying that the last two books are greatly flawed; the adverb cuts both ways. The prosody is violent, the enterprise is desperate, but the work is not clumsy. The poet is paying his kind of absolute attention to *scrannel* sounds, to use the word from *Lycidas*.

Social decorum as it existed at Cambridge when he went to England in 1936 must have seemed trustworthy to him (although his taste never failed him worse than when he wrote about those days in *Love & Fame*). Manners in the larger sense were for him an agreed-on language, an established position from which you could negotiate with accuracy toward or away from human intimacy. Without such fixes (taking the term from navigation) the maneuver is more perilous than with them. He must have picked up the reassuring starchiness of his British spelling and idiom at this time. To the end he would speak of having been *in hospital,* he spelt honor *honour,* he would have addressed an insulting letter *Jerry Rubin, Esq.* Society and its language were for him still a tissue of contracts, however much in flux, however headlong in decline. Once when he wanted to swear at a good man who had with considerable justification asked our party to leave his restaurant, Berryman called him an *insolent inn-keeper,* indicating outrage at the specific breach of contract he felt he had suffered.

I think that day in Vermont he had been speaking against the promiscuous honesty that is preferred to conventional manners today, an honesty that is often no more than an eva-

sion of the social predicament. It pretends to candor but
doesn't care enough about the particular human engagement
to look you in the eye, doesn't seem to recognize that all honest engagements are negotiations, *ad hominem* negotiations
that require the expense of attention. And it is this kind of
attention that distinguishes Berryman's poems. They meet
the eye, they pay you that courtesy.

And calculated rudeness, an element of the Berryman rhetoric, is possible only for the mannerly. It works in terms of
contracts and just deserts:

> Many a one his pen's been bad unto,
> which they deserved
>
> *(261)*

Expressions of contempt in modern literature often smack of
self-contempt, contempt for the human tribe. Berryman's
contempt is for aberrations from the inherited good manners
of the tribe. "I saw in my dream the great lost cities, Machu
Picchu, Cambridge Mass., Angkor . . . " (197). It is a curious fact about modern poetry that many of its large figures
have been men of enormous intelligence (we couldn't have
made good use of Tennyson) supported by enormous reading,
and that they want to restore rather than overthrow traditions. With our lesser poets, it has mostly been the other way
around —average intelligence, average or below-average liter-
acy, and enormous radicalism. The radicalism often seems, by
comparison with Pound or Auden or Berryman or Lowell,
naive.

Lowell or Auden could control a tone of insolence like
Berryman's in "The Lay of Ike" (23), but not many other poets
today have the cultural premises to make it hold. The poem
posits an underlying patriotism, the regularly invoked patriotism of John Adams, perhaps. (It follows the Song called
"Of 1828," which quotes Adams's dying words.) It rests on a
historical mannerliness that makes its goosing of a president
serious. It is funny but it's no joke. We are made aware of a
heritage that President Eisenhower is being insulted for *not*
being aware of. It is a vulgar, telling statement of expectation
from one of the last of the unreconstructed patriots.

On the Sunday morning at the end of that weekend at Goddard there was an easy discussion among poets and student

poets—I think it was billed as a symposium—in the living
room of the guest-house we had stayed in. Berryman was in
good form, despite the fact that for four days he had been
without the sedative (*my quiet pills,* he called them) he took
during those last months when he was not drinking. He was
wonderfully attentive, in the way I had seen him in the classroom at Bread Loaf. The talk was set in motion by Paul
Nelson, the poet who teaches at Goddard. His quiet good
sense set an unpretentious tone for an event that might well
have become competitive. Of the poets who had been there
for the weekend I think only Galway Kinnell had left before
this final session. I remember that Louise Gluck, Michael
Dennis Browne, James Tate, Barry Goldensen, Marvin Bell,
Geof Hewitt and Charles Simic were still there.

After Nelson had thanked the poets, he turned the discussion over to Berryman, who surprised me by introducing me.
I was not an invited member of the weekend but John's guest.
One of the things he said about me was that I understood
Frost better than anyone else and had survived him, the way
he (Berryman) understood and had survived Yeats. I said a
poem I knew by heart and read one out of my journal. He
asked for one I had written about Frost, but it simply would
not come to me and I petered out after a few lines. Then John
said, why doesn't everyone in the gathering of poets say what
he thinks he has done best? It was a good half hour or so then;
unusual human warmth came of that quite characteristic act
on the part of a man who is often described as arrogant. The
poets were completely open with one another, modest before
their calling with a modesty that John had laid on us.

At the end a student, a young woman, read a strong, not
altogether controlled surrealist poem, and John responded.
He spoke about break-through works, and said that the first
section of his *Homage to Mistress Bradstreet* had been a kind of
"first best" for him—too long, but exciting as a first. He
called it a "crisis poem." It was a phrase he had used earlier in
the weekend, talking in wide generalizations about *The
Dream Songs*. The first 384 are about the death of his father,
he said, and number 385 is about the illegitimate pregnancy
of his daughter (an infant in arms at Thanksgiving, 1962,
when the poem can be dated). "I am interested only in people

in crisis," he said. "When I finish one, I enter on another." (I incline to agree with a student of his work, Deborah Melone, who was present at the Sunday morning meeting, that in this reference to the final Dream Song, as often in talking about his poems, he was trying on a new meaning that had suggested itself to him, or in this case been suggested to him, after the fact. When the poem was written, I think, the opening words—"My daughter's heavier"—referred to the process of growth, suggesting the process of mortality.)

I think now that the most important persuasion we shared—I a virtually unread, instinctive, gregarious man, Berryman one of the most learned, intellectual and lonely I've known—was a view about people in crisis. It amounts to a qualified optimism, in his case ultimately a Christian optimism, about crisis as a medium of grace, if an agnostic can put it that way. We both believed that there is an appropriate response to anything that befalls a human being, and that the game is to find and present that response.

Robert Frost's "The Draft Horse," a poem John asked me to say that morning at Goddard (he knew I had it by heart, as I didn't have my poem about Frost), is a poem about the mystery of response to crisis, implying, I think, that the response of love can render evil impotent. Berryman makes a response to it ("Lines to Mr. Frost") in his final collection, lines from one poet at rest, now, to another, concluding, "I was almost ready to hear you from the grave with these passionate grave last words, and frankly Sir you fill me with joy."

The night before I picked him up at Hartford, he had endured a crisis in his hotel there and had written, or anyhow started writing, the astonishing religious poem called "The Facts & Issues." It begins,

> I really believe He's here all over this room
> in a motor hotel in Wallace Stevens' town.

It contains the lines about his friends quoted first in this reminiscence. It ends with the baffling spectacle of a man fending off torrents of a grace that has become unbearable. It is a heroic response to that crisis, as I think his death was too.

As we drove toward Vermont the next afternoon, he told me that he had telephoned his wife that night and asked her (at 4

A.M. again) to tell him "of any act of pure and costly giving" in his life. "I can't stand any more luck, I can't take any more. Neither heaven nor hell—rest, when it's over." I am a bad journalist and an agnostic besides, but I wrote that down that night, in Woodstock, and pray now that it is so for him.

III

Berryman's Poetry

Secret Terror in the Heart

JOSEPH WARREN BEACH

The coming of World War II was naturally the occasion for much earnest reflection on the subject of fear. But in my reading of poetry provoked directly or indirectly by the catastrophe of war, I was impressed with the fact that fear seldom made its appearance as the animal reaction to physical danger, either in the trenches or still less in the accidents of travel at home. Almost always what the poets were concerned with was the generalized moral fear to which men are subject on searching their hearts; the political and economic aspects of contemporary history giving way to what we may broadly call its "spiritual" aspects.

Thus it is in several reflective poems of John Berryman written in the crucial years 1939 and 1940, to be found in his *Poems* (1942) and *The Dispossessed* (1948). In "The Dangerous Year" (1 March 1939) he begins with the thought that we have so far in the United States "come safely with our children, friends," though trying at a distance

> To make out the intentions of that man
> Who is our Man of Fear

The Man of Fear is presumably Hitler, at least on the surface level of meaning. But it may be that he is intended on a deeper level to mean ourselves. For Berryman goes on to ask whether our sense of safety is not temporary and in the end illusory. It is time, he says, to forget the tinsel of our Christmas trees,

---

Excerpted from William Van O'Connor, ed., *Obsessive Images* (University of Minnesota Press, 1960), pp. 83–88. Italics in Berryman's poetry are Beach's.

91

> Forget the crass hope of a world restored
> To dignity and unearned dividends.
> Admit, admit that now *the ancient horde*
> *Loosed from the labyrinth of your desire*
>   *Is coming as you feared.*

The dangers and miseries of the war become a symbol for all
the dangers and miseries to which men are subject and which
are the fruit of their own desires. Thus the perilous world situation of our times is at bottom a spiritual condition for which
we are personally responsible. And he goes on to say that,
while we need courage to meet the situation, courage is not
enough. What we most need is spiritual insight.

> It's time to see how far you have been blind
> And try to prop your lids apart before
>   The midnight of the mind.

This same solemn moral is further developed in "A Point of
Age" (dated Detroit 1940). The somewhat cloudy theme of
this poem is the need for a young man to move on from the
city of his adolescence in strenuous ("Odyssey") pilgrimage
toward some more mature and spiritually satisfying goal. At
the end of the first section he says it is late and time to start:

> Settle the civic woe, deal with your dear,
> Convince the stranger: none of us is well.
> We must *travel in the direction of our fear.*

I cannot pretend to explain all his meaning in this context.
But he is clearly suggesting that we are all suffering from
some spiritual malady; and in saying, "We must travel in the
direction of our fear," he is doubtless carrying out the logic of
the earlier poem. The evil that we fear is the fulfillment of
our own wishes, and our spiritual quest must lead us toward
the discovery of that within us to which we have been blind.
The traditional hero, formidable to his enemy, is not what is
here required, when in the violence of the storm he begins

> The climb, the conflict that are your desire. *

---

* In the later version of this poem in *The Dispossessed*, it has been variously,
and not always happily, "improved"; and this line appears without the helpful
comma: "The climb the conflict that are your desire."

This line can best be understood by referring back to *The Assent of F6*, where the "climb" is essentially represented as a means of facing the underground fears of the several climbers in the very act of facing their overt fears, and where the final chorus declares of one of the dead climbers:

> Free now from indignation,
> Immune from all frustration
> He lies in death alone;
> Now he *with secret terror*
> And every minor error
> Has also *made Man's weakness known.*

David's climbing was motivated by his liking for his fear. "Being frightened was his chief pleasure in life." For Berryman's hero, presumably, the fear in the climbing was prized because it makes man's weakness known, and so leads to a salutary self-knowledge. The poet goes on to ask:

> The animal within the animal
> How shall we satisfy? *With toys its fear,*
> With incantation its adorable trust?

Obviously not, is the answer. What will satisfy the questing hero at any rate is a knowledge of himself. And he takes the world conflagration for symbol of the moral conflagration that rages in the individual.

> All that a man has wished and understood
> Is fuel to the holocaust he lives:
> It spreads, it is the *face of his desire,* *
> *The tongue teeth eyes of your will and of mine.*

Here again one fancies one can trace an interesting line of filiation in literary symbolism leading back by three stages from Berryman to Joseph Conrad. Holocaust is "a burnt sacrifice; a sacrificial offering in which the whole is consumed by fire" (Webster). And the conflagration described by Berryman, caused by our desire and will, is instrumented by the destructive element of fire. In *The Ascent of F6*, perhaps under the influence of the Abbot on the mountain, the leading climber expresses himself in highly religious terms: "Oh, You

---

* In *The Dispossessed,* "It spreads, it is the famine of his desire."

who are the history and creator of all these forms in which we are condemned to suffer, to whom the necessary is also the just, show me, show each of us upon this mortal star the danger that under His hand is softly palpitating. Save us, save us from the *destructive element of our will,* for all we do is evil." Thus Michael Ransom, in the course of the climb, of the conflict that was his desire. "Destructive element" is indeed an image provocative of many different meanings. For Stephen Spender in his volume of criticism *The Destructive Element,* it denoted one idea, and it denoted still another to Stein, in *Lord Jim,* who said: "In the destructive element immerse." It is at least amusing to consider the several possible suggestions in literature lying back of Berryman's holocaust that was "the tongue teeth eyes of your will and of mine."

In still another early poem, "At Chinese Checkers" (Grand Marais, 1939), Berryman was much occupied with the topic of fear. Playing at Chinese checkers with young people, he asks himself how we should

> counsel the unhappy young
> Or young excited in their thoughtlessness
> By game or deviltry or popular song?

And then he goes on to say most cryptically:

> Too many, blazing like disease, confess
> In their extinction *the consuming fear*
> No man has quite escaped: the good, the wise,
> The masters of their generation, share
> That pressure of inaction on their eyes.*

Here, alas, one finds oneself almost hopelessly baffled in one's effort to read some plain meaning in these lines. How much in this is symbol and how much literal fact? Are the "blazing" and "extinction" literal or figurative? Do they refer to young men in ordinary civil life or to young men gone to lose their lives in war? And what is the "pressure of inaction on the eyes" of the good and wise? Does it mean that in the present holocaust of passions (the war in Europe), the good and wise are forced to inaction by their consciousness that all military action is immoral? All that seems clear is that the *consuming*

---

* In *The Dispossessed,* "This pressure of inaction on their eyes."

fear which no man has quite escaped is that moral horror of thinking men at the sight of a world immolating itself on the altar of its own unholy passions.

What makes it peculiarly difficult to make sense of these lines is that nothing in the context, the action of the poem, serves to throw light on these seemingly irrelevant observations. Perhaps it is in this poem that one is most conscious of Berryman's besetting sin—sin against the reader (a scornful disregard for communication); sin against poetic art, for which he has so great a talent if he would only not so hide it under a bushel. It is a many-faceted matter. There is, to begin with, the hopeless confusion between the direct and the oblique modes—between the literal and the figurative. There is the way of putting things together without indication of their relevance to one another. And this involves the habit of allusion, not to things of public note as in Eliot so much as to things known only to the poet and a few intimates—we might call it the private allusion. And along with these and related to them is Berryman's proneness to the eccentric and individual use of words, "dictionary words," as where a little later he says that, bewildered, he sees

> burnt faces rise and fall
> In the recapitulation of their urn.

All this one writes in sorrow; for even in the course of this perversely obscure poem there are strains of arresting music, touches of real feeling, and an imaginative development that would add up to something important if the poet did not constantly so insist on being "different."

I will not try to list all passages in Berryman relevant to our theme, but content myself with one further example, from a poem later than the others considered, "Rock-Study with Wanderer." This is to be found in *The Dispossessed,* and apparently refers to the period immediately following the end of the war, when our foreign officers were still being gay in Europe, though that continent was no more now than a "ravished doll," while poets and thinkers had not yet found any reason to be more complacent with the state of the world, either political or spiritual. This present poet scans the horizon for signs of a political order more conformable to his ideal than any we have seen in the century of the great wars.

> When shall the body of the State come near
> The body's state stable & labile? When
> Irriding & resisting *rage & fear*
> Shall men in unison yet resemble men?

For readers who do not have at their elbow an unabridged dictionary, I will note that according to Webster, *irrid* is obsolete for *deride,* and that for *labile* the definitions most applicable here are not "liable or prone to slip," nor yet "unstable in emotion or behavior," but rather "characterized by adaptability to change or modification," or, more simply, "plastic."

A Bright Surviving Actual Scene: Berryman's Sonnets

WILLIAM MEREDITH

Also there was Laura and three-seventeen
Sonnets to something like her . . . twenty-one years . . .
He never touched her. Swirl our crimes and crimes.
Gold-haired (too), dark-eyed, ignorant of rimes
Was she? Virtuous? The old brume seldom clears.
— Two guilty and crepe-yellow months
    Lise! be our bright surviving actual scene.

                                    (Sonnet 75)

Berryman's *Sonnets* are his least interesting and significant book of poems, about as uninteresting and inconsequential as *The Comedy of Errors.* If readers like myself who admire Berryman's work immoderately would rather read the *Sonnets* than most books of modern poetry, we would still rather read the rest of the master's canon than these brilliant, slightly private, occasionally puppyish *tours de force.* They were not written for us, although a few may have been contrived after the fact to clue us in on the end of the love affair which they recount. (The end of a love affair is apt to be characterized by

---

William Meredith, "A Bright Surviving Actual Scene: *Berryman's Sonnets,*" *Harvard Advocate* (spring 1969): 19–22.

silence or extreme prosiness. A poet will change the subject
sooner than talk about it:

> The weathers changing. This morning was cold,
> as I made for the grove, without expectation,
> some hundred Sonnets in my pocket, old,
> to read her if she came. Presently the sun
> yellowed the pines & my lady came not
> in blue jeans & a sweater. I sat down & wrote.
>
> *(115)*

So the book ends. The final sonnets repress, as they narrate
it, a despair which we can judge, in the light of the story we
have overheard, to have been a wasting away in bleakest
prose.)

The introductory poem, which appears to be a Dream Song
of about Book VII chronology, tells us that the object of the
poems is to remain a secret, and why the poems themselves
may now be first imprinted, in Elizabethan phrase on the title
page:

> He made, a thousand years ago, a-many songs
> for an Excellent lady, wif whom he was in wuv,
> shall he now publish them?
> Has he the right, upon that old young man,
> to bare his nervous system
> & display all the clouds again as they were above?
>
> As a friend of the Court I would say, let them die.
> What does anything matter? Burn them up,
> put them in a bank vault.
> I thought of that and when I returned to this country
> I took them out again. The original fault
> will not be undone by fire.
>
> The original fault was whether wickedness
> was soluble in art. History says it is,
> Jacques Maritain says it is,
> barely. So free them to the winds that play,
> let boys & girls with these old songs have holiday
> if they feel like it.

A non-addicted person is permitted to be momentarily put
off by the Dream Song dialect of the opening lines. The poem

is surely a rather in-group joke to preface what is a non-Henry, or at most a proto-Henry work. But it is a lovely song, and interesting for at least two reasons as a commentary on the book.

In the first place, it reverses the decision of privacy cleanly taken in two of the sonnets. 87 opens:

> Is it possible, poor kids, you must not come out?
> Care you for none but Lise, to whom you cry?
> Here in my small book must you dance, then die?

and concludes, "pomp's not for pioneers." Sonnet 47, raising the issue of the double-talker, the *utraquist* as Berryman precisely names him, implicit in illicit love, seems to make clear that the sonnets are a secret truth in a situation where love and honor are incompatible—a truth not to be spoken:

> How far upon these songs with my strict wrist
> Hard to bear down, who knows? None is to read
> But you: so gently . . . but then truth's to heed
>
> (47)

The poem alludes to Lancelot's story, as 109 compares the lover's situation ironically ("Some horse-shit here, eh?") to Tristan's, and 55 to Aeneas' with Dido—three stories of love where privacy is essential.

The Note at the front of the *Sonnets* does not warn us, as the Notes prefacing both volumes of *Dream Songs* warn, that the characters and events are imaginary. There is not even a suggestion that this introductory poem is protected, through its Dream Song identity, by the general Dream Song *caveat* against autobiographical reading. Notwithstanding its opening hyperbole, the poem *sounds* literal. Not many lyrics, even in this time of ravens, can digest a bleak sentence like

> I thought of that and when I returned to this country
> I took them out again.

What seems to me the second very curious thing about the opening poem is this unconcern about calling the work fiction. A reader who prefers *romans à clef*, or a reader who simply doesn't like poetry as much as he likes lower forms of gossip, is apparently licensed to get right to work misreading the book. This is the more curious in the light of Berryman's unusually sharp protest against such readings of *The Dream Songs,* protests that do not at all have the usual air of having been dictated by the publisher's lawyer.

But if we read the introductory poem with sufficient care, these contradictions are resolved. The reason the private poems can be made public now, and the process which defends them against biographical voyeurs, is set forth in the last six lines. The question is asked "whether wickedness is soluble in art" and it is answered (barely) yes. The artist's imagination confers a faultless reality on faulty experience— a reality behind which we feel (in Eliot's phrase) it is not mannerly to inquire, or behind which it is simply not relevant to inquire. All the time, these poems were *poems.* If they once served as love-letters, that is now irrelevant. Poor young Berryman (like poor Shakespeare) had no more despair than to write *sonnets* when he was deep in love and trouble. "So free them to the winds that play,/ let boys & girls with these old songs have holiday/ if they feel like it."

But people who have seen Berryman plain, along with people who read *Life,* know that there is the most literal correspondence between events recited in the 385 Dream Songs and events in his life and times. The alchemical solution that alters them is poetry. Most of us suffer and occasion calamities like Henry's, none of us could *imagine* them like Henry. So the hairy Minneapolis so-called real Berryman is being quite honest when he protests that the work is "about an imaginary character (not the poet, not me) named Henry, a white American in early middle age sometimes in blackface, who has suffered an irreversible loss and talks about himself sometimes in the first person, sometimes in the third, sometimes even in the second. . . ." (The very nebulousness of person is revealing: as the events are transformed, the protagonist of the events undergoes changes of identity like some of those in science fiction—Berryman has written a fine science story—and like many in myth.) Our actual lives are not soluble (meaning redeemable) in art, but the life an artist can imagine—a life selected, understood, *paid for*—is shrived, and ascends to another world from the history that suggested it. The last six lines of this introductory poem may be more convincing legally, because more explicit philosophically, than the prose disclaimers in *The Dream Songs.*

II

Among the artifices that have turned the faults of that old young man into poetry none is more important than the sonnet form. Symmetrical, decorous, dragging after it all our classy fantasies of Renaissance Italy and England, it is a form nobody younger than Yeats and Frost has been able to do much with except to make cheap reproductions. The purer Petrarchan form, used for this sequence but avoided by Shakespeare, is the more arbitrary, requiring quadruple rhymes for the octave and a structural division of the poem into parry and riposte. To ask the average modern poet to tell a story in Petrarchan sonnets would be like asking a modern sculptor to make his statement with a cookie-cutter.

Berryman seems to have embraced the form for three principal reasons. He has a genuinely and powerfully intellectual view of experience, so that literature and life are of equal intensity to him, are held in a steady equilibrium. To such a sensibility, an overwhelming love constitutes an allusion to the literature of overwhelming love. If the sonnet was the key that unlocked this riddle for Petrarch, Wyatt, Shakespeare, it would suggest itself to him. Secondly, as a man of vivid self-consciousness, he needed a pose (other than his scholarship and his clownish self-mockery which encrust the poems with wit) which could mount a serious passion. The comparison of himself to Renaissance poet is serious and accommodates the intellectuality and the self-mockery. Thirdly, and this is perhaps only to project my own experience about the working of symmetrical form, to subject unruly or incomprehensible experience to the requirements of such form forces the sensibility to look at the experience in fresh ways. As a painter steps back from the easel or a sculptor walks around his platform, a poet can look at his subject, without *staring* at it, only if he can make it move. Satisfying the prosody of such an inflexible form as the Petrarchan sonnet will make an experience move to the point of contortion, in the hands of a skillful poet, and kill it off in less than skillful hands. The wildness of Berryman's feats of association is certainly not caused by formal exigencies. It is a natural wildness which may have been fostered here by an uncommonly pig-headed form.

Variations of the form are chiefly of a variety that is itself traditional, the extension of the final line to double or almost double length (4, 5, 49, 75, 76, 78, 103) (Berryman has spoken of George Meredith and Hopkins as among the English poets who felt that "we don't have enough *room* in an English sonnet, as against the Italian 11-syllable line"); and the occasional and once systematic (11) use of assonance instead of rhyme. Accents to indicate stressed syllables are scattered, for the most part helpfully, throughout the book, as in *The Dream Songs*. Anyone who has heard the poet read will recognize that he has exercised considerable restraint in recording the stresses he feels in language. The printed accents are almost solely concerned with establishing *the sound of sense*, as Frost called it, and not (as in Hopkins) with establishing metrics.

III

Berryman's work breathes with the intellectuality of an alert and scholarly mind. His use of books is the opposite of what we mean by the term bookish. Often his allusions revive the violence of an imaginary event by some highly original violence of syntax. Identifying his rival (the Excellent lady's lawful husband) with King David's rival Uriah the Hittite (Bathsheba's lawful husband), the poet condenses into one flashing line the story (II Samuel 11) of how David sent Uriah into the vanward of the army, exposing him to certain death:

> Whom undone David into the dire van sent
> I'd see as far
>
> *(21)*

The line is a reference to Milton, too, I suppose, whose latinisms and inversions accompany intensities of feeling, either to support or mock them, throughout the book:

> let there be two
> Only, "in that dream kingdom": I would have you
> Me alone recognize your citizen
>
> *(36)*

> Marble nor monuments whereof then we spoke
> We speak of more
>
> *(40)*

There is a good deal of Hopkins, also, not only in heavily alliterated and internally rhymed lines, but in a nervous, freighted syntax more reminiscent of "The Wreck of the Deutschland" than of Henry's speech problems:

> I prod our English: cough me up a word,
> Slip me an epithet will justify
> My darling fondle, fumble of far fire
> Crackling nearby, unreasonable as a surd,
> A flash of light, an insight . . .
>
> (66)

Another kind of echo, of Hopkins's pyrotechnic sound, occurs in two lines which seem to be the first appearance of Berryman's blackface persona (foreshadowing a line from the 72nd Dream Song: "Henry's perhaps to break his burnt-cork luck"):

> Burnt cork, my leer, my Groucho crouch and rush,
> No more my nature than Cyrano's
>
> (100)

Though one need not look for an influence here: even more than Hopkins, Berryman in the *Sonnets* and since has sought out tongue-twisting infelicities of language and made them felicitous.

There are difficulties of syntax and lexicon, and frequently of allusion, in most genuinely original poetry. But the *Sonnets* for the most part carry their own elucidation. Like *The Dream Songs*, they are self-contained experiences making up a larger whole. If you don't happen to know the lyrics by Cummings, Propertius or Pound referred to in no. 27, or if you don't want to look up *syncrisis*, the poem is nevertheless quite accessible, free of the tone and strategy intellectual put-down that announce false intellectuality. Any reader knows he is reading a pretty piece of calculated and affectionate seduction literature (though the reference to three letters owed to Pound is an example of what I mean by puppyish).

> In a poem made by Cummings, long since, his
> Girl was the rain, but darling you are sunlight
> Volleying down blue air, waking a flight
> Of sighs to follow like the mourning iris

Your shining-out-of-shadow hair I miss
A fortnight and to-noon. What you excite
You are, you are me: as light's parasite
For vision on . . . us. O if my syncrisis
Teases you, briefer than Propertius' in
This paraphrase by Pound—to whom I owe
Three letters—why, run through me like a comb:
I lie down flat! under your discipline
I die. No doubt of visored others, though . . .
The broad sky dumb with stars shadows me home.

(27)

Sonnet 25 is the only one Berryman let stand alone, publishing it separately some 15 years ahead of the book. It consists of a single but complex dramatic metaphor. He may have singled it out, at a time when he was still not convinced that the work as a whole had been absolved by art from autobiographical fault, as the poem which best enacted the drama of deception that is the theme and plot of the book. The sonnet appeared in *Poetry* in 1952.

Sometimes the night echoes to prideless wailing
Low as I hunch home late and fever-tired,
Near you not, nearing the sharer I desired,
Toward whom till now I sailed back; but that sailing
Yaws, from the cabin orders like a failing
Dribble, the stores disordered and then fired
Skid wild, the men are glaring, the mate has wired
Hopeless: locked in, and humming, the Captain's nailing
A false log to the lurching table. Lies
And passion sing in the cabin on the voyage home,
The burgee should fly Jolly Roger: wind
Madness like the tackle of a crane (outcries
Ascend) around to heave him from the foam
Irresponsible, since all the stars rain blind.

(25)

The image of sea or sea-peril occurs more than once in the book, sometimes archaicly or decoratively, a Renaissance device:

> alas
> With what soft thought for me, at sea, and sore?
>
> *(10)*

or

> since the chrisom caught me up immersed
> I have heard nothing but the sough of the sea
> And wide upon the open sea my friend
> The sea-wind crying
>
> *(72)*

But more thematic to the plot are these lines, striking across the division between octave and sestet:

> locked in, and humming, the Captain's nailing
> A false log to the lurching table. Lies
> And passion sing in the cabin on the journey home.
> The burgee should fly Jolly Roger

A word about the plot here. Scattered throughout a sequence of 115 love-letters are some 20 or 25 that give physical facts and circumstances in the progress of the emotional history that is the real plot. Thus we learn for instance of the lovers' meeting (16, 70, 106); the pine groves where they tryst (11, 64, 68, 71, 95, 115); of certain episodes in their adulterous deception (21, 25, 33); of accesses of doubt and misgiving (56–57, 82–83); the decline of the affair (96, 97, 101, 107); and something like a denouement, a break in tone anyhow, marking the end (110 *et seq.*). (That Berryman did not entirely mean to hide the fact that the final four poems were added at a later date—if it is a fact—may be corroborated by the fact that those poems, like *The Dream Songs*, have initial capitalization only where it coincides with prose capitalization.)

A glance at the outline of the story reveals that it is a Racinian tale of conflict. The hero is not racked by love only, he is torn between love and honor. There are a number of powerfully erotic poems, among them nos. 3, 9, 70 and 71. But for every intensely felt erotic passage there is at least one similarly intense expression of abhorrence for deception. It is a moral drama. This is one of the reasons these poems involve the reader emotionally. (The absence of any moral component is why a lot of recent love poems, detailing the lover's erotic acts and equipment, are less involving, unless embarrassment can be called a form of involvement.) The speaker's disguises strike him as trivial instances of a pervasive deceit:

> I am dreaming on the hour when I can hear
> My last lie rattle, and then lie truly still.
>
> (31)

>   Strange, warningless we four
> Locked, crocked together, two of us made sneaks—
> Who can't get at each other—midnights of freaks
> On crepitant surfaces, a kiss blind from the door . . .
> One head suspects, drooping and vaguely sore,
> Something entirely sad, skew, she not seeks . . .
>
> (33)

> . . . I am this strange thing I despised; you are.
> To become ourselves we are these wayward things.
> And the lies at noon, months' tremblings, who foresaw?
> And I did not foresee fraud of the Law
>
> (45)

> If the rain ceased and the unlikely sun
> Shone out! . . . whom our stars shake, could we emerge
> Trustful and clear into the common rank,—
> So long deceiving?
>
> (57)

> Heiress whose lovely holding lie too forkt for truth
>
> (76)

> Your hypocrite hangs on the truth, sea-sore
>
> (98)

The obsession with honor in a situation incompatible with it may be one of the forces throwing Berryman's associations—of image and of diction—always toward Elizabethan England and Renaissance Italy. A line in Dream Song 42, years later, would read:

> We dream of honour, and we get along.

The hero of the *Sonnets* dreams of honor as he makes out, and he is wracked and puzzled, as is any honest man, at the discrepancy between his circumstances and his ideals. The poem is dramatic because we want his honor to get home safe.

IV

Berryman's virtuosity with language is greater than any other poet's now writing in English except for Auden. Lowell, who shares their intellectual force, is not as playful as either Auden or Berryman. Language is clearly a source of amusement to Berryman. At the darkest moments of his poems, language confers a gaiety "transfiguring all that dread," in Yeats's phrase. The *Sonnets* are full of puns and transfixed clichés. Their intended privacy may have seemed to license this, and Berryman may have taken courage from this informal, private success to go on to the larger use of vulgar wit which nails *The Dream Songs* home to our moment.

> Pyromaniacal whispers . . .
> the mere
> Lick and a promise of a sweet flame curled
> Fast on its wooden love
> (6)

> Hurry! till we, beginning our eternal
> Junket on the winds, wake like a ton of Styx.
> (46)

> —the water's fine, come in and drown.
> (58)

> Parrots are yattering up the cagy mind
> (12)

> Weekly lamented, weakly flung aside
> (50)

> . . . The *mots* fly, and the flies mope on the food
> (53)

Many lines seem to have been uttered just to make a glad noise:

> Troubled and drumming, tempting and empty waves
>
> *(12)*

There are between ten and twenty words in the book that
will send a humble reader to the dictionary, from which he
will return exhilarated, they are used so nicely. Two poems
(23 and 103) are primarily concerned with vocabulary—that's
their *subject,* though they are love poems.

Over the whole work hovers the grace of wit. If *The Dream
Songs* are the funniest poetry of our time, their author seems
to have got into that way of taking himself and his experience
in this long bout with love and honesty. And the reason his
wit is so funny may be, as I have suggested, precisely because
it is private—jokes intensify in proportion as they enjoy the
economy of in-jokes; absurdity accrues. Perhaps this sonnet
late in the sequence is funnier for our having watched the
protagonist, proto-Henry, bring his sense of pedantry to a
comic pitch. (The story takes place in a college town.)

> Darling I wait O in my upstairs box
> O for your footfall, O for your footfall
> in the extreme heat—I don't mind at all,
> it's silence has me and the no of clocks
> keeping us isolated longer: rocks
> did the first martyr and will do to stall
> our enemies, I'll get up on the roof of the hall
> and heave freely. The University of Soft Knocks
>
> will headlines in the *Times* make: Fellow goes mad,
> crowd panics, rhododendrons injured. Slow
> will flow the obituaries while the facts get straight,
> almost straight. He was in love and he was had.
> That was it: he should have stuck to his own mate,
> before he went a-coming across the sea-O.
>
> *(107)*

V

When the *Sonnets* first appeared, reviewing them against a
750-word limit, I find I wrote: When Berryman says in an introductory note that they "have nothing to do, of course, with
my long poem in progress, *The Dream Songs*," he isn't being

quite accurate. They reveal the poet's mastering of the taut, flexible technique of that work in progress.

I hope the present remarks and illustrations have expanded that view, without suggesting that the *Sonnets* are to be thought of as apprenticework or background-reading. They hold up, like *The Comedy of Errors*, which Shakespeare might have insisted has nothing to do with *Measure for Measure*.

Only once in the *Sonnets* does the lover have a fourteen-line dream. It will serve to conclude an essay facing in two directions, looking at the *Sonnets* as a small miracle and as annunciation of bigger ones to come.

> I dreamt he drove me back to the asylum
> Straight after lunch; we stood then at one end,
> A sort of cafeteria behind, my friend
> Behind me, nuts in groups about the room;
> A dumbwaiter with five shelves was waiting (some-
> thing's missing here) to take me up—I bend
> And lift a quart of milk to hide and tend,
> Take with me. Everbody is watching, dumb.
>
> I try to put it first among some worm-
> shot volumes of the N.E.D. I had
> On the top shelf—then somewhere else . . . slowly
> Lise comes up in a matron's uniform
> And with a look (I saw once) infinitely sad
> In her grey eyes takes it away from me.
>
> (79)

No Middle Flight

BERRYMAN'S *HOMAGE TO MISTRESS BRADSTREET*

Stanley Kunitz

Hover, utter, still
A sourcing   whom my lost candle like the firefly loves.

The ambitiousness of John Berryman's poem resides not so
much in its length—it runs to only 458 lines—as in its material and style. This is no middle flight. Despite the discrepancy in scale, the manifest intention of the poet inevitably
recalls that of Hart Crane in *The Bridge:* to relate himself to
the American past through the discovery of a viable myth, and
to create for his vehicle a grand and exalted language, a language of transfiguration. If Berryman has been less fortunate
than his predecessor in his search for a theme and a language,
his failure nevertheless, like Crane's, is worth more than
most successes.

The historical justification for Berryman's return to Anne
Bradstreet as "a sourcing" seems clear enough. As the first
woman to write verse in English in America—*The Tenth
Muse, Lately Sprung Up in America* appeared originally in England in 1650—she survives in the annals of our literature,
companioned always by her florid title. To imagine her as the
symbolic mother-muse of American poetry is, however, to

Stanley Kunitz, "No Middle Flight," *Poetry* 90 (July 1957): 244–49.

stretch the point, as Berryman himself is well aware, for the
mediocrity of her performance is too blatant.

> . . . all this bald
> abstract didactic rime I read appalled
> harassed for your fame
> mistress neither of fiery nor velvet verse. . . .

It is the life, the spirit, rather than the work, to which Berryman pays his homage. In a sense Anne Bradstreet prefigures
"the alienated poet" with whose image we are all too familiar
in our own time. The rugged environment of Massachusetts
Bay, first glimpsed at eighteen, was scarcely of the kind to appeal to this fastidious, well-bred young English lady, despite
her devotion to her so-much-older husband Simon, eventually
governor of the colony, to whom she bore in due course eight
children. "Pioneering is not feeling well." Modeling her style
on DuBartas and Quarles, she sought refuge in her versifying
(some 7,000 lines in all) and meanwhile labored to recreate in
her immediate circle some of the lost amenities of the polite
tradition. Her many descendants include Oliver Wendell
Holmes, Richard Henry Dana, and Wendell Phillips. Obviously, in a consideration of the American heritage, Anne
Bradstreet is not to be dismissed lightly; but just as obviously
she cannot easily be cast in an heroic mold. Part of the imaginative sweat of Berryman's poem is produced by his wrestle
with his subject.

Berryman opens with an invocation to Anne Bradstreet
which gradually flows into her own speech: her crossing on
the *Arbella,* nostalgia for England, remorse that at fourteen
she found her heart "carnal and sitting loose from God," her
punishment by the pox, Simon's reciprocated love for her despite her "sorry face," and now belatedly the bearing of her
first child. In the mid-section the contemporary poet, or his
creative spirit, engages in what can only be called a love-
dialogue, a passionate confessional on both sides, with the
ghost of Anne. In the third part, devoted largely to a recital of
domestic woes, steeped in the odor of the body's decay, Anne
resumes her narrative. While the children grow, "the proportioned, spiritless poems accumulate"; father throws "a saffron
scum"; "baby John breaks out"; illness and death are ubiq-
uitous attendants ("this our land has ghosted with our dead");

her married daughter Dorothy, mother of nine, declines and is "inearthed"; Anne herself is beset by rheumatic fever and dropsy; in her mortal delirium she leaps to God. The poem closes with a three-stanza coda in which the poet bids farewell to Anne. "I must pretend to leave you. Only you draw off/ a benevolent phantom."

Berryman's poem seethes with an almost terrifying activity, as must be evident even in the fragmentary phrases I have already quoted, where the peculiar energy of the language compels attention. Time and time again the medium comes powerfully alive, packed with original metaphor and galvanic with nouns and verbs that seem interchangeably charged with inventive excitement. At his best, in his moments of superlative force and concentration, Berryman writes with dramatic brilliance: "I am a closet of secrets dying," or again, " . . . they starch their minds./ Folkmoots, & blether, blether. John Cotton rakes/ to the synod of Cambridge." *Homage to Mistress Bradstreet,* I began by saying, is a failure, for reasons I must proceed to demonstrate, but it succeeds in convincing me that Berryman is now entitled to rank among our most gifted poets.

After at least half-a-dozen readings, in which many of the difficulties of the text and the form have been resolved, I still retain my first impression that the scaffolding of the poem is too frail to bear the weight imposed upon it. To put it in other terms, the substance of the poem as a whole lacks inherent imaginative grandeur: whatever effect of magnitude it achieves has been beaten into it. The display of so much exacerbated sensibility, psychic torment, religious ecstasy, seems to be intermittently in excess of what the secular occasion requires; the feelings persist in belonging to the poet instead of becoming the property of the poem.

> I am a man of griefs & fits
> trying to be my friend. And the brown smock splits,
> down the pale flesh a gash
> broadens and Time holds up your heart against my eyes.

In particular, the love-duet in the central section tends to collapse into a bathos somewhat reminiscent of Crashaw's extravagant compounding of religion and sex. Anne speaks:

—Hard and divided heaven! creases me. Shame
is failing. My breath is scented, and I throw
hostile glances towards God.
Crumpling plunge of a pestle, bray:
sin cross & opposite, wherein I survive
nightmares of Eden. Reaches foul & live
he for me, this soul
to crunch, a minute tangle of eternal flame. . . .

a male great pestle smashes
small women swarming towards the mortar's rim in vain.

Intent on "leaguering her image," the poet interrupts Mistress Bradstreet's flights with protestations of devotion that strike me as being curiously incongruous: "I miss you, Anne." . . . "I have earned the right to be alone with you," etc., to which she at length replies, "I know./ I want to take you for my lover." It is presumptuous to be arbitrary about matters of taste and tone, but I cannot gainsay that I find such lapses damaging. The explanation for them is not that the poet suffers from emotional compulsions— these are the very fountainhead of art—but that he has been unable to canalize them totally into the creative process, with the result that they appear as extraneous to his fiction instead of subsuming it.

From the beginning of his career Berryman has been concerned with the problems of his craft. In the prefatory note to twenty of his poems first collected in *Five Young American Poets* (1940) he wrote:

> One of the reasons for writing verse is a delight in craftsmanship—rarely for its own sake, mainly as it seizes and makes visible its subject. Versification, rime, stanzaform, trope are the tools. They provide the means by which the writer can shape from an experience in itself usually vague, a mere feeling or phrase, something that is coherent, directed, intelligible.

In his new work, as I have already indicated, Berryman has evolved, for his language of rapture and of the "delirium of the grand depths," a dense and involuted style which in its very compression and distortion is best adapted for the production of extraordinary, not ordinary, effects. There is much

that is extraordinary in his poem, often as a consequence of
the magnificent conversion of the ordinary, but it is in the
nature of the long poem that it must sweep into its embrace
certain phenomena whose virtue is to be what they are, to re-
sist transubstantiation—and here Berryman is tempted to inflate what he cannot subjugate. "Without the commonplace,"
remarked Hölderlin, "nobility cannot be represented, and so I
shall always say to myself, when I come up against something
common in the world: You need this as urgently as a potter
needs clay, and for that reason always take it in, and do not
reject it, and do not take fright at it."

A portion of Berryman's vocabulary and most of the idio-
syncrasies of his technique can be traced back to Hopkins,
witness such lines as these, spoken by Anne in the crisis of
childbirth:

> Monster you are killing me Be sure
> I'll have you later Women do endure
> I can *can* no longer
> and it passes the wretched trap whelming and I am me
> drencht & powerful, I did it with my body!

But Hopkins, to be sure, would have known better than to
let the last phrase get by. (Hysteria is not an intensity of tone,
but a laxness, a giving in. By the time Anne has pressed out
her child—we are spared few of the physiological details—we
must be prepared to accede to the premise that never has
there been such an excruciating, such a miraculous birth,
and we boggle at the superfluity of the assault on our disbelief.)

In his uncompromising election of a language of artifice
Berryman, like Hopkins, does not hesitate, for the sake of the
emphasis and tension he aims at, to wrench his syntax, invert
his word-order. The rewards of his daring are not to be mini-
mized. The opening stanza, for example, seems to me to move
with beautiful ease and dignity; the tone, the pressures, delicately controlled; the details small and particular, but the air
charged with momentousness:

> The Governor your husband lived so long
> moved you not, restless, waiting for him? Still,
> you were a patient woman. —

> I seem to see you pause here still:
> Sylvester, Quarles, in moments odd you pored
> before a fire at, bright eyes on the Lord,
> all the children still.
> "Simon. . . ." Simon will listen while you read a Song.

But when the dislocations have nothing to recommend them beyond their mechanical violence, the ear recoils:

> Out of maize & air
> your body's made, and moves; I summon, see
> from the centuries it.

> They say thro' the fading winter Dorothy fails,
> my second, who than I bore one more, nine.

If we examine a pair of lines from Hopkins,

> When will you ever, Peace, wild wooddove, shy wings shut,
> Your round me roaming end, and under be my boughs?

we can see that the older poet, however radical his deflections from the linguistic norm, keeps mindful of the natural flow and rhythms of speech, which serves him as his contrapuntal ground.

Throughout his poem Berryman handles his varied eight-line stanza, derived perhaps from *The Wreck of the Deutschland* and composed in a system of functional stressing adapted from Hopkins's sprung rhythm, with admirable assurance. Few modern poets, I think, can even approximate his command of the stanzaic structure. The alterations of pace through his juxtaposition of short and long lines are beautifully controlled; and the narrative-lyrical functions are kept in fluid relation, with the action riding through the stanza, which nevertheless preserves intact the music suspended within it.

Homage to Mistress Bradstreet can bear the kind of scrutiny that an important poem exacts. The flaws are real for me, but the work remains impressive in its ambition and virtuosity. Other poets and critics, it should be noted, have been far less qualified in their praise than I. Both Conrad Aiken and Robert Fitzgerald have not hesitated to apply the epithet "classic" to it. Robert Lowell has called it "a very big achievement." And Edmund Wilson has acclaimed it as "the most distinguished long poem by an American since *The Waste Land*."

The book is handsomely designed and printed, with drawings by Ben Shahn.

Screwing Up the Theorbo

HOMAGE IN MEASURE
TO MR. BERRYMAN

JOHN FREDERICK NIMS

John Berryman's homage to Anne Bradstreet, three hundred
years ago touted (by her brother-in-law) as The Tenth Muse
Lately Sprung Up in America, has been as highly acclaimed
as the work of the poor lady herself. Many readings over many
weeks have left me of many minds about it: it seems magnificent and absurd, mature and adolescent, grave and hysterical,
meticulous and slovenly. Critics whose judgment I respect
more than my own have heaped it with superlatives; their ret-
inue is an honorable one, and I am quite possibly wrong not to
be among them.

What kind of poem is this? To start with the trifles that, in
Michelangelo's saying, make perfection: Berryman's fifty-
seven stanzas have normally an eight-line pattern that, as in
The Wreck of the Deutschland, has a final alexandrine riming
with the first line. Hopkins allows himself only three rimes
and observes them rigorously; Berryman, in his slacker
stanza, takes four, and will settle for identical rime, oblique
rime, or assonance. Whereas Hopkins does not once shirk the
obligations of the form, Berryman sometimes evades them, es
pecially toward the close of the poem, where there are stanzas
that accept the challenge of the rime not more than half the
time. Occurring where they do, the many unrimed lines seem
a sign of flagging interest or concern rather than a deliberate
unravelling such as we find in "After Apple Picking." Even
so, this is a live and dramatic form, with lines of three and

John Frederick Nims, "Screwing Up the Theorbo: Homage in Measure to
Mr. Berryman," Prairie Schooner 32 (Spring 1958): 1–7.

four stresses climaxed by a pivotal couplet in pentameter, and
with a three-stress line that poises the final alexandrine.
There are fine effects too: the dominant and ambiguous
"still," a key word in the poem, riming with itself (like
"cristo" in the *Divina Commedia*) in the first stanza, in a significant stanza halfway through, and again in the final stanza;
the shrill rimes of the tortured stanza 19; the unrimed "howl"
dissonant at the end of stanza 21.

Though the stanza recalls Hopkins, the rhythm is not particularly "sprung"; if we want a term we might fancy it, with
its slabs of spondees and bergs of reversed feet, as "jammed"
or "floe'd" rhythm. At times Berryman takes us for a fine,
teeth-rattling ride over the trochees, but in general this is a
grave, still, crabbed rhythm, occasionally so free that he can
insert whole lines of Anne Bradstreet's verse or even prose
without noticeably disturbing his pace. So in stanzas 7, 13,
and 14. The last three lines of stanza 8 are a prose quotation
adapted to the stanza by transposing pentameter and alexandrine. Without the élan, vigor, or confidence of sprung
rhythm, this rhythm is excellent for certain cramped grating
effects of its own.

With it the diction is in harmony: tense, nervous, crabbed,
agonized, by turns numb and hectic. There are majestic lines:

> Outside the New World winters in grand dark
> white air slashing high thro' the virgin stands

lines of strange and evocative charm:

> Succumbing half, in spirit, to a salmon sash
> I prod the nerveless novel succotash—

lines that might have been written by Tourneur:

> One proud tug greens heaven

or by Webster:

> "Mother,
> how *long* will I be dead?" Our friend the owl
> vanishes, darling, but your homing soul
> retires on heaven, Mercy . . .

(cf. *The White Devil*, III, iii: "What do the dead do, uncle? . . . When do they wake?") Particularly in the talk with

or about children there is sweetness and grace. But too often
there is a grim working of lips and jowls: stretches of god-
awful jawbreaking blether. Language is lashed sadistically,
racked and hip-sprung, broken on the wheel. Why, for a
small example, is the folk-lilt of "Jack-in-the-pulpit" crushed
into "Jack's pulpits"?—a phrase for the chunky tongue and
the tin ear. Sometimes English is written as if it were Latin:

> so were ill
> many as one day we could have no sermons

or worse:

> Jaw-ript, rot with its wisdom, rending then;
> Then not.

There are too many gobbets of undigested Hopkins:

> I can *can* no longer. . .

(cf. Hopkins's "Cry *I can no more.* I can . . . ") or

> Consuming acrid its own smoke. It's me

(cf. Hopkins's "Bitter would have me taste; my taste was me")
or

> Shy, shy with mé Dorothy

There are passages that sound like Hopkins in slow motion:

> He to me ill lingeringly, learning to shun
> a bliss, a lightning blood
> vouchsafed, what did seem life. I kissed his Mystery.

We might use as a text for meditation: "It is not in the least
likely that a truly great style can seriously oppose itself to the
basic form patterns of the language" (Sapir).

But what most puts me off in this remarkable poem is the
fable—so strained that any summary of it sounds like burlesque. And this largely because it runs counter to common
sense, which, as Hopkins wrote when shown "a strained and
unworkable allegory" by the young Yeats, "is never out of
place anywhere, neither on Parnassus nor on Tabor nor on
the mount where the Lord preached." The "poet" of the
poem—and it should not be assumed that this figure is the
author or any mask or persona of the author—contemplates

Anne Bradstreet and her environment; he finds her, like himself, a rejected figure that the world "unhands." They belong
therefore—these two in their "lovers' air"—somehow to each
other. Anne begins to speak of the hardships of the voyage and
the settlement, of her poetry, of her turning away from God
who as a corrective awarded her the smallpox, of her marriage
to "so-much-older" Simon Bradstreet, of her child-bed woes,
her illnesses and ennuis. Abruptly the poet addresses her in
Shelleyan tremolos: he and Anne, soul mates and body mates,
belong in bed together. Touched and flattered, she savors to
the full the glamor of this sexy evil. She invites him to touch
her smallpox scars, exclaims with pleasure when he does. She
is both abandoned ("Kiss me") and prim ("That once"). He re-
sponds to her "talk to me" by calling to her attention the New
England spring, all damply burgeoning with fertility symbols,
"Ravishing, ha," she admits, but yet forbidden. "I am a sober-
sides; I know." Then resorting to throaty italics: "I *want* to
take you for my lover," though it's "madness." The poet, after
an appeal to some Byzantine icons, makes a kind of
Dowsonish general confession. She protests with solicitous
indignation. They discuss religion. She is increasingly carried
away by a temptation increasingly sexual and therefore (it is
hard to say whether poet or poetess is, *au fond*, more Cal-
vinistic) increasingly "a black joy." Women, and she among
them, are almost helpless before the tyranny of sex:

> a great male pestle smashes
> small women swarming toward the mortar's rim in vain.

About to yield, she resorts to a last desperate prayer which
saves both:

> torture me, Father, lest not I be thine!

In this swart poem there is much sex but little love (except
parental love): even God works by "torture" rather than, as in
Hopkins, by the sudden thunderbolt that dazzled Paul or the
"lingering-out sweet skill" that won Augustine. But with this
prayer we leave the panting sexual hothouse and, in one of
those flashing transitions which are among the marvels of the
poem, are in the world of slipshod domestics and prattling
children. These grow up, Anne's father dies, she herself, "ill-
er . . . oftener," grows old and dies; and the poet, materializ-

ing again to see her interred, meditates on the methods of
modern war and our cooling planet. His valedictory addresses
her as "a sourcing   whom my lost candle like the firefly
loves."

Confronted with these events, I cannot suspend my disbelief long enough to take these lay figures seriously. And I
cannot help wondering about the nature of Mistress Bradstreet's attraction for the poet. It is not the fact that she
too is touched with the sacred fire; he cannot conceal the contempt he feels for all her "bald abstract didactic rime" that he
reads "appalled." What he seems to be making is the appeal of
lonely men in shirt-sleeves: he, the real poet, and she, so
much manquée, are in the same melancholy barque, cast
adrift by an unappreciative world. In herself she seems not a
very cogent figure of the poet as exile, this Tenth Muse, "a
woman honored and esteemed where she lives."

And though the historical "sourcing" of the poem should be
irrelevant, I cannot forget it. If the historical Anne Bradstreet
was not "unhanded" by her world, still less was she unhappy
in her husband and in need of extramarital consolations from
a ghostly poet who barges in like the young man carbuncular.
Anne's most passionate rimes were written to her husband:

> If ever two were one, then surely we.
> If ever man were lov'd by wife, then thee;
> If ever wife was happy in a man,
> Compare with me ye women if you can.

But the poet is understandably cool toward a lover bound to
Anne by so bourgeois a tie; he accuses "so-much-older" Simon
(who was about twenty-five when he married his teenage
bride) of being unsympathetic to her literary labors. The ac-
cusation has no particular basis; it seems that even Anne's
own father, a hornier-handed puritan than Simon, himself
wrote verse.

The poet's passion for the body of his poetess is strange too
in that (in spite of some lovely lines on her lost beauty) he prefers to dwell on physical aspects not normally the object of desire: her disease, her "cratered" skin, the cracking vertebrae,
"wretched trap," and unruly colon of her childbed experiences, her retchings, her broodings on her naked body, her
"pustules snapping," her rheumatic joints, her "body a-

drain," her dropsical arm and wrecked chest, her hangnails
and piles. *Oh Beatrice, dolce guida e cara!* The poet describes
his beloved much as Dante describes the figure of nauseating
sin or the punishment of certain damned souls. (It is revealing to compare Beatrice and Anne Bradstreet as *figurae*.)
Though the beliefs are irrelevant (or almost so) to the success
of the poem, it seems to me that here he is pumping a bit too
glumly for his bias, so that what we get is a sort of depressing
propaganda for the view that the flesh is evil: the qualm of
love the poetess longs for is described as being like the qualm
of smallpox. Even the beauty of flowers becomes dangerous
and forbidden: "Ravishing, ha, what crouches outside ought."
The historical Anne, puritan or not, has a more franciscan attitude; she can write of the beauty of nature:

> Rapt were my senses at this delectable view
> . . . .
> If so much excellence abides below,
> How excellent is He that dwells on high,
> Whose power and beauty by his works we know
> . . . .
> That hath this underworld so richly dight.

The nervous puritanism of this "homage" is evident if we
compare Berryman's description of the voyage with actual records of the passengers—not as a literary judgment on the
poem but as a key to its mood. The poem has it that

> By the week we landed we were, most, used up.
> Strange ships across us, after a fortnight's winds
> unfavoring, frightened us;
> bone-sad cold, sleet, scurvy; so were ill
> many as one day we could have no sermons;
> broils, quelled; a fatherless child unkennelled; vermin
> crowding and waiting; waiting.

John Winthrop's *Journal* tells a different story. The "strange
ships" were friendly, but even before that was known "It was
muche to see how chearfull and Comfortable all the Com-
panye appeared, not a woman or Childe that shewed any
feare." The weather was cold, yes; but they had warm clothes
and the sense to put them on. Though it was windy and rainy,

Winthrop often mentions, with something like exhilaration, "a fine gale," "a handsome gale," "a merrye gale in all our sailes." Even when the storms were at their worst "through Godes mercye, we were verye Comfortable, and fewe or none sicke . . . mr. Philipps preached twice that daye." The sermonless day prominent in the stanza above was immediately after their departure; it seems to have been quite exceptional. "It hathe pleased the Lorde to bringe vs hether in peace . . . we had a Comfortable passage," Winthrop wrote his son. The arrival seems to have been a delight: "faire sunneshine weather, and so pleasant a sweet ayre, as did muche refreshe vs, and there came a smell of the shore like the smell of a garden." A few days later they supped ashore "with a good venyson pastye, and good beere." From the poem this is all censored out— the cakes and ale, the venison and beer—by a lugubrious puritan selectivity; one would never guess that, as Morison says, "there was plenty of fun aboard." In Berryman's stanza everything is tense, numb, shivering, painful. There is no reason the world of a poem, even of a poem about a historical figure, should reproduce the historical world—the point of my comparison is to indicate how the poem is conceived: in the key of *dour*.

When not hunched on his gloomy soapbox under the cadaverous raven, Berryman can perform brilliantly. Witness how he brings to vivid life the Henry Winthrop episode, so drably described in the records: "The very day on which he went on shore . . . walking out . . . to view the Indian wigwams, they saw on the other side of the river a small canoe . . . none of the party could swim but himself; and so he plunged in, and, as he was swimming over, was taken with the cramp, a few rods from the shore, and drowned."

> And the day itself he leapt ashore young Henry Winthrop
> (delivered from the waves; because he found
> off their wigwams, sharp-eyed, a lone canoe
> across a tidal river,
> that water glittered fair & blue
> & narrow, none of the other men could swim
> and the plantation's prime theft up to him,
> shouldered on a glad day
> hard on the glorious feasting of thanksgiving) drowned.

And with what deftness he has worked into the texture of the poem hints from the work of Anne Bradstreet herself (these not identified in the notes):

Motes that hop in sunlight

is suggested by one of her verse letters to her husband:

every mote that in the sun-shine hops.

and stanza 40—

I pare
an apple for my pipsqueak Mercy and
she runs & all need naked apples, fanned
their tinier envies.
Vomiting trots rashes

—is a reminiscence of lines on childhood in *The Four Ages of Man*:

My quarrels not for diadems did rise
But for an apple, plum, or some such prize
. . . .
What crudities my stomach cold hath bred
Whence vomits, flux, and worms have issued

The pleasant lines in stanza 42 about wiggling out a child's tooth seem suggested by a line in the same Bradstreet poem. The strange line in stanza 51

and holiness on horses' bells shall stand

which the notes refer simply to Zech. 14:20 is actually Anne's rephrasing of the biblical line near the end of her *A dialogue Between Old England and New*. A number of such little authenticities will unfortunately be lost on most readers. One of the neatest is the combined botanical and astronomical allusion of stanza 31, quite in the manner of Bradstreet's *The Four Seasons*, in which every month is tagged with its proper zodiacal badge:

Venus is trapt—
the hefty pike shifts, sheer—
in Orion blazing.

As for the notes themselves—one wonders. A few are shifty-eyed: the poet's sudden amorous irruption prompts the following:

> One might say: He is enabled to speak, at last, in the fortune of an echo of her—and when she is loneliest (her former spiritual adviser having deserted Anne Hutchinson, and this her closest friend banished), as if she had summoned him; and only thus, perhaps, is she enabled to hear him.

Preposterous prose; I assume the author, ashamed of the shabby trick he is pulling here, is burying his blushing face in folds of evasive style. Anne Hutchinson her closest friend! This is the kind of impious fraud that drugstore historical fiction goes in for. Is there any reason for thinking that Anne Bradstreet, who lived at Ipswich during the few years the brilliant and tragic Anne Hutchinson (*there* is an Anne to conjure with!) was at Boston, ever met her "closest friend"?

The note on "brutish" in stanza 42 is mistaken: it is not "her epithet for London" but for Sodom (which does not stand for London). London, in the passage the notes point to, is "stately" and "our great Britain's glory." A trifle, but if the author thought it was worth having a note about—? For the rest, the notes are a bit chic· a reference to Klee, to Baron Corvo, to movie serials, to Fuchs's collections of engravings, and so forth.

In summary, I myself cannot see this as a great poem, though it has magnificent passages. Its successes and failures are dramatized by the first and last stanzas. The grave melody of the first is impressive, unforgettable. But in the last the sense of strain necessary to inflate this flaccid myth, the awareness of having nothing, ultimately, to say about it leads to the contortion and flabbiness of the utterly unmemorable last lines, which the dubious syntax, the shady Dante allusion and the archaic vocabulary do nothing to shore up. Throughout the poem I find this alternation of strength, gravity, even nobility with a shrill hectic fury, a whipped-up excitement, a maudlin violence of *mal protesi nervi*. A suitable invocation for the bad passages would be the lines of Francis Quarles, one of Anne's favorite poets:

>Rouse thee, my soul, and drain thee from the dregs
>Of vulgar thoughts; screw up the heighten'd pegs
>Of thy sublime theorbo four notes higher

In part Berryman's gallant failure (a better thing than many tidy successes in the magazines) is related to his double focus: purportedly concerned with Anne Bradstreet, his poem is really about "the poet" himself, his romantic and exacerbated personality, his sense of loneliness, his need for a mistress, confidante, confessor. One might think there would be more satisfactory candidates for this triple role among the living. Myth too is common sense, offspring of flesh and blood; Berryman, in his dealings with lovesick ectoplasm, has too little human reality to sustain his myth—screw up the sublime theorbo as he will.

Living with Henry

ADRIENNE RICH

The mind as dream-world. The intellectual, literate mind, the civilized. The mind that gets more and more expert at assimilation, self-protection, perfecting its distant early warning system against the violence of the world and the extreme creations of art. If tragic, or disturbing, art was ever curative, the viruses have developed drug-resistant strains. The worst moments of the best and unhappiest minds alive can hardly scandalize, let alone transfigure any more.

The dream world that conforms the pain of others to comfortable theory; that will perform the most delicate, insane intellectual contortions to avoid personal risk or vulnerability—this is the world of mind most threatened by the realities of poetry.

John Berryman can't complain that he is insufficiently admired. For many, he is *the* master poet of this half-century—perhaps the last master poet for a while to come, the last for whom a certain kind of technical daring and inventiveness combine with historical certainty and total awareness of our language and our tradition. But our ability to read—to read ourselves into—the 77 *Dream Songs* or the 308 published late last year, has some relation to our own willingness to risk body and mind in the real world. Terrible risks have gone into making this poetry. Like their hero, durable and battered Henry, *The Dream Songs* are open everywhere; open, at the risk of total breakdown, to nothing less than the life that breathed them: its black vistas, grotesque fantasies, errant affections, memories, lucid indignations, true loves.

Adrienne Rich, "Living with Henry," *Harvard Advocate* 103, no. 1 (spring 1969): 10–11.

I keep going to Godard films and thinking of Berryman. No neat aesthetic parallels, just two kinds of experience which often seem to intersect. The passion both have for exemplary or portent-bearing figures from the old Western culture, which appear and disappear throughout a Godard film or a stretch of Dream Songs:—e.g., on the one hand, Velásquez, Emily Brontë, Saint-Just, the postcards in *Les Carabiniers;* on the other, Schubert, Kafka, the Spanish Armada, Piazza Navona, Autun cathedral. Godard's camera panning past a high-tension wire with its yellow sign: DANGER DE MORT. The character in *Weekend* who says: "We're not in a novel—we're in a movie, and a movie is real life!" *The Dream Songs*—both volumes—aren't literature, they are poetry; and poetry is real life.

As Berryman grows freer and freer, through the second volume, there are fewer poems which seem terrific in their singleness (though I'd name, for a start, nos. 100, 116, 125, 161, 192, 210, 216, 218, 234, 238, 258, 259, 368, and the last, shatteringly juxtaposed two). Rather, the sense of the Long Poem on which he has been insisting accumulates to fulfillment. The whole thing is working at once, with a dynamic that is, as he wanted it—

> strange
> as the world of anti-matter
> where they are wondering: does time run backward
> which the poet thought was true . . .

In a sense *The Dream Songs* want a more than linear reading. And in this, too, they are beyond literature.

Fame, etc. As a "white American in early middle-age" who served time at Harvard and then at Cambridge University, and who earns his bread as a university teacher, Berryman's Henry lives close to the intellectual dream-world. He takes that risk and plays with it: the White House reception, the *TLS,* the National Book Award, the *New York Times* obituary, the tokens of Establishment fame and Establishment sell-out, inhabit his mind neither as objects of pity nor terror.

Another directory form to be corrected.
Henry did one years & years ago for *Who's Who*.
wasn't that enough?
Why does the rehearsal of the public events of his life
always strike him as a list of failures, pal?
where is childhood

from which he recovered, and where are the moments of love?

What he takes seriously is another matter.

A lone letter from a young man: that is fame.

No poetry of our time has taken the human creature, the moments of love, more seriously, more to heart. Henry feels oddly responsible—not merely, with dogged tenderness, for wife and child and friends: somehow it is he, with all his inadequacies, who must lash himself to the mast and endure for his fellows:

Dance in the gunwales to what they cannot hear
my lorn men. I bear every piece of it.
Often, in the ways to come,
where the sun rises and fulfills their fear
unlashed, I'll whistle bits.
Through the mad Pillars we are bound for home.

At the same time there is no lipservice to a stylish *agape:* the morality is concrete and precise. It takes the courage of the affections to write:

Pakistan may Pakistan, well, find;
or not.
Henry couldn't care less.
—Mr Bones, cares for all men!
—Overloaded. It is my country   in my country only
cast is our lot.

Which is a far cry from the cop-out cliché about loving individuals but not the human race; and far from the privatism of the university.

Berryman, polyglot. A new language is evolving in the heads of some Americans who use English. Some streak of genius in

Berryman told him to try on what he's referred to as "that god-damned baby-talk," that blackface dialect, for his persona. No political stance taught him, no rational sympathy with *negritude*. For blackface is the supreme dialect and posture of this country, going straight to the roots of our madness. A man who needs to discourse on the most extreme, most tragic subjects, has recourse to nigger talk. "Arrive a time when all coons lose dere grip" . . . early in the 77; most flaboyant, most broad blackface. Later, more complexly: the muted, the whispering "Come away, Mr. Bones." Come away! Shake-speare's English and some minstrelly refrain meet, salute and inform each other.

And we are all experiencing this, those of us who want to write poetry and not set-pieces. English is not a language any more; there is no standard American language. Over and against the purities of a Brecht, a Louis Aragon, a Pasternak, the security of a native tongue, of a Dictionary, we have this mad amalgam of ballad-idiom (ours via Appalachia), Shake-speherian rag, Gerard Manley Hopkins in a delirium of syn-tactical reversals, nigger-talk, blues talk, hip-talk engendered from both, Miltonic diction, Calypso, bureaucratiana, pure blurted Anglo-Saxon. The English (American) language. Who knows entirely what it is? Maybe two men in this dec-ade: Bob Dylan, John Berryman.

How much can a Long Poem be? Before the invention of liter-ature, poetry *was* film and theater, rock-beat and the 6 o'clock news, as well as religion and tribal memory. At the other end of time, I stand in Doubleday's bookstore on Fifth Avenue and read the golden letters on the wall: "In the highest civiliza-tion, the Book is still the highest delight." That was Emerson, "disgusting Emerson" according to Berryman ("wisdom in every line, while his wife cried upstairs"). The Book as sym-bolic object, totem, religious fetish, the Book as automatic trigger of a string of cultural reflexes: the Book as weapon of oppression as much as of liberation; the Book as a dualism of soul and body, physical object and psychic catalyst;—what-ever it has become for us, highest delight I should guess it is not. The shadow of the Boston Athenaeum, of Emerson and Margaret Fuller under one roof, pushing literary documents under each other's bedroom doors, the cerebral self-congrat-

ulation of the Transcendental-Abolitionist spirit, still hang
palely round the American academy; but the book as evasion
of life has its days numbered.

"These poems are meant to terrify and comfort," says
Berryman—and they can, they will, to the extent that we are
accessible to them, can meet their demands as the demands of
experience, often in perplexity and frustration, but also with
some existential gaiety.

The 308 new Dream Songs dispose finally of the possibility
that Berryman might be merely a master technician writing
mad, wicked confessional verse. The 77 *Dream Songs* often
seemed, in their knotted language, their bruised accents, like
a brilliant, furious contest against demons, a poem of exorcism. The 308 new songs, more open, more naked, more various, more compassionate, are above all a great love poem, and
a poem of victory. At the end of the *Opus Posthumous* which
opens the book, Lazarus-Henry is at the point of digging his
way back into the grave from which he has been exhumed.
Throughout the book,

> He feels his death tugging within him, wild
> to slide loose & to fall:

deaths occur around him—one early and traumatic death
memory, the deaths and suicides of friends and strangers who
were also poets. Yet continually threaded through the songs
are the living—

> The lovely friends, and friends the friends of friends
> pursuing insights to their journey's ends
> subtle & steadfast:

the work alive in him, the vital force itself—

> I seem to be Henry then at twenty-one
> steaming the sea again in another British boat
> again, half mad with hope:
> with my loved Basque friend, I stroll the topmost deck
> high in the windy night, in love with life
> which has produced this wreck.

Throughout, Henry is engaged in an act of resistance: this,
finally, is the plot of the poem.

When worst it got you went away I charge you
and we will wonder over this in Hell
if the circles communicate.
I stayed here. It's changing from blue to blue
but you would be rapt with the gold hues, well,
you went like Pier to another fate.

I never changed. My desire for death was strong
but never strong enough. I thought: this is my chance,
I can bear it . . .
            Come hunt me, ancient friend
and tell me I was wrong.

The poem accumulates in an immense tension, between
death that appears and reappears as his toy, his dream, his
rest, the subject of so many songs, the persistent seducer—
and the generous, indignant sense of life—one man's life
gathering many to it, cherishing, wounding, forgiving, the
life of the human creature doomed to love. It is no accident
that on the last two pages of the poem, in the last two songs,
destructive violence and healing tenderness, death and love,
lie pressed together, face to face.

Berryman's Songs

PHILIP TOYNBEE

John Berryman and Robert Lowell—both around fifty this
year—have become the most prominent American poets since
the recent deaths of Robert Frost, William Carlos Williams,
and Theodore Roethke. Of Berryman's last long poem,
Homage to Mistress Bradstreet, Edmund Wilson wrote that it
was "the most distinguished long poem by an American since
The Waste Land." Lowell, Allen Tate, and Conrad Aiken have
all added praises of the same order, and so have our own Mr.
Kermode and Mr Alvarez. A poet is important, in his own
time, if he is generally thought to be important, and by this
criterion there is no doubt whatever that Mr. Berryman deserves attention.

The first thing to be said about his poetry is that though he
has become increasingly obscure in his later work he has always remained an immediately appetizing poet. He is accessible even when he is not intelligible. Here, for example, is the
verse which opens that dense and difficult poem *Homage to
Mistress Bradstreet*:

> The Governor your husband lived so long
> moved you not, restless, waiting for him? Still,
> you were a patient woman—
> I seem to see you pause here still:
> Sylvester, Quarles, in moments odd you pored
> before a fire at, bright eyes on the Lord,
> all the children still.
> "Simon." Simon will listen while you read a Song.

Unless we are well prepared for it this is not an opening
which offers an easy entry into the sense of the situation, yet

Philip Toynbee, "Berryman's Songs," *Encounter* 24 (March 1965): 76–78.

it is a beguiling opening none the less. We acknowledge a
strongly individual tone and the authority of a poet who has
learned to know exactly what he is doing and why he is doing
it. The new sequence of poems (nearly all of them are in three
verses of six lines each) is far more obscure than *Homage to
Mistress Bradstreet,* and the tone has changed from the faintly
biblical and archaic to the violently modern and demotic. Yet
here, too, the first verse has an unusual power to excite and
encourage a new reader:

> Huffy Henry hid   the day,
> unappeasable Henry sulked.
> I see his point—a trying to put things over.
> It was the thought that they thought
> they could *do* it made Henry wicked & away.
> But he should have come out and talked.

The new poem is much more freely written than the earlier
one. Its rhymes are irregular; its meter expansive. It is altogether an open poem, while the earlier one was tightly
closed in on itself. The method is something like Meredith's
in *Modern Love*—a dreamy sequence of events and reflections
surrounding a central figure but not always directly concerned with him. Henry, a projection, at very varying dis-
tances, of the poet himself, emerges and disappears
throughout the sequence, a figure of fun or pity or disap-
proval. "Mr. Bones"—apparently the death which Henry
fears—is a secondary character with whom he engages at
times in sinister and ludicrous fragments of dialogue. The
poem is so obscure that no reader will avoid being lost in it for
much of the time; until the inevitable key is supplied from
some English faculty somewhere. Yet the poem remains pleasantly suggestive, at the least, even where its lines make only
the vaguest suggestion of sense to us. We feel all the time that
new possibilities of verse are being offered us. Here are a few
verses which may help to give a flavor of Berryman's latest
method:

> Ol' Henry then Mount Henery he scale:
> or rather fail, being his own Laval—
> who he? Sir Vertigo!—
> to peak that Everest of old snow.

Instead he tumble nimbly down hisself
und wed a lush; for cash.

Ha ha, fifth column, quisling, genocide,
he held his hands and laught from side to side
a loverly time.
The berries and the rods left him alone less.
Thro' a race of water once I went: happiness.
I'll walk into the sky.

God's Henry's enemy. We're in business. . . .
    Why,
what business must be clear.
A cornering.
I couldn't feel more like it.—Mr. Bones,
as I look on the saffron sky,
you strike me as ornery.

Henry he not see the constellations.
He was his own light, or something glowing.
Henry may be going
one day down that pit of deep damnation.
"I can lick any mansize stargazer:
Mr. Bones, I amaze you?"

Henry sats in de plane & was gay.
Careful Henry nothing said aloud
but where a Virgin out of cloud
to her Mountain dropt in light,
his thoughts made pockets & the plane buckt.
"Parm me, lady." "Orright."

    The verses are not consecutive, which does Mr. Berryman
an injustice. What may prove to do him a greater injustice is
that two of them were written by me, taking a few minutes for
each verse, and a few more for brushing up; or down. Assuming that the imitation verses escape ready detection, something *must* surely have been suggested to the poet's
disadvantage. It is not a trick that one could have played on
Yeats or Eliot when their best feet were forward, and it does
at least throw a certain doubt on Allen Tate's belief that
Berryman's poetry "cannot be imitated."
    My own strange and sad feeling is that he is a poet whose
evaporation rate is very high indeed. His early verse was

mellifluous, easy to understand and pleasing; but much of it is
fairly obvious pastiche of other contemporaries; and it suffers
from the fatal defect, as to survival, of being easy in sentiment as well as in expression. The well-known "Ball Poem,"
for example, could easily be transcribed into a sentimental
popular song about the incurable sadness of a little boy losing
his ball. "Boston Common" reveals, under the surface rhetoric, a depressingly trite meditation on history and present
time. Worse than this, I have found that my many readings of
Mistress Bradstreet since its first appearance here in 1959 have
reduced that initially exciting poem to something a good deal
less than it seemed.

These readings have reduced, first of all, the apparent origi-
nality of the diction and the form. The influences of Hopkins
and Dylan Thomas, evident from the first, have become by
now almost unbearably oppressive. The subject itself seems
more and more arbitrary. Was it chosen, this oblique narrative
of a poetess who was also one of the earliest settlers in New
England, simply because of its alluring exoticism? Mr. Berryman demonstrates in the course of the poem that Anne
Bradstreet was herself a very bad poet. He is paying, of
course, a tribute to courage, and this is not a trite theme, but,
on the contrary, one of those "eternal commonplaces" which
are the proper subjects of much ambitious poetry. And no
doubt, too, he was genuinely excited, as any poet might be, by
the harsh temerity of that particular pioneering community.
Yet as the apparent difficulties of the poem resolve themselves
most of them are seen to be of that irrelevent kind which are
simply due to the poet having acquired information—in this
case biographical information—which the reader is unlikely
to possess.

Similarly, when the Dream Poems emerge into the light of
day it is often into a common light indeed. Generalizations,
for example, leap out of the exotic turmoil from time to time
with a rather sickening thud: "However things hurt, men
hurt worse." "Women is better, braver." "Death is a German
expert." The obvious jokes are well below *New Yorker* standard: "My psychiatrist can lick your psychiatrist," "and something can (has) been said for sobriety/but very little." There

are "shocking" juxtapositions which are painfully corny, as in
these opening lines of poem 66:

"All virtues enter into this world":
A Buddhist, doused in the street, serenely burned.
The Secretary of State for War,
winking it over, screwed a redhaired whore.

A whole poem is devoted to a sardonic attack on Eisenhower
which contributes nothing at all to our feelings about that de-
plorable president.

Of course it is true that the sequence of the poems, and the
apparently arbitrary choice of subjects, have been carefully
thought out by the poet and will reveal, in time and with outside help, a sense and a "point" which no reader can yet dis-
cern. There seems, for example, to be a Christian message
running through *The Dream Songs,* and this may become
more explicit both with time and study and with the further
series of poems which are promised. Yet I feel bound to suspect that there will *not* emerge a sense of that inevitable union
of means and meaning which we receive from all good poetry.
I feel bound to suspect that Mr. Berryman has wrapped up an
untranscended poverty of thought and feeling in a form which
may excite but cannot feed his readers.

Yet this does not mean that this poet is meretricious as a
man or futile as a poet. In his search for new means he remains excitingly suggestive. This particular combination of
one kind of demotic speech—much of it joke-negro—with a
deliberate narrative confusion and a deliberate obliqueness of
public reference remains stimulating even when its matter
and its particular application have become suspect. In one
way Pound was a very different kind of poet from Berryman:
what lay behind *his* obscurities and technical innovations was
not a meditative triteness but an insane message, or command. Yet it may be that Berryman will prove to have done as
great a service to the poets of his own time as Ezra Pound did
for the poets of fifty years ago and ever since. There is a wry
nobility in this role—to have achieved comparatively little for
or by oneself and yet to have been the means of liberating
other poets and enabling them to succeed where the innovator

has himself failed. Perhaps Eliot's insistent gratitude to Pound contained something of this sad, and never expressed, recognition.

The first and the fourth of those quoted verses were not written by Mr. Berryman.

Gaiety & Lamentation

THE DEFEAT OF JOHN BERRYMAN

D o u g l a s   D u n n

Most of those who have written on John Berryman's poems
have found it reasonable to assume that his work poses—even
postures—as "difficult." It has been considered a poetry for
which certain clues must be known beforehand in order to
gain access, let alone understanding. Martin Dodsworth's article, in *The Survival of Poetry,** was called "John Berryman:
An Introduction," suggesting, by its title and method, that
here was a poet who must be subjected to elementary critical
exposure before any attempt by a less critical public to read
him. And Edward Mendelson's contribution to the subject is
called "How to Read Berryman's *Dream Songs,*"† the implication being that readers have stumbled, or misunderstood, in
the past, and that more than a chair (not the university kind)
and a copy of the books is required.

The problem is partly Berryman's fault. He complained in
prefaces and in interviews that his work was discussed in
wrong ways, that critics missed the point. As well as that,
readers, and critics, especially British ones, have been put off
by Berryman's syntax and orthography. Even worse, his scholarly affectations, his cultural reach, not only manifest themselves in poems as allusive details, but are held by some to be
the stiffening in a larger theological argument. Few British
readers can take *that* seriously. These indifferent reactions are

---

Douglas Dunn, "Gaiety & Lamentation: The Defeat of John Berryman," *Encounter* 43 (August 1974): 72–77.

*   Faber and Faber, 1970.

†   In *American Poetry Since 1960,* ed. Robert B. Shaw (Carcanet Press, 1973).

the grumbling of an Age without vision. They can be held to one side. What must be asserted about Berryman's work is its humanity. Berryman himself may have thought that beside the point too; but it is what, in my opinion, is strongest in his poems.

Christopher Ricks writes that "*The Dream Songs* can't but be a theodicy,"* which means they constitute a defense of God's goodness in spite of the disasters and pain inflicted on the poet who makes the defense. I don't see that. There is so much blasphemy and doubt in *Dream Songs* that its religious dimensions come across as an absence of faith, as spiritual torture. Of Henry, the protagonist of *Dream Songs*, Berryman said in a published conversation with Richard Kostelanetz:†

> The point in Henry was to investigate a man with many op-portunities, far more than those allowed to the lover in the *Bradstreet* poem—many chances to observe and see what peo-ple of various nations are like, and what they do and are, and so on. Now Henry is a man with, God knows, many faults, but among them is not self-understanding. He believes in his enterprise. He is suffering and suffering heavily and has to. That can't be helped. And he has a friend, Mr. Bones, but the friend is some friend. He's like Job's Comforter. Remember the three who pretend to be Job's friends? They sit down and lament with him, and give him the traditional Jewish jazz— namely, you suffer, therefore you are guilty. . . . Well, Hen-ry's friend sits down and gives him the same business. Henry is so troubled and bothered by his many problems that he nev-er actually comes up with solutions. and from that point of view the poem is a failure. . . .

The religious correspondences are obvious enough; but for the theodicy argument to stand, Berryman would have had to admit to a "solution," to a positive religious attitude. Throughout his work, Berryman had said earlier in the con-versation, there "is a tendency to regard the individual soul under stress." But to claim this as a religious intention, in *The Dream Songs,* is to take matters too far. Professor Ricks de-tected an aspect of Berryman's interests which was only to be-

---

* *Massachusetts Review,* spring 1970.

† *Paris Review,* winter 1972.

come positive and dominant in *Love & Fame* and *Delusions, Etc.*

Part of Ricks's theodicy argument is a comparison between Tennyson's *In Memoriam* and *Dream Songs*. Dedicated to "the sacred memory of Delmore Schwartz," lamenting the fates of Jarrell, Blackmur, Roethke and other friends, cherishing dozens of precious literary and cultural heroes, *The Dream Songs* is undoubtedly haunted by elegiac feeling. But Berryman's own ploy with Henry, described in his words above, ought to complicate purely elegiac or religious definitions of the work. The poem appears to me cast on lines closer to Byron's *Don Juan*.

One can justify that suggestion in several ways. First, the nature of the poem's construction, its insinuation of spontaneity, a writing according to the pressures of the day whether actual or remembered, its frequent comedies, and its use of musical-sounding verse for loosely narrative functions. Second, in place of satire, Berryman's temperament found literary elegy more natural. The proximity of the two kinds is probably closer than those uninterested in classical forms realize. Both literary satire and literary elegy tend to lament the imperfections of an Age, and the injustice of Fate. Yet mere suggestion of antecedents, while it might help provoke an understanding of Berryman's literary temperament, is more likely to emphasize that *Dream Songs* is a hybrid, a modern *poem*, and, in the context of Berryman's career of thoughts and feelings, one phase of his life's argument.

Berryman's life-in-his-poems has been probed, about as far as is decent. The poems ask for this. Autobiography was an adjunct of his understanding of Fame. But Henry is so unanimously accepted as Berryman himself that the imaginative function of the person-who-behaves-like-the-self in a poem has been neglected.

The self-as-subject is one of the problems raised, not only by Berryman's work, but by many contemporary poetries, those of Plath and Lowell in particular. Michael Berryhill, in an interesting essay, * hints at a solution to the problem as it concerns Berryman. He refers to the idea of "couvade" in

---

* "The Epistemology of Loss" in Richard J. Kelly, *John Berryman: A Checklist* (Scarecrow Press, 1972).

Dream Song 124—"Couvade was always Henry's favorite custom . . ."

As well as its meaning in anthropology, "couvade" also means "to brood, to do nothing." Both meanings are important in Berryman's work. There are many references to helplessness, inactivity, the state of being impractical and inert, bogged down in thought and considerations. And the degree of empathy, of "being another," which is involved in the anthropological meaning—when a man takes to an intuitive simulation of childbearing during his mate's real pregnancy—is exactly the degree of sympathy Berryman enacts, not only towards other people, but to Henry. Berryman is not Henry; but Henry *is* Berryman. Yet Henry, I speculate, is produced imaginatively, by a process in which psychological and imaginative necessities are satisfied together, not only as a cipher, or mask, through which Berryman can speak, but as, if you like, a "poet's friend." Out of his real self, Berryman drew another person who is, intuitively, and perhaps for psychological reasons I cannot pretend to understand, as like the real Berryman as makes no difference.

Whether this process results in a creation that can be called a "literary device" is questionable. It appears to be more personal, more to do with the nature of the poet's mind, and the consolations it needs to compensate for solitude and the nature of what he knows about himself. It could also be said to be fundamental in a poetry in which the self is exploited through imaginative recreations—as in Jarrell's monologues. Jarrell, writing "The Woman at the Washington Zoo," could have said, as Berryman did of his student in Dream Song 242—

> When she got
> control, I said "What's the matter—if you want to talk?"
> "Nothing. Nothing's the matter." So.
> I am her.

The writing here is even like Jarrell's. But in Berryman's circumstances, the implications of personal interchange, of a dangerous benevolence, are even more interesting, because more original. They are taken even further. Consider the despair, the predicament, of a man whose disciplined and large intellect allowed him to create an imaginary friend out of himself, whose fears, guilts, doubts and escapades he could describe and condemn. And is not that despair, that predicament, the substance of Berryman's writing? More than that, though. Is it not also a consequence of Berryman's creation of "other-Berryman," of Henry, that we consider the psychology behind it as perhaps an extreme instance of the dilemma of the contemporary poet, brought partially into the open, as it is here, by poetic form, by a technique which can be tentatively explained in psychological terms? Or the dilemma of a contemporary poet willing to face up to the turbulence of his life, of lives in general, in the context of what Valéry called "the most difficult of all the arts"? For Berryman never allowed his personal difficulties to intrude on an enduring fascination with metrics and all the stylistic problems of poems.

Homage to Mistress Bradstreet shows the beginnings of this psycho-technical literary feat. Berryman creates an imaginary life out of a real life, manufacturing predicaments said to be Anne's and her lover's, but personal to Berryman, invented by him, and to which he can respond—

> O all your ages at the mercy of my loves
> together lie at once, forever or
> so long as I happen.

It is also in *Homage to Mistress Bradstreet* that Berryman's "crumpled syntax" first makes itself obtrusive. His interest in a distinctive grammar dates from much earlier. In *Love & Fame,* he records the impact of a sentence from a review by R. P. Blackmur, read in the mid-thirties while still an undergraduate—

> "The art of poetry
> is amply distinguished from the manufacture of verse
> by an animating presence in the poetry
> of a fresh idiom: language
>
> so twisted and posed in a form
> that it not only expresses the matter in hand
> but adds to the stock of available reality."
> I was never altogether the same man after *that.*

More interestingly, Berryman says in his *Paris Review* interview that Saul Bellow's *Adventures of Augie March* gave him the inspiration for *Homage to Mistress Bradstreet*. Berryman probably meant this in the sense of creative impetus, the will to contribute to an exciting phase of American writing. The nature of Bellow's long and brilliant novel is pertinent, too. For one thing, it is delivered in the first person. *Augie March*, says Sidney Finkelstein, "has something of the character of a farewell to social responsibility," which is replaced by a sense of the world as absurd. Its damage can be held off by unscrupulousness, by laughter, by participation in absurdity, garrulously flowing with the world's tide as a means of staying sane on one hand, and of critically observing the nature of realities as the other objective. Such a stance, in poetry, avoids omniscience and hasty indignation.

Merely to recognize the world as absurd does not preclude suffering. Berryman's is a poetry of pain. It is about dying, about thwarted life, in which gaiety and lamentation, in almost equal proportions, or merged, seem equally pointless. Suicide is pondered so often in Berryman's poems that the opening sentence of Camus's *The Myth of Sisyphus* echoes with unsurprising inevitability—"There is but one truly serious philosophical problem, and that is suicide." Those who, like Claude Mauriac, considered Camus's theory of the absurd an argument which helped lead them from the spiritual confusion with which they had been struggling, testified, and still testify, despite the fresh popularities of Marxism, to the political and spiritual agonies of the times.

More and more it seems that the absence of a unifying intellectual system, one which possesses all the virtues of a humane philosophy, is responsible for the tortuous self-examination of writers. The European psyche and intelligence have had radical socialisms and fascisms to hang on to, as well as usually more placid religious or nationalist orthodoxies and conservatisms. Positive demands for political resistance have also been made. Yet the American writer has been unable to face these options with quite the same confidence; or, rather, quite the same version of the lack of it. He has been forced to rely on himself, fearing, as did Berryman, "the increasingly fanatical Americans" but unwilling to enter that same arena on an opposing platform, except that of the self-as-art—

> Take my vices alike
>
> with some my virtues, if you can find any.
> I stick up like Coriolanus with my scars
> for mob inspection.
> Only, dear, I am not running in any election
>
> I am not my gifted egomaniacal ally N. Mailer
>
> The *sorrows* of the Hero, Alexander's.
> The terrors of the Saint,—
> most people feel okay! Thoreau was *wrong,*
> he judged by himself.
>
> When I was fiddling later with every wife
> on the Eastern seaboard
> I longed to climb into a pulpit & confess.
> Tear me to pieces!
>
> Lincoln once wrote to a friend "I bite my lip & am quiet."

As a search for an individual and spiritual haven in which he could wait for the inevitable with an honest resignation, Berryman's poetry is a fair sample of a continuing phenomenon, albeit in his case magnified by genius. He writes about what it is like to possess formidable intelligence in a society where all aspirations appear negative, or frustrated from the start. His intelligence appears to have had no objective beyond that of writing poems. He recoils from public worsening, but not publicity. Personal disasters repeat themselves or return in shuddering, nerve-racking memories. His past is full of grief—his father's suicide, the deaths of his friends, his affairs and marriages. His drinking continues. His lapses of sanity come and go and recur. Yet all the time it is a poetry of waiting, a poetry of impending solutions, which were to come in the religious poems that close *Love & Fame,* and constitute much of *Delusions, Etc.* Early in *The Dream Songs,* we get

> It is in the administration of rhetoric,
> on these occasions, that—not the fathomless heart—
> the thinky death consists;
> his chest is pinched. The enemy are sick,
> and so is us of. Often, to rising trysts,
> like this one, drove he out
>
> and the gasps of love, after all, had got him ready.

> However things hurt, men hurt worse. He's stark
> to be jerked onward?
> Yes. In the headlights he got' keep him steady,
> leak not, look out over. This' hard work
> boss, wait' for The Word.

If Berryman was waiting for the imminence of the conditions on which he could be granted religious faith, parallel
with this sometimes bitter, sometimes humorous, sometimes
agonized patience, he also expected his own premature death.
It is a death that arises from thinking, knowing, and the inability to do—"Henry was morbid, inactive & a child to
Angst. . . ."
Not only does he imagine Henry writing as dead, but in
Dream Song 90, op. posth. no. 13, an elegy for Jarrell, he says

> The panic died and in the panic's dying
> so did my old friend. I am headed west
> also, also somehow.

One can long for one's own death, almost as a point of eti-
quette, when writing an elegy for a beloved friend. Berryman
would be drawn to that; his powers of identification, his "cos-
mic sympathies," would expect it of him. Yet he takes his own
death seriously, with morbid humor, rescuing Henry as an act
of perseverance, as a will to continue against odds, even if the
gesture is unconvincing. The fourteen "op. posth." poems,
pretending to be from beyond the grave, contain some of his
finest writing. Dream Song 86 shows his masterful abilities as
a mimic, a provider of voices, the work of a great poetic dramatist. It is to the service of *speaking,* of emphases and cir-
cumlocutions, that his unusual syntax is put.

Never able to collect his senses into a Stoic reasonableness,
Berryman's confused and solitary *Angst* is not typical of ex-
tremity, of being different from others, but of everyday passions he had to live with. "The ordinariness of the days was
what it was all about," says Saul Bellow in his gently incisive
memoir that prefaces *Recovery,* Berryman's posthumous and
incomplete novel, in its own right a remarkable dramatization
of the agonies of alcoholism. His poems are so close to a sense

of life, an imparting of truth complete with the bias of technique and personality, that they have the true flavor of fiction.
An enormously comprehensive and unsentimental pathos
slips out of his work, complicated and perplexing. We realize
that although it may all be about ordinary Berryman, it generalizes itself, it has compass.

His generous humanity is neglected by those who shy away
from the oddness of his voice, or the grotesque inventions of
his imagination. "Lunatic exotica," they say. "Why, he always
puts in an ampersand, and never writes 'and.' How can *that*
be good?" But Berryman has much to say, wisely and with
pleasure, of the human condition, as in Dream Song 264,
which begins

> I always wanted to be old, I wanted to say
> "O I haven't read that for fifteen years"
> or "my copy of that
> seems in the usual course to have gone astray"
> or "She—that woman moved me to young tears,
> even Henry Cat."

The seriousness with which Berryman engaged with the
problems of writing, of achieving a contemporary idiom as a
matter of priority, is what marks him off from most British
talents. At times, his erudition on the subject of styles, prac-
tical though it was, is inhibiting. In his *Sonnets* especially,
though elsewhere too, he courts the traditions of writing as
self-consciously as he seeks the truths of experience. The tension in such a method is familiar from the modernism of Eliot
and Pound. It is no novelty.

Yet Berryman's appreciation of creativity is a despairing
one. It does him no good in the midst of his troubles. It even
helps to make them. "The original crime," he wrote— "art,
rime." Later in *The Dream Songs* he amplifies on this,

> Wait the lime-pits for all originators,
> wounded propped up to be executed,
> afterwards known as martyrs,

a view which appears to be in abject opposition to the facetious confidence with which he refers to his "large work,

which will appear, and baffle everybody." But the willingness to amaze, to annoy and put off stride, is a consequence of his perception of "originators" as inevitably fated to sordid "execution," followed by indecently swift and philistine canonization.

Alienated writers, i.e. all contemporary writers with a proper knowledge of what contemporaneity is, do not seek repose. They know it will not be granted on the honest terms of art. It would involve compromise with ideologies, communist or capitalist (as they are practiced); and, by compromising, they would subordinate the freedom inherent in the nature of art to totalitarian decision on one hand, and the freedom to buy and sell on the other. Instead, a poet like Berryman looks for revenge in the name of art, and longs for the reform of caricatured cultural processes in societies which uphold them as constituent parts of their order. That, or something like it, is a fundamental position behind Berryman's work. He is a political poet without politics.

Of the struggle to work against pressures of personal and artistic difficulties, he wrote,

> Hunger was constitutional with him,
> women, cigarettes, liquor, need need need
> until he went to pieces.
> The pieces sat up and wrote. They did not heed
> their piecedom but kept very quietly on
> among the chaos.

"But kept very quietly on"—Berryman felt it necessary to say that formality and mannerisms, habitual skill, controlled his personal disintegration for literature. He took personal and artistic pride in being both self-consciously *maudit* as well as accomplished, "the steadiest man on the Block" for some things.

In Dream Song 310 he began, "His gift receded. He could write no more." Plagued with literary exhaustion at several points in his life, in this poem it leads him to consider Goethe's advice to idle "when no theme presents itself." He then modulates to German literature generally. Kafka provides him with,

> Henry, monstrous bug, laid himself down
> on the machine in the penal colony
> without a single regret,

just as Kafka gave him the first line in the previous quotation. Other literature is a catalyst to his despair. He is the victim of his reading. His worries metamorphose it to life in his imagination. His quandaries multiply. He inserts himself into other writers' images; or into images from films (Dream Songs 7 and 9, for instance); or into the idiom of blues singers and jazz musicians,

> we will blow our best,
> our sad wild riffs come easy in that case . . .

posed against the idiom of Elizabethan drama.

Demotic American culture and the "valiant art" of literary and musical heroes are all part of his wayward mixture of styles, which he enjoyed to blend and contrast. "This writing," he appears to say, "is like the varieties of the world, its madnesses. Drive-ins and Hölderlin; cigarettes and Kafka; high-yaller whores and the duel between John Day and Henry Porter; Strindberg and blues; Humphrey Bogart and St. Anselm."

Avoiding pomposity, Berryman's sense of humor is the sort, he said, "fatal to bardic pretension." A sweep as mundane, carnal and sacred as Berryman's, so many things at once, not only deflated any tendency to indulge in high rhetoric—giving us a "monotonous sublime" that pretended not to be monotonous—but heightened his serious moods, adding an awkward earnestness. It was all part of his *performance,* a bravado of both high and low spirits.

Enraptured by self-destructive necessities, Berryman sought consolation in theology, literature and philosophy; and these became part of the rapture. Final consolation arrived in the form of Catholicism, a religion he had known as a boy. Of God, he writes with an idiom and simplicity of reverence reminiscent of Stevie Smith—

> You have come to my rescue again & again
> in my impassable, sometimes despairing years.

> You have allowed my brilliant friends to destroy themselves
> and I am still here, severely damaged, but functioning.
>
> Unknowable, as I am unknown to my guinea-pigs:
> but how can I "love" you?
> I only as far as gratitude & awe
> confidently & absolutely go.

His religious poems in *Love & Fame* are intended to "criticize backward" the earlier, scandalous sections; and, presumably, the carnality, comedy and religious doubts of *Dream Songs* as well. The religious conscience which had said of a Saint's Day—

> We celebrate her feast with our caps on,
> whom God has not visited—

converted the invisible God of appeal to one palpably of rescue. His new spiritual situation demanded penitence, which he says he couldn't muster, not even for the promise of glory. Berryman may have discovered faith, and its attendant certainties; but a nervous edge, an incompletion, was to remain. Nor was his language to be greatly altered in these later poems. It is still "mixed" and quirky in "The Facts & Issues."

Berryman's manic grasp at salvation and safety can be respected; at least, it is by me. Yet I cannot help but count myself among those whom Berryman realized would not "buy" his answers, those whom Berryman said were "deluded," who will say in return Berryman was "deluded" too. Poets are tricked by their emergencies. Their talents are stunted and held back by an insurmountable political and spiritual impasse. Mere decision is insufficient to overcome it. No idealism, no forecast, no vision; they have somehow become unclean. Poets can still rise out of their miseries to mourn and condemn large tragedies, for which there is a monstrous appetite—the Camps, Viet Nam, Ulster. But to alter the psychologies that make them possible?

To move even tentatively in that direction calls for such an active participation in the atmosphere of the times, a comprehensive literature of insult and recommendation, that its difficulty withholds poets from the attempt. "Alienation" is now a commonplace. We take it for granted that a poet walks in a different direction from that of the society he lives in. "How could it be otherwise," we ask, "when only commissars, lairds, captains of industry, the rich and the subservient, are satisfied by existing orders?"

It is probably true to say not only that poets like Berryman, ambitious poets who honor poetry by attempts at odyssey and who picture "the individual soul under stress," become alienated from external society, but that the man who writes grows to despise the man who lives. The whole business ends in the agony of attempting to salvage one's own soul, in turning one's back on the profane; and in seeking, not to embody or criticize, but to worship the unknowable, in a tragic evasion of causes.

What of the world Berryman turned his back on, which defeated him? Of death and the "extremist poets," Lowell, in his glowing and affectionate memorial to Berryman in the *New York Review of Books*, said—

> Were they killed, as standard radicals say, by our corrupted society? Was their success an aspect of their destruction? Were we uncomfortable epigoni of Frost, Pound, Eliot, Marianne Moore, etc.? This bitter possibility came to us at the moment of our *arrival*. Death comes sooner or later, these made it sooner.

His late conversion—not his death, which is Berryman's business—involved a partial "rescue" which is more significant than a claim that God intervened on his behalf, his own literal understanding of it. He willed it. It proves the honesty of his anguish at the cruelty of the world, the competition without kindness. Yet it derives from fatigue. Poets, defeated by their material, withdraw into their own exhaustion. Those who read their work, without the slightest intention of allowing it to bother them, look at this exhaustion, at the poet, a pitiful heap of vices, exasperations and hopes, and call the heap an illustration of "the strength of the human spirit," mentioning, perhaps, "the alienation of the artist," because they have been told. The world suffers no loss at the death of a poet. It paid little attention to him when he lived. There appears to be no end to the defeats poetry must continue to face.

♉

Berryman's Long Dream

Denis Donoghue

John Berryman has now completed the long poem, *The Dream Songs*, begun in 1955. The first part of the dream was published in 1964 as *77 Dream Songs*. Songs 78-385, the middle and the end, are given now as *His Toy, His Dream, His Rest*.

In Song 354 Mr. Berryman writes three stanzas of sardonic meditation on the problem of the long poem. "The only happy people in the world," he sings, "are those who do not have to write long poems." An unwritten essay is called "The Care and Feeding of Long Poems." The poet planned to consult President Johnson on the problem, during his ten seconds in the receiving line at the White House. But the invitation reached him too late, an ocean away, in Ireland. So the problem persisted, until the poet resolved it in his own way. His own way; not Eliot's way in *Four Quartets*, Williams's way in *Paterson*, Pound's way in the *Cantos*, or Hart Crane's way in *The Bridge*. It comes to a question of form; how to be free and law-abiding at the same time. Or how to ensure that the whole poem is greater than the sum of its parts. In the twentieth century a poet feels incomplete, apparently, until he has written a long poem. He wants a mighty reach, a span, everything implied and encompassed, not merely one little poem and then another little poem. Mr. Berryman's answer was to conceive a diary, a dream diary, in which the dream would allow the poet every desirable kind of freedom, and law could be acknowledged in the movement of time, the insistence of years, decay, death. It is always an open question, how free a poet should be in his poem. Perhaps the answer is: as free as he needs to be. But in extreme cases the price is high.

Denis Donoghue, "Berryman's Long Dream," *Art International* 13 (March 20, 1969): 61–64.

Mr. Berryman's case is extreme. On the understanding, perhaps, that one *Song of Myself* is enough, he decided to hand over his entire dream world to an invented character called Henry, not to be confused with John Berryman, author and poet.

> The poem then, whatever its wide cast of characters, is essentially about an imaginary character (not the poet, not me) named Henry, a white American in early middle age sometimes in blackface, who has suffered an irreversible loss and talks about himself sometimes in the first person, sometimes in the third, sometimes even in the second; he has a friend, never named, who addresses him as Mr. Bones and variants thereof. Requiescant in pace.

Amen, indeed. Mr. Berryman is hard on those readers who think that Henry Pussy-Cat is just a pet name for John Berryman; he is impatient. Has he not assured us that H.P. and J.B. are two, not one? Has he not arranged to send H.P. into death before the long dream is over, so that the last dream songs are sung by a Lazarus, come back to tell all? Is not this enough? Thus far, the case is simple. When we read of Henry on LSD, we do not think of Mr. Berryman as a devotee of acid. And so on. For my own part, I have no difficulty in accepting the invented character Henry as distinct from his maker in the 77 *Dream Songs*. I might have confused them in the dark. But as the dreams continue in the new and last book, the identity of Henry as distinct from J.B. becomes harder to take. "Edgy Henry" begins to collapse into his poet, and the poem begins to sound like the *Song of Myself*. This would not matter if it were a different kind of poem.

On the first page of the first dream song we read, stanza 3:

> What he has now to say is a long
> wonder the world can bear & be.
> Once in a sycamore I was glad
> all at the top, and I sang.
> Hard on the land wears the strong sea
> and empty grows every bed.

Three voices, two lines each, speaking in one stanza. The first voice is objective, the poet introducing his character, giving the gist of his theme. The second voice may be received as

Henry's voice, recalling the good times, sycamores and songs. But the third voice is different from either; it is generic, representative, apocalyptic, Mankind rather than any particular man, Henry or J.B. or anyone else. In this third voice the feeling is universal rather than local; it is consistent with the first and second voices, but distinct, as if its experience were the history of the world rather than the fate of a man. It is my understanding that these three voices are nearly as many as the poet requires for his long poem: the unidentified friend who addresses Henry occasionally as Mr. Bones uses an Al Jolson voice and a chocolate idiom to admonish his white American friend, but beyond that degree he is hardly distinguished from any other figure, silent, sympathetic, watchful. So the three voices are nearly enough.

It is my impression that Mr. Berryman first practiced this procedure in an early story called "The Imaginary Jew" (1945). The Gentile hero, by a great reach of sympathy, becomes an imaginary Jew, fights the Jew's battles, accepts insult. At the end he says to himself:

> In the days following, as my resentment died, I saw that I had not been a victim altogether unjustly. My persecutors were right: I was a Jew. The imaginary Jew I was was as real as the imaginary Jew hunted down, on other nights and days, in a real Jew. Every murderer strikes the mirror, the lash of the torturer falls on the mirror and cuts the real image, and the real and the imaginary blood flow down together.

A Gentile who becomes an imaginary Jew by an act of sympathy is perhaps as complete as a modern man can be. The corresponding power in poetry is the dramatic imagination. Mr. Berryman is not a dramatist, but he is gifted in dramatic narrative, as in *Homage to Mistress Bradstreet*, where several voices are distinguished, each bearing its proper burden, its own history. The three voices heard in the first song are also practiced in the poem to Anne Bradstreet. Sometimes the words on the page carry Anne's voice, her experience, her character; sometimes different words, with a different rhythm and a different syntax, carry her husband's voice. And sometimes Anne's husband is enabled to speak, as Mr. Berryman says in a gloss, "at last, in the fortune of an echo of her—and when she is loneliest . . . as if she had summoned

him; and only thus, perhaps, is she enabled to hear him."
Often, in the same poem, what we hear is the poet's voice,
leading our feeling, helping us to feel more deeply, more rele-
vantly. Often, too, the voice we hear is generic, distant, im-
perious, as if God were to speak of his servant Anne.
Sometimes, to end his list, the poet speaks for Anne, knowing
that, poet as she was in her own need, she often failed to
speak for herself, or spoke haltingly, lacking one of the gifts.

So to the dream songs of an imaginary Jew. The hint is given
in Song 48, where we read of

> a Greek idea,
> troublesome to imaginary Jews,
> like bitter Henry, full of the death of love . . .

Or again in Song 310:

> Henry, monstrous bug, laid himself down
> on the machine in the penal colony
> without a single regret.

Monstrous bug; that is, Gregor Samsa in Kafka's *Metamorphosis*. Laid himself down; that is, the officer in Kafka's *In
the Penal Colony*. At this stage Henry has only to name a victim, and he becomes that victim. The corresponding gesture
in the poet has the effect of sacrificing a single voice, John
Berryman's voice, for the sake of other voices. The poet gives
up his egotistical sublimity, accepting the modest role of medium. He becomes a shell, through which the sea speaks. In
Song 38 the poet Robert Frost is invoked as "the quirky medium of so many truths." A comic version of the poet as medium
is given in Song 143, the poet as vaudeville man: "Honour the
burnt cork." Hazlitt said of Shakespeare that "he was nothing
in himself; but he was all that others were"; an ideal state,
endless humility, toward which the inventor of Henry strives,
in principle. In principle, in theory, and in the practice of the
77 Dream Songs, where the grace of humility receives many
poetic favors. In these poems the content may be drawn, for
all I know, from Mr. Berryman's own experience. He may indeed have seen a woman, "complexion Latin," filling her compact and delicious body with chicken paprika; he may have
seen Paul Muni in *The Prisoner of Shark Island;* his mother

may have said to him, "Ever to confess you're bored means you have no Inner Resources." It may be so. But in these well-tempered songs the poet has imposed upon these experiences a particular test; he has not merely transcribed them as remembered. Rather, he has tested them, sending them away to reside in another character, Henry, and receiving them back only when they have survived the journey. That is to say: even if these are his own experiences, he has tested them as if they were newly invented. Actual experience has always one advantage; it does not need to be invented. But to transcribe the experience is one thing; and it may not be enough. There is another way; to begin by depriving the experience of its advantage, and then to insist that it must earn any merit to be assigned. The merit is earned by subjecting the experience to new trials, different from those mysterious trials which it survived by coming into time and history. We say that these new trials are aesthetic, but that is only another way of saying that, for poetic purposes, history is not enough. There is also art.

This is why we attend to virtues and vices in poetry only to the extent that they are now, at last, verbal; they have survived their own element and now they have established themselves in a new element, words, grammar, syntax, rhetoric. Often when we attend to a phrase, a line, a stanza in a poem, we delight in its finesse, its propriety; knowing that this perfection is the second and later grace, the first being perhaps a moral perception, the adjudication of acts and sufferings in the world before these have become verbal. Mature art is the process of a double establishment, the result of a double test. I think of Mr. Berryman's Song 16, beginning "Henry's pelt was put on sundry walls." The poem is apparently indebted to an aphorism by (I think) Gottfried Benn: "We are using our skins for wallpaper, and we cannot win." The sentiment is congenial, however rueful, because it endorses Berryman's notion of the poet as society's scapegoat, its chosen victim. The poem is concerned with the cost of public victory in private defeat. Cocktail bars are gorgeously furnished, clothed with the richest wallpaper, because a poet's skin is ready. In Sealdah Station "some possessionless / children survive to die," and therefore "the Chinese communes hum." The song ends:

> Two daiquiris
> withdrew into a corner of the gorgeous room
> and one told the other a lie.

Perhaps it is enough to receive this in the witty terms in
which it is given. But even if the experience is recalled rather
than invented, it is not merely transcribed. Indeed, it would
be useful to ponder the relation between the experience and
its final establishment in the words. I have no information on
its first establishment, apart from the liberty of an amateur
guess. My guess is that the experience was either actual or
virtual; such incidents are common. Perhaps the first stage
began and ended there, as a minor incident. The second stage
began, I continue to guess, when the poet introduced the incident into a poetic rhythm already partly rehearsed, a
rhythm of the public and the private worlds, set off one
against the other. In another cadence, this might set the pretentious public world against the even deadlier facts of the
case. For this purpose it would be necessary to reduce the par-
ticipants; as by calling two people two daiquiris. It would then
be proper to give the public setting in terms grand and false:
the two daiquiris "withdrew into a corner of the gorgeous
room." And then the bare private truth: "and one told the
other a lie." The second establishment, then, is an act of the
imagination, conspiring with certain possibilities in diction,
syntax, and rhythm. History and fact are not enough.

   The procedure is strict, the aesthetic abstemious. I shall
argue on the evidence of the later songs that Mr. Berryman
found the rules too hard, and sought an easier course, at some
cost to the poems. The long dream began with Henry already
ill, at a loss, defeated; the game is up. In Song 28 he says, "If
I had to do the whole thing over again / I wouldn't." Song 29
has all the bells saying, "too late." So Henry's letter to the
world, reasonably enough, is a rejection slip, a curse. The bad
gangs thrive. Nature is good, but man is not: "Pleased, at the
worst, except with a man, he shook / the brightest winter
sun." There is still time for another song, a fine gesture: "But
the snows and summers grieve & dream." For the rest, Henry's life is a crash program, a holding operation so long as the
operation holds. There is a plot of sorts: Henry down to the
grave and, briefly, back again. But increasingly, as the night

darkens, the singer wearies of the rigor, the discipline of the
dramatic imagination. If Wordsworth got away with the egotistical sublime, why not Henry, why not Mr. Berryman? The
change comes, as a matter of aesthetic insistence, in Song
141:

> Duly he does his needful little then
> with a chest of ice, a head tipping with pain.
> That perhaps is his programme,
> cause: Henry for Henry in the main:
> he'll push it: down with anything Bostonian:
> even god howled "I am."

Anything Bostonian is genteel, proper, Jamesian (Henry). In
Notes of a Son and Brother James said that Boston seemed
"more expressive than I had supposed an American city could
be of a seated and rooted social order, an order not complex
but sensibly fixed." To Henry, no tolerable order is sensibly
fixed; the self, responsible to nothing in Boston, howls, "I
am." Song 133 says, "It seems to be solely a matter of continuing Henry / voicing & obsessed." The data, Henry decides in
Song 148, "were abundantly his / or if not, never." Increasingly, as the voicing continues, everything becomes not
itself but a function of Henry's obsession. In Song 219 he re-
bukes Wallace Stevens for lifting the metaphysics so high that
the physics is lost. For himself, in Song 370, he claims em-
pirical innocence, "not a symbol in the place." But in fact the
self is the only center, and the circumference is derived from
that center. Whitman, "the great Walt," is properly invoked.
The structure of the poem is glossed in Song 293, "not
cliffhangers or old serials / but according to his nature." I take
this to mean: down with any structure Bostonian, objective,
independent. The structure comes from within, or it does not
come at all. There is no classic order among the materials;
order is to be imposed rather than discovered. In Song 305 the
aesthetic procedure is given as attention to the means rather
than the end; presumably because a projected end implies a
classic order waiting to be unfolded. The means: what else
but to work according to one's nature. That is to say: anything
goes, if it comes from within. Another version turns up in
Song 311:

> Hunger was constitutional with him,
> women, cigarettes, liquor, need need need
> until he went to pieces.
> The pieces sat up & wrote. They did not heed
> their piecedom but kept very quietly on
> among the chaos.

This is ingenious. A poet, living in various degrees of chaos, dissociates himself; allowing to each fragment its corresponding voice. The fragments scream; that is, sing. The whole man, undissociated, is to be found as the sum of his parts; as *The Dream Songs* is the sum of 385 separate songs. The pieces are sanctioned by a nature which is their sum; the more diverse the pieces, the greater the nature. This is not Whitman's way. Whitman's aesthetic implies that the self is the sum of its experiences, not the sum of its dissociated fragments. In Whitman the self is not dissociated, the self is deemed to be whole at any and every moment. The experiences are diverse; as one experience follows upon another, the receiving self is enlarged. But the self is never understood as a fraction; it is always a whole number. The history of the self is the history of its possessions; what it possesses is an ever increasing body of experience. As the experiences accrue, the self expands. So the self corresponds with the world by sharing its procedures; accumulation, addition, arithmetic, possession. In Mr. Berryman's poems the self is heard in fragments. The poet's hope is that as the poems proceed, page by page, the fragments will be so various, so compelling, that only a unified sensibility could emerge, at the last.

Perhaps this goes part way to account for Mr. Berryman's characteristic syntax. He does not run to Whitman's long line, the loose line of feeling. Whitman's syntax is the mark of his confidence: he knows, trusting himself, that he can go along with his experience in any direction; his confidence is expansive because the world is promise. But the world is a threat, to Mr. Berryman; it has made no promise. Everywhere in *The Dream Songs* the world is an obstacle, a troublemaker; it takes away more than it gives. Landscape is often charming, but man's deeds are vindictive. Men walk the earth, it appears, to thwart Henry, finally to break him in pieces. So Mr. Berryman's typical syntax, especially in the later songs, is intensive rather than expansive; he favors the short line, the isolated perception, as a form of defense or reprisal. Normally the sentence features the bare report, with an air of finality; doom accomplished. Only the voice, constitutionally in need, breaks silence and keeps the show going. After such knowledge, the long dream proposes, there is very little to say; but that little is better than nothing. So: say it. Repeat it, if it helps to fend off the void:

> In sleep, of a heart attack, let Henry go.
> The end of tennis. The beginning of the dark.
> The beginning of the wagon.
> It is the onward coming terrifies.
> Now at last the effort to make him kill himself
> has failed.
>
> Take down the thing then to which he was nailed.
> I am a boat was moored on the wrong shelf.
> Love has wings & flies.

This is more like Roethke's syntax than like anything in Whitman; and for good reason. In Roethke as in Mr. Berryman the only hope is to shore a few fragments against one's ruin. The life of a modern poet is representative; that is, vestigial. The only distinction that is relevant is the distinction between those few fragments and the other thing; nothing, Nil. A corresponding syntax is likely to be aggressive, defensive; it captures one thing here and another there, and it holds on to its possessions. The poet lives by his nature, that is, by his constitutional needs.

We come back to Henry, upon whose needs Mr. Berryman insists. I have argued that in the middle and later songs it has become increasingly difficult to take Henry seriously as a character distinct from his maker. It is not a question of the materials; though it is easy to demonstrate that, for the most part, Henry's experience in fiction coincides with Mr. Berryman's experience in fact. Often, the occasion of a poem is the arrival of the postman with a letter or this week's issue of the *Times Literary Supplement*. In Song 293 the poet refers to the "hotspur materials" of his Book VII, but most of them are, at least in Hamlet's sense, common. The following is a short list of motifs: fear, lust, irritation, "ensamples violent," travel, Death, Death, Death, poetry, rest, marriage, divorce, sex, daughters, butterflies, lectures, money, prizes, fame. More specifically: there are poems about Mr. Berryman's friends and colleagues, Randall Jarrell, Delmore Schwartz, Roethke, Robert Frost, R. P. Blackmur, William Carlos Williams, Yvor Winters; poems about Eisenhower's presidency, an M.L.A. meeting in Chicago or New York, a BBC TV show in which the star was the poet John Berryman, the co-star his daughter, a year lived in Dublin, the misery of Vietnam, Sylvia Plath's suicide, John F. Kennedy, Hemingway, Jonathan Swift, W. B. Yeats; even Christine Keeler. Song 23 interpolated "O Adlai mine." Much of one's life is what the postman brings. No, it is not a question of the materials. But Mr. Berryman claims to give these materials to his man, Henry, and that this makes a difference. There is an established aesthetic tradition to support the claim: its most distinctive modern adepts are W. B. Yeats and Ezra Pound. Yeats says in *Estrangement* that "there is a relation between discipline and the theatrical sense." "If we cannot imagine ourselves as different from what we are and assume that second self, we cannot impose a discipline upon ourselves, though we may accept one from others. Active virtue as distinguished from the passive acceptance of a current code is therefore theatrical, consciously dramatic, the wearing of a mask." This is the text we need: it is the application of the theatrical metaphor to the common idea of a creative imagination. In such cases the imagination is creative because it imagines forms of life different from its own, and assumes those forms. The process is continuously dramatic, interrogative. The relation between discipline and the theatrical sense is based upon the fact that, given the theatrical sense as described, the self may ignore itself, may ignore its own nature. Whitman extends his nature by adding to its experiences. Yeats extends his nature the other way, from within; not by adding to the materials, but by conceiving different ways of receiving them. The multiplicity is active within, not without. The discipline is active within, not without. Pound's theory of the *persona* is more or less the same as Yeats's, so far as it is a genuine theory at all. In practice, Pound's imagination is not remarkable in a theatrical way; it does not naturally operate by conceiving several different selves. It is too authoritarian for that. The result is that when Pound proposes a *persona*, distinct from himself, the distinction is highly doubtful; as in *Hugh Selwyn Mauberley*. Mauberley is like Mr. Berryman's Henry in the later stages of *The Dream Songs;* he is not, in Yeats's sense, a mask, he is merely a disguise. There is a difference. A figure disguises himself for his protection, not for self-discipline. Behind the disguise he is the same as ever, and he is determined to remain so. The last thing he wants is to change. He does not propose to extend his nature; he proposes to defend it. This applies even more to Henry than to Mauberley. In *Mauberley* Pound tries to detect the meretricious elements in his man, and fails largely because he is not gifted in self-detection. But in the later songs the gap between Henry and his maker is closed: Mr. Berryman's effort to maintain a distance is perfunctory. The hotspur materials are the same materials, and there is no sense of a receiving self different from his own.

Mr. Berryman has proposed to himself the discipline of dramatic character, but he has not, in the later songs, accepted its obligations. The first result is that discipline is intermittent and haphazard. Yeats's method, if fully endorsed in practice, would ensure discipline at every moment. Mr. Berryman's discipline is not ensured. Sometimes it is provided by a sense of poetic achievements different from his own, and the pressure of a literary tradition. Song 171 accepts the relevance of Waller's poem "Go, Lovely Rose"; so Waller's feeling is a witness, a presence which must not be disgraced. In Song 285 the discipline comes, for the moment, from within; its sign, the ironic use of an elaborately learned idiom:

> Much petted Henry like a petal throve,
> his narthex let the girls & pupils in,
> aptotic he remained
> Henry's own man, when he squirmed not in love,
> fifty pressures herded one discipline:
> the sun shot up, it rained,
> weathering Henry kept on his own side,
> whatever in the name of God that side was.
> And he struggled, pal.
> Apricate never: too he took in his stride
> more than most monsters can . . .

And so on, for another stanza. Let us say that Henry, on a transatlantic liner, has avoided shipboard romance and is pleased, with reservations natural in the circumstances. Narthex: several meanings, including a tall plant, a perfume case, but especially that part of an early Christian church which was reserved for monks or for women. So: he lets women in, but only under controlled and innocent conditions. Aptotic: referring to a noun that has no distinction of cases; or to languages that have no grammatical inflections; transferred now to a poet, a language-man resistant, unyielding, retaining his virtue. Apricate never: never exposed to the sun, never basking in the sun with the stripped-down girls. The stanza is not momentous, but it has something of that wit which Eliot described in his essay on Marvell: "a tough reasonableness beneath the slight lyric grace." The note of wit is here the mark of discipline. In other moments Mr. Berryman has accepted discipline from other sources. In the *Homage to Mistress Bradstreet* two of the finest occasions accept other voices. In stanza 13, "I found my heart more carnal and sitting loose from God" is taken from Anne's *My Dear Children*. In stanza 33 a wonderful phrase, "Wan dolls in indigo on gold" is taken from Baron Corvo's *The Desire and Pursuit of the Whole*.

It is my impression that in the later songs attention to other voices has receded. Increasingly, there is one voice, doctrinaire, edgy, magisterial. The question is: what does the change denote? It may be innocent; meaning merely that Mr. Berryman found the pretense a bit of a bore, Henry a nuisance, after a while. Or it may mean that, as the poems proceeded, Mr. Berryman found that the sole indelible interest was his own emotion. Hotspur materials, hotspur emotions. Santayana, writing of Whitman and Browning as barbarians, said that the barbarian is one "who regards his passions as their own excuse for being." Is it not true that, in the later poems, Mr. Berryman came to feel thus tenderly for his own passions, so that nothing beyond their constitutional need seemed real or potent? Keats spoke of the egotistical sublime as Wordsworthian; it was Wordsworth's way of coloring every natural form with his own sensibility. At one extreme, such an artist comes to feel that the natural event is nothing, his own sensibility everything.

So the later Berryman is Wordsworthian, at least in his

new character. But it is necessary to distinguish further, since this way of poetry includes the best as well as the worst in Mr. Berryman. The relation between passion and perception is never easy to specify. There are occasions on which the passion takes the form of energy surrounding the perception; perception is the center, passion the circumference. There are other occasions on which the perception is merely ostensible, and the real center is the passion; where the perception is entertained for the sake of the passion. In Song 321, for instance, Mr. Berryman composes a loud invocation to Ireland, with much talk of Connolly, Pearse, Joyce, Yeats, Swift, Synge, O'Casey, Kavanagh, and Clarke. The poem is crude by any reckoning; it is a bad poem. But in fact it is not a poem about Ireland at all, despite the heroic names; it is about John Berryman and his high horse. The natural forms, the historical references, are merely occasional; they are hired to serve the poet, to let him mount the horse. Obviously it makes no difference to the poem, and no improvement, if we agree to call the horseman Henry rather than Mr. Berryman. In Song 385, on the other hand, while the mode is still Wordsworthian, the direction of feeling is something other (I give the poem entire):

> My daughter's heavier. Light leaves are flying.
> Everywhere in enormous numbers turkeys will be dying
> and other birds, all their wings.
> They never greatly flew. Did they wish to?
> I should know. Off away somewhere once I knew
> such things.
>
> Or good Ralph Hodgson back then did, or does.
> The man is dead whom Eliot praised. My praise
> follows and flows too late.
> Fall is grievy, brisk. Tears behind the eyes
> almost fall. Fall comes to us as a prize
> to rouse us toward our fate.
>
> My house is made of wood and it's made well,
> unlike us. My house is older than Henry;
> that's fairly old.
> If there were a middle   ground between things and the soul
> or if the sky resembled more the sea,

> I wouldn't have to scold
>   my heavy daughter.

The reference to Henry is perfunctory; the play is not a
Henriad. Rather, our poet is speaking *in propria persona,* husband and father, poet, too, representative man. The first
stanza is all reverie, the mind moving easily, picking its way
by association, one sound calling to another: heavy daughter,
light leaves; flying, dying. "They never greatly flew"; in context, after 384 poems in which success and failure were pondered, the sentence is more evocative than it would be
elsewhere. Recall in *Ulysses:* "They flew. Where to? Paris and
back. Newhaven–Dieppe. . . ." (I speak from memory.) For
the moment, the words stand for all forms of loss, including
the irreversible loss from which the whole enterprise began.
From loss to genial success: Ralph Hodgson is hardly a heavy-
weight success, no Shakespeare, no Dante. But for that very
reason he is invoked here, to mark the easy happiness available to those good people who accept what they are given by
the gods. Hodgson is memorialized in Eliot's *Five-Finger Exercises* as the delightful owner of a Baskerville hound, unnum-
bered finches and fairies, and 999 canaries. It is proper, in
reverie, to let the name come as it will, mediated through
Eliot's little poem. It is not a time for heavy guns. The key
word in this stanza is *fall,* the poet intones it thrice, noun,
verb, noun; surrounding it with a correspondent rhyme, "too
late," "our fate." Eliot persists in the background, mainly
through the recollection of Gerontion enforced by the first
lines of the last stanza here: in Eliot's poem, "My house is a
decayed house." In Mr. Berryman's poem the house is firm,
we are the decay. In the last lines the intimations of loss and
fall are translated into immediately domestic terms: the tone
is not apocalyptic, though it might be so if the same losses and
falls were violently sensed. Mr. Berryman's "sense of an ending" is gentle, the lines—it is proper to say—are beautiful. In
the reading, according to the print, we are to hover between
"middle" and "ground"; or rather, we are to feel the gap while
stretching across it. The stretching is desire, the fact is the
gap. The poet longs for a mediating ground, first, between
things and the soul; and then he longs for a structure of correspondence and analogy, one thing linked to another. The old

continuity of things is lost. There are gaps everywhere; as now between loving father and heavy daughter. Surely this poem is not the work of a barbarian: the poem is all perception, surrounded by feeling. The feeling is not on show, on parade; it comes into the lines only because it attends upon perceptions which could not appear without that favor. The end is good.

ॐ

Cagey John

BERRYMAN AS MEDICINE MAN

WILLIAM WASSERSTROM

No doubt the situation of the writer in America has always been difficult,
his responsibilities always enormous. But they are even more extreme now
because everything seems to be turning in on him at once. The mass soci-
ety in which he lives is becoming even more massive, more monolithic,
devious, and even more anxious to swallow him up whole. At the same
time, the under-forces he can sense at work are more violent, more de-
structive, and more impossible to contain or deny. And the certainties have
become fewer. . . . Even the dominant creed of modern America, that of
psychoanalysis, helps only to thrust the artist more deeply in on himself.
So he is left alone to play out by ear his art, his identity, and even his
society on the page in front of him.

A. ALVAREZ

I

With Theodore Roethke's death, Randall Jarrell's and Delmore Schwartz's, three of the half-dozen superbly endowed
poets of the American middle generation are now gone. Those
who remain, John Berryman, Karl Shapiro, Robert Lowell,
survive in the state of touch-and-go. Although it is no longer
helpful to speak of this as a condition of the literary life in
America, the matter is dramatic enough to warrant mention
and to require, someday, sorting out. Survival itself, however,

William Wasserstrom, "Cagey John: Berryman as Medicine Man," *Centennial*
Review (summer 1968): 334–54.

despite disease and gloom, is impressive too. And for all the cachet and power lately come to Lowell and to the Lowell circle at the *New York Review of Books,* it is less Lowell's endurance than Berryman's which must be celebrated. For it is Berryman's genius that contrives a poetry which blends the twin modes of work and purpose common to all American arts today—measure and balance on the one hand and, on the other, a scarcely controlled explosion of immoderate passion. In William Burroughs's fiction, Norman O. Brown's criticism and Berryman's verse, 77 *Dream Songs,* we are confronted by accomplishment of quite a new kind, the attainment of New Apocalyptists, cooked and raw, a ritual ceremony of revelation so fierce and intricate that their work most perplexes those whom it most enchants.

Despite the attention lavished on Berryman's songs, despite a Pulitzer Prize and a unanimity of opinion on the poet's gifts, there are two opposing general views on Berryman's art. Some see artifice where others find innovation, footwork not choreography—as if these poems represented the mind of still another camp follower of apocalypse, a sort of death-of-god man or one of Warhol's Chelsea boys. Those who contend that the poems express a failure, not a feat of language, ascribe this to a defeat of the American artist's will to enact the role of a public poet in a society whose quality and tone must defeat any poet's will. Clotted in the act of utterance, it is said, Berryman does not fuse arcane learning and mother wit, formal speech and demotic. Rather, he resorts to idiosyncrasy and inversion, quirks and tics of diction which exhibit a mind at the end of its tether and do not display means to unlock those fetters which jail the mind.

Negative opinion at its harshest, Philip Toynbee's essay in *Encounter* (March 1965), turns on that critic's effort to "throw a certain doubt on Allen Tate's belief that Berryman's poetry 'cannot be imitated.' " Toynbee offers five samples of Berryman's method, remarks that these are "not consecutive, which does Mr. Berryman an injustice," then confesses that "what may prove to do him a greater injustice is that two of them were written by me, taking a few minutes for each verse." Although in six or twelve lines nearly anyone can seem to imitate almost anybody, the gambit would be more arresting if Toynbee were charier, warier, in its use. For a similar trick opens a later essay, a review of Mary Renault's *The Mask of Apollo* in the *New Republic,* and therefore tends to throw a certain doubt on the utility, for literary criticism, of a reviewer's gimmick.

Toynbee's essay is useful as a point of departure, not for its show of audacity but for its judgment, given in the form of a suspicion, that in the end "there will *not* emerge a sense of that inevitable union of means and meaning which we receive from all good poetry." For what in fact distinguishes Berryman's poetry is the invention of truly audacious means exactly suited to his meaning. Regard the four epigraphs which open the book. The initial one ("THOU DREWEST NEAR IN THE DAY") stands alone. Unidentified, it is followed, next page, by a trio of lines, the first also unascribed but written in Negro dialect ("GO IN, BRACK MAN, DE DAY'S YO' OWN"); the second (". . . I AM THEIR MUSICK") is drawn from *Lamentations* 3:63. And the third ("BUT THERE IS ANOTHER METHOD") is taken from an unnamed work by the South African reformer and fantasist Olive Schreiner. Short, flat, these seem to offer disjointed, not sibylline learning, and properly mystified, we know that a certain amount of detective work is in order.

What it yields is extraordinary. "GO IN, BRACK MAN . . ." turns up as the epigraph in a book on the history of blackface minstrelsy in America, Carl Wittke's *Tambo and Bones* (1930). Olive Schreiner's comment is taken from a work which has long haunted Berryman, *Dreams* (1914), where Miss Schreiner defined two ways in which artists customarily depict "truth." The first, of which she disapproved, she named the "stage method": people behave as puppets of the creator's will, character is cut and dried, problems are devised so that solutions can be found. "But there is another method—the method of life we all lead. Here nothing can be prophesied. There is a strange coming and going of feet. Men appear, act and re-act upon each other, and pass away. When the crisis comes, the man who would fit it does not return. When the curtain falls, no one is ready. When the footlights are brightest, they are blown out: and what the name of the play is no one knows."

Olive Schreiner was a shrewder theorist than practitioner of literature: her notion of a "stage" method corresponds to the technique Abram Tertz condemns in the essay on socialist realism, and that "other" method corresponds to the technique Tertz approved, the literature of phantasmagoria. Hearing her speak about coming and going of feet, performances of the unnameable, we naturally think of Beckett. But it is not just a prescience of literary cunning which Berryman admires in Miss Schreiner. Both she and that other exemplary lady to whom Berryman has committed himself, Anne Bradstreet, are women in whom a passion for things of the spirit is suffused by a compassion for the life of flesh. Indeed, the color of spirit is in Berryman's view livid flesh. And it is Anne's skin "cratered" by smallpox, the "body a-drain" with its "pustules snapping," which he loves. That identical matters engage Olive Schreiner's sympathy too is evident in a dream-vision, "The Sunlight Lay Across My Bed," where the dreamer finds herself in a place inhabited by people who suffer all the least supportable forms of physical grief. Unaccountably, the more nastily bruised their bodies are, the more intense is the light they exude. "I had thought that blindness and maimedness were great evils," she says, marveling that in this "strange land" men convert pain into energy. Awaking, she realizes that her mission is to celebrate, without rant or romantic illusion or heroic pose, the vitality of life in men mutilated but unmastered by earth. This was the "music" she would henceforth sing: "I was glad the long day was before me."

Better equipped now to take up the clues offered by Berryman's epigraphs, we recognize in these a filigree of signs which specify a coherent pattern of purposes within the 77 songs. "I AM THEIR MUSICK" links the book *Lamentations* with Olive Schreiner's book *Dreams*. "BUT THERE IS ANOTHER METHOD," which connotes a particular principle of literary creation, leads to the line from minstrelsy, "GO IN BRACK MAN, DE DAY'S YO' OWN," where dialect alone identifies exactly whose plight and passion and grief and pain are sung by whom on which stage in accord with what mode of performance. Applying a similar technique of argument to the dedicatory epigraph, "THOU DREWEST NEAR IN THE DAY," *Lamentations* 3:57, we infer that the cycle as a whole, for all its hodgepodge of association, is single-minded in pursuit of one theme: Fear not. "THOU DREWEST NEAR IN THE DAY THAT I CALLED UPON THEE: THOU SAIDST, FEAR NOT."

If all this sounds as much like an exercise in mathematical proof as criticism of verse, part of the reason is that Berryman has in fact introduced a system of arithmetic notation into his numbers and thereby turned the fact of number into a main issue within the very form of the verse. The 77 songs are distributed among three sections—26, 25, 26. With nine exceptions, each poem is 18 lines in length, arranged in three verse paragraphs each six lines long. The nine exceptions must be deliberate, for Berryman resorts to the most patent subterfuges of dilation in order to vary a pattern which could easily conform to standard. And the standard itself is very tidily signified by a cue, at once arithmetic and thematic, present in the central epigraph, *Lamentations* 3:63—the 77 *Dream Songs* offers three sections of poems, six verses per stanza, three stanzas per poem.

Berryman's taste for mystification is thus supported by a mystique of numerology—a mystique which is the more firmly bolstered by the poet's reliance on a Biblical book which is itself gnomic in form and function. Not only does *Lamentations* mourn the fall of Old Jerusalem and therefore supply a paradigm for Berryman's lament, fall of our New Jerusalem, but also each of its sections develops an alphabetical acrostic. The third section, the one on which Berryman draws, is unique in that it elaborates three verses around its letter instead of the one verse per letter usual in the other sections. That is, *Lamentations* 3 has 66 verses; the other two sections have 22 verses each. There may be a touch of alphabetic play in the 77 songs, represented by the number of poems placed in each of its segments. But Berryman's ingenuity is spent on an exercise of wider range. For a more impressive intersection of form and meaning occurs when we restore, from *Lamentations* 3:63, that half which Berryman has left off: "Behold their sitting down, and their rising up: I am their musick." In this restoration we accomplish nothing less than the connection of minstrel show and holy text. Tambo and Bones rise and sit in response to questions from the Interlocutor, who plays straight man to their end men. He is the one through whom the two speak. He is their music and they are of course his. Berryman, casting himself in the role of interlocutor, in this way devises a secular language and music no less intricate than the sacred. The poet conceives a "method" which will

recreate the downs and ups, the debasements which degrade
and the passions which inspirit the lives of mutilated men,
American Negroes, "Henry" and "Bones," who convert pain
into song.

The place of minstrelsy on Berryman's stage cannot, however, be this neatly disposed of. For minstrelsy represents the
climactic and synoptic solution to the poet's "long, often back-
breaking search for an inclusive style, a style that could use
his erudition," Robert Lowell says, and "catch the high, even
frenetic, intensity of his experience, disgusts and enthusi-
asm." Before it is possible to decide whether or not this solution works, it is necessary to acquire a little of Berryman's
erudition—that is, search out where diverse clues lead. The
second Dream Song, for example, called "Big Buttons, Cor-
nets: the Advance," leads to Daddy Rice, Thomas Dartmouth
Rice, a white actor who in the 1820s and 1830s "sang and
jumped 'Jim Crow,'" Berryman explains, in dedicating this
song to the memory of that man. Impersonating a plantation
Negro, dressed in patchy pants and ragged shoes (wearing,
according to some reports, a vest with buttons made of five-
and ten-dollar gold pieces), he wheeled and turned and
jumped "windmill fashion." Throwing weight alternately on
the heel of one foot and the toe of the other, he chanted comment on the movements of his dance:

> This is the style of Alabama
> What they hab in Mobile,
> And dis is Louisiana
> Whar de track upon de heel.

From Long Island to Indiana, from "Kentuck" to "ol Mis-
sissip," I "weel about, and turn about, and do jis so" and
"Eb'ry time I weel about, I jump Jim Crow": Step and fetch it
if you can! Because ways of jumping Jim Crow varied from
place to place—"De Georgia step" went according to "de double rule of three"—part of the point of Rice's song and dance
was to display nuance within the first wholly original and authentic form of folk art to be developed within the American
experience. But whatever these steps and rules were, Rice's
impersonations served as the model and mainspring for minstrels and minstrel shows of later decades. Shortly after Rice
introduced his dance, in 1828, blackface actors banded to-

gether, first in pairs and later in diverse combinations which somehow implicate a rule of three: "two banjoists and one dancer; one banjoist and two dancers; one fiddler and two dancers; one banjoist, a dancer and a singer." Rice himself, dancing solo, remained the most popular of all blackface performers in Great Britain and the United States. He was able to fill the American Theatre on the Bowery even on the "fifty-seventh night" of his "original and celebrated extravaganza . . . on which occasion every department of the house was thronged to an excess unprecedented in the records of theatrical attraction," according to an advertisement dated November 25, 1833.*

Within ten years of this date the Virginia Minstrels had been formed. Four white men in blackface sat onstage in a semicircle, turned partly toward the audience and partly toward one another, fiddle and banjo flanked by tambourine and bones. Their show was divided into two parts and both parts alternated ensemble play with solo act—song, skit, dance in no certain order. During the 1850s and later, at a zenith of popularity, the classic form of minstrelsy was fixed by two groups, Bryant's Minstrels and Christy's Band of Original Virginia Minstrels. Christy's three minstrels performed on banjo, violin, tambourine, bones, triangle—and "they all played double." Both this troupe and Bryant's presented a three-part entertainment which opened with a chorus and grand entrance. Then the interlocutor, in white lace and full-dress, said "Gentlemen be seated" and exchanged jokes with Tambo and Bones, dressed in blackface, swallowtails and striped trousers. Part 2, the olio, ended with a hoedown in which each member of the company did a solo turn. What happened in Part 3 is not clear—or not clear to me, anyway, for specialists differ in their opinions. It was probably ragout again, spiced by skit, farce and sketch based on subjects drawn from plantation life.

Most of their stuff is lost, but the cakewalk remains alive still, a dance step which, LeRoi Jones contends in *Blues People*, originated as a Negro parody of white high manners in the

---

* I am duty bound to remark on this conjunction of 3 and 57, for it coincides with the number of Berryman's dedicatory epigraph, *Lamentations* 3:57. It may be coincidence, too, that "The Last Dream Song: 161" was published on November 25, 1965.

manor house. Because the cakewalk seems to develop from
black caricature of white custom, Jones wonders what response is appropriate to a white company which, unaware of
self-mockery, offers Stepin Fetchit as straight burlesque of
the black peasantry. "I find the idea of white minstrels in
black-face satirizing a dance satirizing themselves a remarkable kind of irony—which, I suppose, is the whole point of
minstrel shows." Amplifying this idea, Jones claims that parody in black minstrel shows was directed against whites.
Wearing stagy blackface to cover their true color, Negro minstrels in the 1870s exploited the deepest resources of private
and communal life—folk speech, song, dance, game and
play—in order to devise a form of public entertainment
which would please both sets of audiences. Whereas white
minstrels in blackface merely exposed their own folly, Negro
minstrels in blackface, anticipating Genet, created a black
travesty of white burlesque and thereby cut deep into the double life of both races. *

Black minstrels accomplished something really momentous, Jones thinks, by mocking white audiences with a music,
true jazz and classic blues, until then unknown outside shan-
tytown. And it is precisely in the use of similar materials that
Berryman has introduced matter no less fateful for English
prosody. Blues, which spring "from no readily apparent Western source," are customarily pieces in twelve bars: "each verse
is of three lines, each line is about four bars long. The words
of the song usually occupy about one-half of each line, leaving
a space of two bars for either a sung answer or an instrumental response." Knowing that Berryman's epigraphs, for example, which are invariably halved, require the reader to supply
that portion of the utterance which the poet has left off, we
suspect that the form of blues and not its idiom alone—minstrelsy itself, not just its stereotypes—is subsumed within the

---

* Jones's views on black minstrelsy are unconventional. It is commonly held
that the popularity of Negro performers on Mississippi steamboats led white
men, first in imitation and then in parody, to adopt blackface. Their success
in turn compelled Negroes to apply burnt cork. But Jones cannot be quite
wrong, as the police helped to confirm in Denver, in October 1966, when
they arrested Negro members of the San Francisco Mime Troupe for per-
forming a blackface minstrel show, "Civil Rights in a Cracker Barrel," satirizing the village villainies of white prejudice in heartland America. The
police decided that the show was "indecent."

very form of Berryman's verse. When the first line of the first
Dream Song breaks, the effect is a sort of syncopation ("Huffy
Henry hid   the day"). But the break elsewhere, as in Song 3,
is intended to exact a voiced response from the reader:

> Rilke was a *jerk*.
> I admit his griefs & music
> & title spelled all-disappointed ladies.
> A threshold worse than the circles
> where the vile settle & lurk,
> Rilke's. As I said,—

There are many examples. But it is Song 2, the one dedicated to Daddy Rice, which crystallizes the full resource-
fulness of Berryman's art. "Le's do a hoedown, gal," in the
second stanza, prepares for the olio of the third stanza, where
Henry goes into his act, does his solo specialty, enacts a black
burlesque of white paraody, performs a cakewalk—a masque
in which Sir Bones speaks from behind his mask a satiric language taken from Negro rhyming slang, the kind of speech devised in order to hide true meaning from the Man, the enemy:

> —Sir Bones, or Galahad; astonishin
> yo legal & yo good. Is you feel well?
> Honey dusk do sprawl.
> —Hit's hard. Kinged or thing, though, fling & wing.
> Poll-cats are coming, hurrah, hurray.
> I votes in my hole.

Cakewalk and masque, blues and slang—these bits and
echoes do indeed banish meaning. Berryman's sense is virtually gone. Paradoxically, its very disappearance must be
taken as a sign of the poet's achievement. Compare Berryman's verses with those of "Old Pee Dee," a song popular but
commonplace in the last century.

> To Boston Part I den sail roun,
> Dey said de Dickens was in town;
> I ax dem who de Dickens was
> Dey sed 'twas massa Pickwick Boz.
> Ring de Hoop! an blow de horn!
> Massa Dickens eat de corn,

Way down in de low ground feeld
3,4 mile from Pompey's hee.

Here too exterior meaning is banished and external sense is
gone. Both Berryman's songs and minstrel songs disdain manifest statement and replace it in the manner of dreams, with a
juxtaposition of images. A dream is tough to crack because it
replaces a conscious conjunction of ideas with an unconscious
disjunction of images which make sheerly irrational sense. A
minstrel song is equally troublesome because it exploits both
principles, conjunction and disjunction, so that its white
(manifest) sense will be one thing and its black (latent) sense
another. And black is at odds with white. In minstrelsy, then,
Berryman found an exact analogue to dream. And in blues he
found a music which permitted him to excise, deliberately,
any connectives which might pull his work toward merely rational order. For it is not, as Leslie Fiedler remarks, Berryman's or Roethke's or Lowell's lucidity and logic we admire but
"their flirtation with incoherence and disorder." And it is
Berryman's distinction that he alone plunges deep into some
public sources of the primitive American imagination in
search of a tradition which represents long immersion in and
mastery of disjunction and disorder.

What distinguishes a dream song, therefore, is not a co-
quetry or a clumsiness of art, as Toynbee argued, but a rather
capital thing, the discovery that American minstrelsy long ago
devised a formula which could transmit the mood of an idea
and simultaneously conceal its reason. This discovery enabled
Berryman to create what Lowell calls a "waking hallucination," the form which unites conscious design and unconscious drift. Design and drift are perhaps clearest seen in
Song 40 whose initial line, "I'm scared a lonely. Never see my
son," an undisguised importation of Negritude, is drawn
straight from the heart of misery incarnate in Sir Bones. The
song itself mourns the lives of all who must "cry oursel's
awake" yet who manage to convert grief into energy, energy
into work, work to survive the lure of suicide and at last, each
day, make "it all the way to that bed on these feet." This song
plainly recalls the theme of Olive Schreiner's *Dreams*. Less
plain but more vivid is its evocation of that great man of blues,

Leadbelly, whose own music is curiously obsessed by exactly
the same theme—interplay of sleeplessness and dream as his
biographer Frederic Ramsey says—which absorbs Berryman.
"Sleeplessness complements the dream," real and unreal are
mixed, "seen and unseen come together," so that in the end
the text and tone of Leadbelly's song can be best described as a
"waking dream."

Whether or not Berryman knows Ramsey's memoir, doubtless he knows Huddie Leadbetter's music. Nor is there any
doubt that he knows Charles Lamb's remark about the sanity
of true genius: the poet dreams being awake, is not possessed
by but has dominion over his subject. And surely Berryman
knows the etymology of "vernacular"—from *verna,* slave born
in his master's house. For in 1963, after many years' labor on
a project whose working title, since 1955, had been *The
Dream Songs,* Berryman said that the poems refer to somebody
"apparently named Henry, or says he is. He has a tendency to
talk about himself in the third person. His last name is in
doubt. It is given at one point as Henry House and at other
points as Henry Pussy-cat." Miss Schreiner, Leadbelly,
Lamb—all are represented in this potpourri of songs by John
the minstrel man who, possessed by his subject, the savage-
ries which mutilate men in our nightmarish world, dreams up
Henry, sans surname, caricature of the American black man,
enslaved in his own house. Mixing formal speech and folk,
high art and pop, John furnishes Henry with the very language and ritual, drawn from the history of the American
white man, which first enabled white to imitate black and
black to parody white. In this way the victim is not possessed
by but achieves dominion over the tyrant; indeed, he transforms himself into the tyrant's savior. "I was a derision to all
my people; *and* their song all the day," says *Lamentations* 3:14,
in paraphrase of virtually everything I have so laboriously
construed till now.

II

Realizing that *The Dream Songs* date from 1955 or earlier, recalling that this period coincides with the period following
publication of Berryman's psychoanalytic study, *Stephen*

Crane (1950), we are tempted to return to that little book in order to discover which of its ideas bear on these songs.* For when Berryman says that the strongest influence on Crane's poetry was Olive Schreiner's "small book of allegories published in Boston . . . *Dreams,*" and says again that the parable and proverbial form of Crane's poetry is traceable to "the Bible and to Olive Schreiner's *Dreams,*" we know that we are placed amid two of Berryman's own sources of imagination and assume instantly that we must add a third, Crane himself.

Stephen Crane is a work both dense and diffuse. Pioneer in its use of Freud to untangle some knotty problems of motive in Crane's life and art, Berryman's work then seemed to refer to Crane alone. Today, reading Berryman's tortuous inquiry into Crane's habit of nomenclature ("the names authors give their characters seldom receive sufficient attention unless the significance of a name is immediately striking"), we are notified that Berryman's own choice of names cannot go unattended. Not all asides hide an issue of moment, of course, but this one rather obviously ties diverse things in a neat packet: "the discovery of Henry's whole identity, by him and by us, comprises the plot of the poem," says William Meredith, to whom Song 36 is dedicated.

The place of "Henry" in Crane's life, the role of "Henry" in Crane's art—these comprise the plot of Berryman's book. Crane's first hero, Berryman contends, "was the African explorer Henry Stanley. Henry is the name of the hero in *The Red Badge of Courage,* the name of *The Monster* and the name displaced at the catastrophe of the Blue Hotel, and we shall come shortly to a Prince Henry [Prince Henry of Prussia] . . . Stephen Crane seems to have had a middle name beginning with "H" which he dropped after 1893, and perhaps it was 'Henry'—a name very common in the family." Straining to make a strange point, Berryman wonders if Crane's friendship with Henry James in Sussex was not due in some way to an affinity of name.

Circumstantial stuff, surely; nevertheless the argument

---

* Long after I had worked out this segment of my essay, Berryman published "Nine Dream Songs" (*Times Literary Supplement,* December 1, 1966). In the first of these, "Op. posth. no. 1," Henry, dying, names among his ancestors "the younger Stephen Crane / of a powerful memory, of pain."

enables Berryman to concentrate on the fiction, *The Monster,* which most cogently reveals the special role of "Henry" in Crane's unconscious mind. The story is a "study of a society's fear, stupidity, persecution" of Henry Johnson, "Negro coachman of a small-town doctor." Brave and good, Henry is "mutilated while saving the doctor's little boy when the house burns." As a result he is rendered "faceless" and harmlessly insane. His fate represents a pattern of action, habitual in Crane's art, which Berryman calls the rescue-and-punishment theme: "for trying to rescue the boy, the Negro is punished with mutilation and idiocy, he becomes a 'monster' and has to hide his no-face." To have no face, to be veiled, understood psychoanalytically, is "to hide one's face, to be ashamed." Although Berryman is certain that "all three figures, father, Negro, son," represent components of Crane's own identity, it is Henry Johnson, veiled and shamed, who serves as "the chief Crane-mask." And shame, the presiding mood of Crane's repressed life, Berryman's psychoanalysis traces to "oedipal elements" in the writer's "rivalry against the father, the wish to be the father."

Although Crane's Henry and Berryman's are not equivalent—Berryman's relation with his own father is not in question—both figures serve as emblems of the black unconscious in American life on which Crane instinctively drew and in which Berryman, along with, say, Norman Mailer or James Baldwin, now discovers matter for exaltation. What is instinctive in Crane, in Mailer sloppy and in Baldwin vague, Berryman's psychoanalysis renders bare and sharp. As Freud provided him with the key to motive in Crane's art, so too did Freud furnish him with a dramatis personae of the inner life. According to rules set down in *The Ego and the Id,* ego is a "poor creature owing service to three masters and consequently menaced by three several dangers; from the external world, from the libido . . . and from the severity of the superego. Three kinds of anxiety correspond to these three dangers," and three kinds of action are performed by the ego as it struggles to dispel anxiety in order to fulfill its trio of functions: "to mediate between the world and the id, to make the id comply with the world's demands and . . . to accommodate the world to the id's desires."

From these permutations of the rule of three ("triads of

Hegel," Berryman says in "Op. posth. no. 1," drawn from
"upstairs and from down," from metaphysics and psychology,
which bolster Henry's determination to serve as "the American Bard"), the poet derives his calculus of character. Instead
of Henry, read ego. In place of id, visualize Bones, end man of
minstrel shows, unruly in the beat of tambourine and rattle of
bones, bobbing up and down, swaying to and fro, sputtering
coarse sayings, shouts and hoarse laughter. Sometimes, like
id, that olio of vulgar and irrepressible want, Bones's black
need bursts his own and even, beyond disentangling, Berryman's bounds. At other times Henry goes into a cakewalk of
mediation: Song 22, "Of 1826," compares the life of America
today ("teenage cancer") with its life on July 4, 1826, the day
when Adams, dying, gasped "Thomas Jefferson still lives"
even as Jefferson, incredibly, that day lay dying too. Although
Adams and Jefferson died, left us in the lurch, Henry lives. "I
am Henry Pussy-cat! My whiskers fly!" Elsewhere Henry is
all but obliterated by "them," superego rampant, those who in
the name and age of Ike "took away his crotch."

> Henry hates the world. What the world to Henry
> did will not bear thought.

Pain so excruciating may not bear thought, but it does enable Henry to accomplish the one act which makes thought
and life bearable, which synthesizes all fragments of the self,
which helps the self to mediate, accommodate, comply and in
this way avoid all menace of extinction. Pulling Henry together, in the last songs of this sequence, "considering, like a
madman," Henry "put forth a book." For all the agony his
dreams portray, Henry is no house cat, no pussyfoot Uncle
Tom who rattles a pair of bones for the general amusement.
He is a tomcat with passion enough (cat house) and guts
enough (outhouse) to make our bones rattle. In echo of Marianne Moore's account of poetry—an imaginary garden with
real toads in it—Berryman conjures out of the materials of
the unconscious an imaginary minstrel show with a real Jim
Crow. Polymorph, magpie, jackdaw, cunning and chattering
bird, Henry performs in song and dance a ritual of exorcism,
a black rite of salvation inside the white skin of his maker
whose identity he disguises with a burnt-cork mask. And if
Henry can do it, reassemble his parts by turning, in Olive

Schreiner's fashion, frightful nightmare into savage song, then "perhaps the unutterable midnights of the universe will have no power to daunt the colour of the soul."

III

Those are the words, derived from the final statement in Crane's story *The Monster,* which Berryman chose to conclude his *Stephen Crane.* And I have imitated Berryman's rhetoric in order to underscore the constancy of his devotion to a consistent set of ideas and images. If, however, the whole affair is treated as a brilliant display of marvelous or misspent gifts, or if we assent to one pronouncement or another—"It is the quality of their journey, not their destination, which is their value"—then all we have is a charcuterie of rime. And that is not justification enough for thirty years' study and experiment in music and mathematics, history and psychology and myth, which prepared the way for Berryman's theory and performance of a master work. However impressive the quality of Berryman's journey may be, far more portentous is the place Henry hopes to go. For he is on his way somewhere, he remarks in Song 76, "Henry's Confession": "I saw nobody coming, so I went instead," says our Rescuer. With this song Berryman himself disappears. "Cagey John" has gone native and, like the composer John Cage, has chosen silence. Having adopted the mask and speech of a primitive, cagey John has pulled Joyce's trick and slipped away, vanished into his work. "Wif a book of his in either hand / he is stript down to move on." Joyce's trick it may be, but it is again Crane whom Berryman selects for his model, Crane's *Maggie,* which Berryman cherishes because in no other work did an American author manage to remain so "persistently invisible behind his creation." Duplicating Crane's feat, cagey John disappears inside "his own mad books."

Inspired by Crane, sharing with Joyce the atavism of a lapsed Catholic who preserves outside theology a passion for trinity—sharing with Joyce too a conviction that the myth-making, dream-making and poetry-making faculties of imagination are at bottom one—cagey John undertakes to transmute secular art into a sacramental rite. For if myth can be said to reach deep down and far back into the history of race, then obviously it parallels the reach of minstrelsy, which goes deep into American racial history. And if the myth of minstrelsy enables Berryman to recreate some of the aims of primitive ritual drama, that form in which "art and life converge, life itself is seen as drama, roles are symbolically acted out" by means of "masks, poems, songs . . . and above all the dance," then the poet can be said to cast himself into the role of ur-poet, medicine man. "In constant danger of breakdown, of ceasing to function, or of functioning fantastically, in ways that were too private to elicit a popular response," the shaman's presence served his people as a daily "reminder that life often balances on the knife edge."

Although in each detail these views might well refer to Berryman, his poetry, his state of spirit, I have taken the remarks from an essay in anthropology—Stanley Diamond's "Plato and the Definition of the Primitive"—not in literary criticism. Almost any anthropological study of the primitive would do. For these ideas today are taken for conventional wisdom by members of a generation taught by Konrad Lorenz, Lévi-Strauss and Heinrich Zimmer, to scour the savage world in order to determine what in the nature of man is original, what is artificial. And Berryman, who some years ago went on a State Department tour of the Far East, whose 77 songs include mention of lotos, Ganges, Bodhidharma and so on, apparently found in Eastern myths some old and subtle sanctions for the transformation of a minstrel show into an imitation of a sacred action designed to purge fear.

For when we recognize what myth it is which best coincides with Berryman's intentions, with the aims delicately implied in the leading epigraph, then we discover why Daddy Rice's dance opens the 77 *Dream Songs*. Farfetched though the idea may seem, it is the dance of Shiva which Berryman hopes we will associate with Jim Crow. Shiva, according to Zimmer's account, is "The Black One," member of a trinity which includes Brahma the Creator, and Vishnu the Preserver. And his "flying arms and legs and the swaying of his torso," crowned by a "masklike" head, are accompanied by mystic utterance, at once holy speech and impenetrable silence, the syllable AUM, Shiva's dream song: "A—is the state of waking consciousness . . . U—is the state of dreaming consciousness . . . M—the state of dreamless sleep." Wearing the brahminical thread which adorns the three upper castes of India, the twice-born, those who inhabit the sphere of history and the realm of eternity, Shiva too dances in time to a double rule of three. Berryman seems to have connected this thread to two of Shiva's four arms, the one which holds a drum symbolizing the beat of time, and the one which is held aloft in the eternal gesture of comfort, of certitude, the gesture *abhaya-mudrā*: Fear not. Making these connections, *The Dream Songs* dispute and dispel the notion, more persuasive to British and Continental critics than American, that poetry cannot work as an agent of therapy or as the reliquary of culture or a surrogate for worship.

Having been exported to India by the American Department of State, Berryman has imported into his poetry those symbols of ritual drama which unite Brahma and Jehovah, the Dance of Shiva and *The Lamentations of Jeremiah*, in a single gesture. I must confess, however, that the role of Shiva in Berryman's art is, though plausible, uncertain. What is certain is that Berryman was drawn to the primitive, as *Stephen Crane* yields its final gloss, by way of Robert Graves.

> Robert Graves, one of the shrewdest, craziest, and most neglected students of poetry living, laid out a theory of the origins of poetry once. A savage dreams, is frightened by the dream, and goes to the medicine man to have it explained. The medicine man can make up anything, anything will reassure the savage, so long as the manner of its delivery is impressive; so he chants, perhaps he stamps his foot, people like rhythm, what he says becomes rhythmical, people like to hear things *again*, and what he says begins to rhyme. Poetry begins—as a practical matter, for *use*. It reassures the savage. Perhaps he only hears back again, chanted, the dream he just told the medicine man, but he is reassured: it is like a spell. And medicine men are shrewd: interpretation enters the chanting, symbols are developed and connected, the gods are invoked, poetry booms.

It was Graves, then, whose theory—joining primordial and present time, dream and song, song and dance, dance and rite, rite and rime—first invited Berryman to plunge into a study of the mythic origins and ritual ends of the arts of imagination. Making this theory his own, Berryman argued that

Crane's poetry must be read as "a series of anti-spells." Today, Graves's skeleton of a theory has been fleshed out by cagey John, the invisible and silent man behind the stage on which a "spellbound," raving, savage Henry and his shaman Bones reenact in dialogue "made-up stories/lighting the past of Henry," stories which cunningly transmute inchoate terror into a booming poetry of the anti-spell. For if a medicine man can be said to invent *poetry* when he casts a savage's dreams into chants which reassure the patient, then a poet can be said to invent a *cure* when he casts his song into the form of a dream which makes manifest the disintegration, death and, in "Op. posth. no. 10," the reincarnation of a people: "Henry may be returning to our life / adult & difficult."

If, finally, it was Graves who set Berryman going, it is Lévi-Strauss's essay "The Effectiveness of Symbols" which tells how far he has come. "In the schizophrenic cure the healer performs the acts and the patient produces his myth; in the shamanistic cure the healer supplies the myth and the patient performs the actions." Cagey John, the schizophrene, disintegrates, disappears, then reappears in the mask of a minstrel man who jumps Jim Crow and thereby supplies the myth which will enable his blues people to understand the "lessen" Bones has up his "slave." Drawing his myth from minstrelsy, his parable from Olive Schreiner, his theory from Graves, his text from *Lamentations*—finding in Freud his cast of characters and in Crane the very model of a quintessential poet—Berryman savages America for its taste for blood.

Not just America, of course. For two songs, "The Translator—I" and "The Translator—II," not included among the 77, take up the trial of Joseph Brodsky, the Soviet poet and translator who in March 1964 was sentenced to five years' labor, psychiatric confinement, as a social parasite.

> Henry rushes not in here. The matter's their matter,
> and Hart Crane drowned himself some over money.

American hands are unclean too, bloody with the murder of poets. Suddenly he decides that it is "Henry's matter after all," the fate of that young man Brodsky

> Who only wanted to walk beside the canals
> talking about poetry & make it.

Deciding that Brodsky's is Henry's matter, Berryman causes
Henry to advance some steps along his way, a way I take to
represent a reversal of the rescue-and-punishment theme
which Berryman contended was the obsession of Crane's unconscious mind. Human matter is my matter. Henry's matter
defines the chief article of belief which underlies Berryman's
making poetry and making poetry the instrument whereby the
world might be healed and whole. We are in each other's
hands who care, says the line which epitomizes Berryman's
gist in *Homage to Mistress Bradstreet*. Fear not.

Berryman's testament. The marvel is that this old testament
represents exactly the sort of conquest over prosody and politics to which both the Beats and Black Mountaineers, two
chief schools of American experiment today, aspire. Allen
Ginsberg chants foul and elegant words in jazzy and cantorial
rhythms. And Charles Olson finds, in the heartbeat and
breadth of speech, a formula which—he hopes—will put
body back into American English. All three in concert. Berryman the medicine man and Ginsberg the zaddik and Olson
the guru, intoning the prophetic voice of poetry, share in common the will to transform and transmit primal human and
American energy, by way of the poem, to the life of the people. Although all resort to "myth," none searches that murky
realm for quick consolation, none replaces the bitter savor of
character for the treacle of archetype. But it is Berryman
alone who has confronted all imaginable demons, learned to
speak their tongue and, like Luther, invented a devilish vernacular which must henceforth invade standard speech.

Berryman

ROBERT PINSKY

To assign part of the poem to a voice or protagonist gives the attributed element a kind of autonomy, however illusory or conventional. Lowell has used that illusion of autonomy as a way to approach elusive or ambivalent judgments of outward matters, values of a cultural or social kind. In John Berryman's poems dramatic devices often seem to work similarly in relation to more wholly inward judgments; the quasi-autonomous element in the poem supplies a way to have one's self-dramatization and yet to judge it—or at least to stand a little apart from it. (Ted Hughes's *Crow* seems to carry this principle even further.)

Stylistically, persona or attribution works for Lowell largely as a way to balance meanings and allegiances in complex masses: in line, sentence, paragraph. As adapted to Berryman's meanings, the equally elaborate screens and attributions seem to free the poet mainly in the matter of diction— making legitimate particular words that in the single authorial voice might be too disparate or flat or maudlin.

So, though the syntactical eruptions of baby-talk or minstrel-talk may seem to have some particular, special implication, Berryman's language seems to me to grow first of all from the poet's need for a vocabulary that does not restrict him or embarrass him. And weight and strength therefore depend not on the words, in a way, but on areas between the words, on the disparities and oddball vacuums:

> . . . close by a smothering southern sea
> spreadeagled on an island, by my knee.

Excerpted from Robert Pinsky, *The Situation of Poetry* (Princeton University Press, 1976), pp. 23–29.

—You is from hunger, Mr. Bones,

I offers you this handkerchief, now set
your left foot by my right foot,
shoulder to shoulder, all that jazz,
arm in arm, by the beautiful sea,
hum a little, Mr. Bones.
—I saw nobody coming, so I went instead.

(*The Dream Songs, 76*)

Perhaps the most important point to be made is that the colloquial words and the gag-words are not the words for which
the extravagant style provides a kind of license or passport.
Rather, the colloquial words help the syntax, the gags, and
the personae in a general effort to admit another kind of
phrase—like "a smothering southern sea"—just as in ordinary talk tough-slangy taglines such as "all that jazz" often
excuse and qualify a phrase the speaker fears may seem too
elevated or pretentious.

But "elevated or pretentious" does not exactly identify the
kind of language that I mean, that I think Berryman originally felt driven to use by his material, and that in turn demanded his method. This kind of language has tended to be
driven out of modern poetry by various pressures: the pressure
toward evocative physical description as being the most essentially poetic use of language, the pressure towards idiomatic,
spoken discourse. The result of these is to put extraordinary,
cramping demands for freshness upon those words—mostly
by necessity "abstract"—which in the ordinary way name the
emotions themselves directly; so, in passages like the following one, the assumed voices and mannerisms provide a more
or less ironic context for late-Romantic diction like "proud,"
"strike . . . from despair," "polished women," "dream
awhile," "flashing and bursting":

Something about this
unshedding bulky bole-proud blue-green moist

thing made by savage & thoughtful
surviving Henry
began to strike the passers from despair
so that sore on their shoulders old men hoisted
six-foot sons and polished women called

> small girls to dream awhile toward the flashing & bursting
> tree!
>
> *(The Dream Songs, 75)*

But it is precisely only the context that is ironic, the weird
manner. The irony is only that of a man in pain assuming dialects and self-effacing tones in torments of embarrassment
and diffidence, as to distract himself. That is, the phrases of
celebration, and the poet's phallic pride in his book, are
meant; the irony constitutes a sort of request for permission to
use such phrases and to express such pride.

To put it another way, the "thing made" represents a return
to the more or less late-Romantic idea of the poem as an irresistible outpouring, an emotional need and lifting-up for writer and reader; but while in some ways an idea like that one
has come round again, largely replacing the mandarin, new-
critical ideas about composition, it is also true that the standards of language which belong to the period of Eliot and Stevens retain their strength. For the subject of pain and survival
Berryman, in *The Dream Songs,* wanted a fluent, ready language which could cover ground rapidly, establishing feelings
without laborious "objective correlatives" and meticulously
"sculpted" phrases. The Swinburnian "smothering southern
sea" of 76 and the adjectival passage of the "six-foot sons" in
75 are the essential tongue of the poems, a sort of forbidden or
ritual language admitted by the surface lingo of the dream-
song manner.

In fact, there is a temptation to see much of modern poetry's history as a series of strategies for retaining or recovering
the elevation of Victorian diction. I am thinking less of the
nineties-ish moments in Pound and Eliot than of such
phrases of aroused and bardic diction as:

> An eagle rejoices in the oak trees of heaven
>
> (JAMES WRIGHT,
> *"Today I Was So Happy I Made This Poem"*)

> We shall see the grave of love as a lovely sight
>   and temporary near the elm that spells the
>   lovers' names in roots
>
> (FRANK O'HARA,
> *"Ode to Joy"*)

> it is true
> That only flesh dies, and spirit flowers without stop.
>
> (GALWAY KINNELL,
> "Freedom, New Hampshire")

The tones of the forbidden language of Arnold and Tennyson, against which modernism (according to one view) reacted, sometimes appear more or less explicitly, as in the last lines of the first Dream Song:

> Once in a sycamore I was glad
> all at the top, and I sang.
> Hard on the land wears the strong sea
> and empty grows every bed.

This same note, similarly associated with a bardic renewing of the past through poetry, appears in Pound's early, pre-Raphaelite poems like "Ballateta" or even, briefly, in the rhymes and diction of "Ash Wednesday":

> The new years walk, restoring
> Through a bright cloud of tears, the years, restoring
> With a new verse the ancient rhyme. Redeem
> The time. Redeem
> The unread vision in the higher dream
> While jewelled unicorns draw by the gilded hearse.

But for Berryman the use (however ironic) of the old poetic diction is not archaizing or momentary. He establishes the context for it and then makes it into a readily available poetic language whose aim is largeness of feeling: to make up in co-piousness and range what it may lack in distinction of other kinds. His subjects—disillusion, remorse, yearning, a de-spairing irritation with boundaries—demanded the some-what sloppy richness of the forbidden tongue.

The point may be more persuasive if I quote all of Dream Song 29 (which seems to me to be one of the most successful) and ask the reader to make a kind of imaginary revision, re-moving Henry and the eccentric syntax, but retaining the words and images and their approximate order—conceiving also, if possible, a background murmur of Tennysonian fig-ures of sound:

> There sat down, once, a thing on Henry's heart
> so heavy, if he had a hundred years
> & more, & weeping, sleepless, in all them time
> Henry could not make good.
> Starts again always in Henry's ears
> the little cough somewhere, an odour, a chime.
>
> And there is another thing he has in mind
> like a grave Sienese face a thousand years
> would fail to blur the still profiled reproach of. Ghastly,
> with open eyes, he attends, blind.
> All the bells say: too late. This is not for tears;
> thinking.
>
> But never did Henry, as he thought he did,
> end anyone and hacks her body up
> and hide the pieces, where they may be found.
> He knows: he went over everyone, & nobody's missing.
> Often, he reckons, in the dawn, them up.
> Nobody is ever missing.

It is true that the approach I suggest is not fair as a whole judgment of the poem; to call attention to the possibility

> Often he reckons them up in the dawn

does not necessarily prove a great deal about the line as actually written. I suggest the exercise to make only a restricted, but important, point: namely, that a contemporary poet has adapted an elaborate mannerism in order to speak simply, that he uses one part of his tradition (the intricate use of a strange speaker) to make available another part of it. That other part, the late-Romantic feeling of the diction, is made clear by a process of mutilation for which I apologize. Anyway, here is a rough outline of the imaginary revision which I suggest as an experiment:

> . . . so heavy that if I had a hundred years
> And more of weeping, sleepless, in all that time
> I could not make it good. Always in my ears
> There starts again somewhere an odour, a chime. . . .
>
> . . . thing in my mind whose still profiled reproach,
> Like a grave Sienese face, a thousand years
> Would fail to blur. . . .

The quaint or grotesque nineteenth-century writer so suggested is not Berryman, of course. To isolate his diction in a context which may suggest its origins does, however, help to define the method of *The Dream Songs*.

The essence of the poem is the violently tormenting regret and guilt; no tears, no madness or violence or vision, will expiate that torment: "All the bells say: too late." In fact, it is not only too late, but too far or too deep, too undramatizable perhaps. Too far beyond action, anyway. In themselves, the Romantically broad emotional terms might imply some outcome of the feeling in the world of action. But Henry, the specialized ironic twitches of dream-song argot, the strange ways of the poem, all imply that this feeling is beyond or apart from action or even dramatic expression. The poet is permanently burdened with the pent-up nature of the feeling, and the style of the poem represents a kind of husk of being, surrounding the emotional essence. The dry, hard sense of circumstance and limit, which seems to rule out tears as well as atrocity, condemns the poet to insomniac meditation. The pressure against such limits creates the oddity of his voice.

The term for a cloak so involved, so egregious, and so arbitrary from some points of view is "mannerism." The vital, difficult question about *The Dream Songs* is whether the manner is finally arbitrary, or justified in some way oblique yet profound.

John Berryman

A QUESTION OF IMPERIAL SWAY

JOHN BAYLEY

Berryman, like Lowell and perhaps more so, is the poet of the time whose size and whose new kind of stylistic being shrugs off any attempt at enclosure. But one thing about both is obviously true. *Life Studies, Notebook,* and *The Dream Songs* show that verses, old-fashioned *numbers,* are still capable of being what Byron wanted—"a form that's large enough to swim in and talk on any subject that I please"—and not only the capable but the imperially inevitable form. Compare their talking verse—dense as lead one moment and light as feathers the next—with the brutal monotony of that dimension of talking prose which Hemingway evolved, and which Miller, Mailer, Burroughs, and others have practiced in their various ways. In *The Dream Songs* and *Love & Fame* Berryman makes that kind of prose appear beside his verse not only doltish and limited but incapable even of straight talking.

Formalistically speaking, curiosity has no place in our reception of the Berryman experience. The medium makes the message all too clear. In spite of all the loose ends of talk, the name-dropping and the facts given, we have no urge to find out with whom, when, why, and what; and this is not a bit like Byron. "I perfect my meters," writes Berryman, "until no mosquito can get through." Let's hope he's right. In every context today we sup full of intimacies. The group therapy of our age is its total explicitness; privacy and reticence have lost all artistic function and status: and so a lack of curiosity is not abnormal in the reader or even unusual. But Berryman seals

John Bayley, "John Berryman: A Question of Imperial Sway," *Salmagundi* 22–23 (spring-summer 1973): 84–102.

off curiosity with a degree of artistic justification against which there is no *ad hominem* appeal.

The implications of these two phenomena—a new verse and a new self in it—seem to me what discussion of Berryman has to be about. There is no point in prosing along with detailed technical discussion of his verse, for its idioms and techniques are all completely self-justifying and self-illuminating.

"Poetry," said Thoreau, "is a piece of very private history, which unostentatiously lets us into the secret of a man's life." The matter would only have been put thus by a North American, at once orphan and contemporary of romanticism. The triumph of Berryman's poetry is that in becoming itself it has learnt how to undermine the apparent relevance to the poetic art of that niggling adverb: by flinging it suddenly on its back he has revealed that utter and shameless ostentation can become the same thing as total form, and virtually the same thing as the impersonality which our knowledge and love of the traditions of poetry condition us to expect. To let us in unostentatiously usually means today to be *confiding*. Elizabeth Bishop makes her Fish her poem, but is at the same time both confiding and self-justifying, as is such a typical poem of Wallace Stevens's final period as "The Planet on the Table." So at the other extreme of length and technique is *Paterson*. These confidences produce the impression that the poet is (to turn Stevens's own words against him) "an obstruction, a man / Too exactly himself." Such confidences cease to be important when they are made by a poet as far back as Wordsworth, but in our own time they are very important because they collapse style, the only thing that enables us to guess at the authority of a modern poet. At the moment they are not "soluble in art" (the phrase from the prologue to *Berryman's Sonnets*) though they may dissolve in time—or the whole poem may.

One thing which that in-other-respects overrated European author Beckett shares with Berryman and Lowell is the masterly inability to confide. None of them is deadpan: indeed all seem very forthcoming, but what Berryman calls "imperial sway" (Pound was "not fated like his protégé Tom or drunky Jim/or hard-headed Willie for imperial sway") manifests in them as a kind of regal blankness: it is not for them to know or care whether or not their subjects are listening.

Berryman cannot be "exactly himself," for he is so present
to us that the thought of the real live Berryman is inconceiv-
able, and scarcely endurable. His poetry creates the poet by a
process opposite to that in which a novelist creates a character. We get to know Macbeth, say, or Leopold Bloom, to the
point where we enter into him and he becomes a part of us;
like Eurydice in Rilke's poem he is *geben aus wie hundertfacher
Vorrat*—bestowed upon the world as a multitudinous product.
Berryman, by contrast, creates himself as an entity so single
that we cannot share with or be a part of him. Such an autobiography as his does not make him real in the fictional sense.
Everything is there, but so is the poetry, "language / so twisted and posed in a form / that it not only expresses the matter
in hand / but adds to the stock of available reality."

That is Blackmur, one of Berryman's heroes: his wisdom
put into a lapidary stanza and three quarters, ending with the
poet's comment: "I was never altogether the same man after
that." *That* is after all, though, a conventional formalistic and
Mallarméan utterance, and the great apparent size of Berryman and Lowell is that they have achieved a peculiarly American breakthrough: the emancipation of poetry from its
European bondage as *chose préservée* and its elevation into a
form which can challenge and defeat the authority and easy-
goingness of prose at every point. As Valéry perceived when
he coined the phrase, Europe can never get over its tradition
that poetry occupies a special place, and that prose has grown
all round it like some rank and indestructibly vital weed, iso-
lating it in an unmistakable enclave. Wallace Stevens con-
cedes the same thing, in his practice, in his Jamesian persona
("John D. Rockefeller drenched in attar of roses" as Mary Mc-
Carthy put it) and in his comment that "French and English
constitute a single language" (exclusive of American presumably). Looking back in England, we see that Wordsworth, the
great seeming liberator, was more subjected than he knew; as
he grew older the "poetic" engulfed him; Coleridge's attempts
to write a "poetry that affects not to be poetry" renounce all
tension, and lack even the circumambulatory virtues of *Biog-
raphia Literaria*. But whatever the difficulties of emancipation
American writers had to overcome, this was not one of them.
Whitman showed the way. Pound, as he says, "made a pact"
with him, and the *Cantos*, no less than *Leaves of Grass*, never

strike us as tacitly admitting that the same kind of thing could
be or is being said in prose.

For one thing, the "I" is wholly different. Coleridge's and
Wordsworth's "I" is usually themselves, the "man speaking to
men," in either verse or prose. Even in such a masterpiece as
Resolution and Independence, "I" is not metamorphosed by the
medium, by the poetry. Hence, even there, the poetry is not
doing its poetic job to the hilt. A prose Wordsworth is, or
would be, perfectly acceptable, but a prose Whitman "I" or a
prose "Henry" Berryman would be intolerable. To make a poetic "I" as free and even more free, as naturalistic and even
more so, than a prose ego, and yet quite quite different: that is
the secret of the American new poetry which appears to reach
its apogee in Lowell and Berryman. By this they show not only
that verse can still do more than prose, but that the more
closely it is involved in the contingent, the more it can manifest itself as the aesthetically and formalistically abolute.

I must return to this point in a moment, but let us first dispose of Berryman's own comments about the "I" of *The Dream
Songs.*

> Many opinions and errors in the songs are to be referred not to
> the character Henry, still less to the author, but to the title of
> the work. . . . The poem then, whatever its wide cast of char-
> acters, is essentially about an imaginary character (not the
> poet, not me) named Henry, a white American in early middle
> age in blackface, who has suffered irreversible loss and talks
> about himself sometimes in the first person, sometimes in the
> third, sometimes even in the second; he has a friend, never
> named, who addresses him as Mr. Bones and variants thereof.

This of course is rubbish in one sense, but in another it is a
perfectly salutary and justified reminder by the author that
when he puts himself into a poem he formalizes himself. To
labor the point again: Mailer is always Mailer, but Berryman
in verse is Berryman in verse. That does not mean that he is
exaggerated or altered or dramatized: on the contrary, if he
were so the poem would be quite different and much more
conventional. Berryman of course deeply admired and was
much influenced by Yeats, who helped him to acquire the
poet's imperial sway over himself and us, but he is not in the
least concerned with Yeats's doctrine of the Masks, and with

trying out contrasting dramatic representations of the self; such a cumbrous and courtly device of European poetry does not go with American directness and the new American expansiveness. Why bother to put on masks when you can make the total creature writing all the form that is needed?

Byron and Pushkin also emphasized the formal nature of their poetic device, often in facetious terms and in the poems themselves—making characters meet real friends and themselves, etc.; Berryman's gambit to emphasize a comparable formalism has a long history. None the less his comments are misleading in so far as they imply something like a dramatic relation between characters and ideas in *The Dream Songs*. The hero of Meredith's *Modern Love* would be as impossible in any other art context as Henry, but he is in a dramatic situation, and in that situation we can—indeed we are positively invited to—judge him, as we judge Evgeny Onegin. And to judge here is to become a part of. The heroes of such poems with dramatic insides to them are not taken as seriously as heroes in prose; they are unstable and frenetic, capable of all or nothing, because we do not get accustomed to them: they appear and vanish in each line and rhyme. None the less they are stable enough to be sat in judgment on, and Berryman's Henry is not. Ultimately, the formal triumph of Henry is that because he is not us and never could be, he has—like our own solitary egos—passed beyond judgment.

The paradox is complete, and completely satisfying. Clearly Berryman knew it. "These songs are not meant to be understood you understand / They are only meant to terrify and comfort" (366). But though it is not dramatic the interior of *The Dream Songs* is grippingly exciting, deep, detailed and spacious. Moreover it is not in the least claustrophobic in the sense in which the world of Sylvia Plath involuntarily constricts and imprisons: on the contrary, like the world of early Auden it is boisterously exhilarating and liberating. It has no corpus of exposition, sententiousness, or pet theory, which is why it is far more like *Modern Love* or *Evgeny Onegin* than the *Cantos* or, say, *The Testament of Beauty*. It never expounds. Another thing in common with the Meredith and Pushkin is the nature of the pattern. Each "Number" is finished, as is each of the intricate stanzas of their long poems, but in reading the whole we go on with curiosity unslaked and growing, as if reading a serial. The separate numbers of *The Dream Songs* published in magazines could not of course indicate this serial significance, which is not sequent, but taken as a whole reveals unity.

The Russian formalists have a term, *pruzhina*, referring to the "sprung" interior of a successful poetic narration, the bits under tension which keep the parts apart and the dimensions open and inviting. Thus, in *Evgeny Onegin*, Tatiana is a heroine, a story-book heroine, and a parody of such a heroine; while Evgeny is, conversely, a "romantic" hero for her, a parody of such a hero, and a hero. The spring keeps each separable in the formal art of the poem, and the pair of them in isolation from each other. I am inclined to think that Berryman's quite consciously contrived *pruzhina* in *The Dream Songs* is a very simple and very radical one: to hold in opposed tension and full view the poet at his desk at the moment he was putting down the words, and the words themselves in their arrangement on the page as poetry. When one comes to think of it, it is surprising that no one has thought of exploiting this basic and intimate confrontation before. (The weary old stream of consciousness is something quite other, being composed like any other literature in the author's head, irrespective of where he was and what he was being at the time.) The extreme analogy of such a confrontation would be Shakespeare weaving into the words of "To be or not to be," or "Tomorrow and tomorrow and tomorrow" such instant reactions and reflections as "Shall I go for a piss now or hold it till I've done a few more lines," or "I wonder what size her clitoris is," or "We must be out of olive oil." Of course there is no effect of interpretation in Berryman; but the spring does hold apart, and constantly, a terrifying and comforting image of the poet as *there*—wrestling in his flesh and in his huddle of needs—while at the same time poetry is engraving itself permanently on the page. It is this that keeps our awed and round-eyed attention more than anything else: our simultaneous sense of the pain of being such a poet, and of the pleasure of being able to read his poetry.

It is also instrumental in our not judging. The poet is not asking us to pity his racked state, or to understand and sympathize with the wild bad obsessed exhibitionist behavior it goes with. These things are simply there, as formal achieve-

ment, and Henry James, that great Whitman fan, would oddly enough, I am sure, have understood and been gratified by
it. He suggests it in the advice he gave to the sculptor An-
dersen about how to convey the tension and the isolation in an
embracing sculptured couple.

> Make the creature palpitate, and their flesh tingle and flush,
> and their internal economy proceed and their bellies ache and
> their bladders fill—all in the mystery of your art.

"Hard-headed Willie" in his magisterial way, and with his
"blood, imagination, intellect running together," might also
have given a clue; but when he says "I walk through a long
school-room questioning" or

> I count those feathered balls of soot
> The moorhen guides upon the stream
> To silence the envy in my thought.

it is well understood that he is doing no such thing. This is
the rhetoric of the moment, not its apparent actuality; the
thought he is silencing and the questions he asks have all
been cooked up in the study afterward. His air of immediate
imperiousness, with himself and us, is a bit of a fraud, and
this seasons our admiration with an affectionate touch of decision. Yeats is the boss whose little tricks we can see through
and like him the more for: all the same, we do judge.

And with Berryman we don't; the spring device forbids it.
How judge someone who while talking and tormenting himself is also writing a poem about the talk and torment? Except
that we know, deeper down, that this effect *is* a formalistic device and that Berryman's control of it is total. And this knowledge makes us watch the taut spring vibrating with even
rapter attention. There is a parallel with the formalism so
brilliantly pulled off by Lowell in *Life Studies,* where the poetry seemed itself the act of alienation and cancellation, as if
poet and subject had died the instant the words hit the paper.
The formal device or emblem above the door framing the two
collections might be, in Lowell's case, a speech cut off by the
moment of death: in Berryman's, a Word condemned to
scratch itself eternally, in its chair and at its desk.

Lowell forsook that frame, and in *Notebook* approaches the
idiom of *The Dream Songs* (I waive any inquiry, surely bound

to be inconclusive, into questions of mutual sympathetic influencing). But in achieving the note of continuing casualness, in contriving to stay alive as it were, *Notebook* remains individual pieces, fascinating in themselves, but lacking the tension that makes *Dream Songs* a clear and quivering serial. The comparison may be unfair, because *Notebook* may not be intended to be a narrative poem, but it shows how much and how successfully *The Dream Songs* is one, and *Love & Fame*. If I am right in thinking that Berryman's aim is to hold in opposed tension and full view the poet and his words, I may also be right in supposing that *Homage to Mistress Bradstreet* was inspired, in the form it took, by the same preoccupation. What seems to have been the donnée for Berryman there was the contrast between the woman as she presumably was, and the poems that she wrote. Berryman's ways of suggesting this are on the whole crude—I do not see how they could be anything else; but the idea obviously fascinates him. Why couldn't her poems be *her,* as he wills his to be him?—the poem celebrates a gulf and a contrast.

> When by me in the dusk my child sits down
> I am myself. Simon, if it's that loose,
> Let me wiggle it out.
> You'll get a bigger one there, & bite.
> How they loft, how their sizes delight and grate.
> The proportioned, spiritless poems accumulate.
> And they publish them
> away in brutish London, for a hollow crown.

Homage to Mistress Bradstreet is far from being a masterpiece; it is a very provisional kind of poem. Its virtues grow on one, but so does a sense of the effort Berryman was making to push through a feat of re-creation for which a clarified version of the style of Dylan Thomas was—hopefully—appropriate. Had Thomas, instead of lapsing into "Fern Hill," been able to write a long coherent poem on a real subject—the kind of subject touched on in "'The Tombstone Told When She Died"—it might have been something like this. But Thomas never got so far. We know from *Love & Fame* that Berryman felt the impact of Thomas early—in Cambridge, England, before the war—found him better than anyone writing in America, and made great use of him, the kind of use a formidably developing poet can make of an arrested one. The superiority of *Mistress Bradstreet* over the poems that are unemancipated from Auden— "World-Telegram," "1 September 1939," "Desire Is a World by Night," etc.—strikingly shows how Auden was far too intellectually in shape to be successfully digested by Berryman as Thomas had been.

The feeling imagination, the verbal love, in fact, of *Mistress Bradstreet,* is most moving; and the image of her reading Quarles and Sylvester ("her favourite poets; unfortunately") is, I am convinced, a counter-projection of the image later willed on us by the grand, fully "voiced" Berryman of his own self at his own desk. Finding his own voice is for Berryman a consummation in which his own self and his poetry become one. Nor would it be fanciful to see this as the climax of a historical as well as of a personal process. Poetry, in its old European sense, *was* very largely a matter of getting out of your own perishable tatty self into a timeless metaphysical world of order and beauty. We have only to think of Spenser scribbling in Kilcomman Castle, transforming the horrors of the Irish reality into the beauties of *The Faerie Queen;* while Donne—often taken as "modern"—is no less a transformer of the casual and the promiscuous into metaphysical fantasy and form.

From Bradstreet to "Henry," who is no mask but a nickname in the formal spousals of poet to reader, is therefore a journey of almost symbolic dimensions, and one which only Lowell and Berryman could have successfully accomplished. Whatever their technical interest and merits, all their early poems were strangely clangorous and muffled, as if a new god were trying to climb out from inside the machinery: they needed the machinery to establish but not to *be* themselves. *Berryman's Sonnets* are brilliantly donnish in the way they cavort around the traditions and idioms of the genre, and it is indeed part of that idiom that there is no inside to them, no personal non-dramatic reality.

> Keep your eyes open when you kiss: do: when
> You kiss. All silly time else, close them to . . .

In combination with such admirable and witty pastiche the gins and limes and so on of the *Sonnets* strike one as mere modern properties, and quite singularly not about what

Berryman is. His use of Donne here is more generous than Lowell's grabbings out of the past; yet if Lowell wears his versions more ruthlessly he does it also more comprehensively.

Their absolute need of at last finding, and then being, themselves, could be seen in the light of Auden's comment: "When I read a poem I look first at the contraption and then at the guy inside it." To both Auden and Yeats it would make no sense to be in search of their own voices. They remain what they were from the beginning. When Yeats says, "It is myself that I remake," he is subsuming guy and contraption under a single flourish, but in fact the continuity between Yeats young and old is unbroken, and so with Auden. There is never any doubt what guy is in the contraption and that he is the same one. I would say, therefore, that there is a radical and important difference, *in this respect,* between the poetry of Auden and Yeats and that of Lowell and Berryman; and, interesting as it is, I would not agree with the conclusion that M. L. Rosenthal comes to in "The Poetry of Confession."* He feels that the Americans "are carrying on where Yeats left off" when he proposed that the time had come to make the literal Self poetry's central redeeming symbol:

> I must lie down where all the ladders start,
> In the foul rag-and-bone shop of the heart.

But that is surely Yeats striking out a new line, apparently turning a somersault but really remaining the same old aesthete and tower-builder who chided the contingencies of this world for "wronging your image that blossoms a rose in the deeps of my heart." Yeats had always affirmed the self: he took it for granted, he did not have to find it: and in "Sailing to Byzantium" he exaggerates almost to the verge of parody the traditional view that seems to start Berryman off in *Mistress Bradstreet:* that "once out of nature" and in the world of art the perishable and tatty self enters a new dimension of being, becomes a poet. What is fascinating about Berryman's enterprise is that starting from "the proportioned spiritless poems" he tries to reconstitute, so to speak, the perishable

---

* *The Modern Poets* (Oxford University Press, 1960). Reprinted in *Robert Lowell: A Portrait of the Artist in His Time,* edited by Michael London and Robert Boyers (David Lewis, 1970).

being who so improbably produced them. That seems to me
the significant American poetic journey—to discover the living ego as it has to be ("I renounce not even ragged glances,
small teeth, nothing")—and it is the exact reverse of Yeats's
pilgrimage. In finding themselves Lowell and Berryman must
indeed renounce nothing, not a hair of their heads, "forever
or / so long as I happen." Such an achievement is a triumph
quite new to poetry and confers on it a new and unsuspected
authority. Thomas Wolfe said something like: "I believe we
are lost in America but I believe we shall be found." Lowell
and Berryman could have nothing to do with the lush fervor
of the sentiment. None the less, in terms of poetry they embody such a faith and justify it.

II

This is indeed glorious but not necessarily satisfactory. Let us
try to see what has been lost as well as gained. My contention
would be that the two poets reverse completely one canon of
the European aesthetic tradition, as represented by Yeats, and
those other European Magi Rilke and Valéry, but in another
way they are willy-nilly bound to it.* Their spectacular
breakthrough into contingency is only possible because of the
other Magi article of belief that things have no existence except in the poet's mind. So that in the iron selfhood the two
poets have created, the most apparently feeble, hasty, or obviously untrue comment, sloughed off from day to day, ac-
quires an imperishable existence when it is unsubstantiated
on the page. The poems in *Love & Fame*, where even the nickname "Henry" has been dropped between us (as nicknames
come to be dropped between old married couples), are apparently bar-room comments on Berryman's past, nothing more,
and the people, events, feuds, and boastings in them are as

---

* Berryman's comment on Rilke in *The Dream Songs* is characteristically
exhilarating.

> Rilke was a *jerk.*
> I admit his griefs & music
> & title spelled all-disappointed ladies.
> A threshold worse than the circles
> where the vile settle & lurk,
> Rilke's. As I said,—

commonplace as the lunch-hour. The lines are like a late Picasso drawing, the realized personality of genius implicit in every flick of the pencil. (One wonders whether Edmund Wilson, who maintained in "Is Verse a Dying Technique?" that modern poetry is the prose of Flaubert, Joyce and Lawrence, had a chance to read them.)

And yet something is missing, the something that might join all these things to life itself. Such a poetry is not "earthed"—cannot be—for it has nothing of the *accidental* and inadvertent in it, no trace of genuine impurity. Art is all trickery, but it is a trickery which can join up with our own lives and dreams, events and responses, our own self-trickery maybe. And can it be that in so meticulously creating the contingent self Lowell and Berryman have had to cut it off from the outside world? That is what I meant by saying that the poet is created here by a process opposite to that in which the novelist creates his characters. The novelist arrives at the reality of the world because his art is not and cannot be fully under his control. He cannot make everything himself: his readers must supply it; and the people and things he writes of will become real not only because his readers are doing a lot of the work themselves but because what he invents will become true by repetition and by being taken for granted; the man he shapes for us on page 2 will have become his own man by page 200. And this is as true of Joyce as of Trollope; it is equally true of much poetry in which "things" and a "world" are created—*Evgeny Onegin* or "The Eve of St. Agnes." But it is not true of Lowell and Berryman, however much they may seem to be putting things and a world before us.

Some time ago, in a book called *The Romantic Survival*, I made a point about the world of Auden's poetry which I still think important, though the rest of the book no longer seems very relevant to me. It is that Auden, following Yeats, had carried the personal and legendary domain of that "Last Romantic" one stage further, creating his characteristically and ominously centripetal world of stylized meaningfulness—derelict factories, semi-detached houses, "the silent comb / Where dogs have worried or a bird was shot." What gave this world its instant authority was its appearance of stern political and social finger-pointing with its actual invitation to conspiracy and relish in the landscape of the evil fairy, the Death

Wish. "Auden has followed Yeats," I wrote, "in showing how
the intense private world of symbolism can be brought right
out into the open, eclecticized, and pegged down to every
point of interest in contemporary life." And yet Auden constantly reminded us—his wittiest spokesman was Caliban in
"The Sea and The Mirror"—that the realities of such poetry
are necessarily mirror realities.

> All the phenomena of an empirically ordered world are given.
> Extended objects appear to which events happen—old men
> catch dreadful coughs, little girls get their arms twisted. . . .
> All the voluntary movements are possible—crawling through
> flues and old sewers, sauntering past shopfronts, tiptoeing
> through quicksands and mined areas . . . all the modes of
> transport are available, but any sense of direction, any knowl-
> edge of where on earth one has come from or where on earth
> one is going to, is completely absent.

The *bien pensants* of contemporary culture have made so
much of the desolating, but also heartening and "compassionate" sense of the pressures of life, of the sheer difficulty of
being oneself, which Lowell and Berryman have conveyed in
their poetry, that a qualification along these lines may be in
order. Auden finds the trick to let out Yeats into a new world
of legend: Lowell and Berryman—on a scale and with a virtuosity of which today only American poets are capable—let
him out in his turn, into a place where "*all* the phenomena of
an empirically ordered world are given," and "*all* the volun-
tary movements are possible." Its very completeness precludes
any attachment to mundane eventfulness— "From a *poet?*
Words / to menace action. O I don't think so." Berryman's remark echoes what Auden constantly reiterates. Theirs is a
breath-taking achievement, with results not at all like Auden,
but I doubt it could have been done without him. As Berryman so engagingly puts it in that superlative *Love & Fame*
poem "Two Organs":

> I didn't want my next poem to be *exactly* like Yeats
> or exactly like Auden
> since in that case where the hell was *I?*
> but what instead *did* I want it to sound like?

Temperamentally, one infers, Berryman could hardly be more
different from either Yeats or Auden. He was "up against it"

in a sense (I take it) unknown to their basically sane and self-centering personalities, but he adapts the mirror world of their invention to sound like what he wants to be. Success is shown by the failure of the alternatives taken by poets in a comparable situation (not of course of Berryman's stature, but that begs the question): the "confidences" of Anne Sexton and the "blown top" meaninglessness of Kenneth Fearing, for example. Berryman takes from Auden not only the mirror world but the wry unswerving knowledge of its use, which adds—as it does in Auden—a further dimension to the meaning of the poem. An instance would be 97 in *The Dream Songs,* which deliberately lapses delicately into gibberish and concludes:

> Front back & backside go bare!
> Cats' blackness, booze, blows, grunts, grand groans.
> Yo bad yōm i-oowaled bo   v'ha'l lail awmer h're gawber!
> —Now, now, poor Bones.

This is not like Lear's fool, clowning to hide desolation and fear, though something like his voice can be heard at times in *The Dream Songs.* It is a humorous, rather than a witty, exploitation of the formal idiom; its camp "blackface" touch not unlike Auden's handling of Jewish Rosetta in *The Age of Anxiety.* Both poets know that they can only move us by means of a sort of carnival exploitation of the mirror world. Caliban, with his virtuoso eloquence, and Rosetta with her day dreams, would be equally at home among the exuberance and desperation of *The Dream Songs.* "A man speaking to men" does not say, as Henry does, "He stared at ruin. Ruin stared straight back." The humor of Groucho Marx, even if corny, also belongs to the mirror world.

And so does the straight talk. We can have no objection to sentiments like

> Working & children & pals are the point of the thing
> for the grand sea awaits
> us which will then us toss
> & endlessly us undo.

or

> We will die, & the evidence
> is: nothing after that.
> Honey, we don't rejoin.

> The thing meanwhile, I suppose, is to be courageous and
>   kind.

because they are less earnest than sparkles from the wheel, and have been so wholly cauterized by contrivance. We can have "a human relation," for what that's worth, with poets far less good than Berryman. We can enter into such and share their feelings in a way impossible with him, for all the openness and Olympianly inclusive naturalness of his method. It is strangely unsatisfactory that in his poetry the poet cannot put a foot wrong. He can go off the air (Auden can too) but that is a different thing. If any technological habit has unconsciously influenced this kind of poetry it may be the record player with its click on and off, its hairline acoustics and relentless sensitivity. Both Lowell's and Berryman's poems have the flat finality of something perfectly recorded, and just the right length for perfect transmission. I notice writing down quotations that they do not sound very good, even when I had admired them as part of the poem: for the proper rigorous effect every word of the poem must be there.

This again excludes the accidental. The tone does not change or modulate, does not sag accidentally or rise with deliberate effort; the "supernatural crafter" is too much in charge, as he gives us an inkling in "The Heroes."

> I had, from my beginning, to adore heroes
> & I elected that they witness to,
> show forth, transfigure: life-suffering and pure heart
> & hardly definable but central weaknesses
>
> for which they were to be enthroned and forgiven by me.
> They had to come on like revolutionaries,
> enemies throughout to accident & chance,
> relentless travellers, long used to failure
>
> in tasks that but for them would sit like hanging judges
> on faithless & by no means up to it Man.
> Humility & complex pride their badges,
> every "third thought" their grave.

Compare and contrast with that the young Stephen Spender's hopefully confiding and altogether by no means up to it poem "I think continually of those who were truly great." Spender gives it away by the touching solemnity of knowing he is writing a poem, a poem about heroes, the truly great. An all too

human poem, as human as the embarrassment with and for
the author that flushes us as we read it, but at least we know
from it what we do *not* feel about those who "left the vivid air
signed with their honor," etc. By patronizing it we engage
with it: by disliking its sentiment we adjust our own. And we
respond to it; it is not a null poem, even though it combines
the inadvertent and the contrived in an unstable state.

   Great as well as small poets are, or have been, rich with
this inadvertence. Keats, writing in halcyon good faith,

> Let the mad poets say whate'er they please
> Of the sweets of peris, fairies, goddesses;
> There is not such a treat among them all,
> Haunters of cavern, lake, and waterfall,
> As a real woman,

seems not to know how it was going to look, or what the reader was going to think, and certainly not how revealing of his
genius the lines are. Byron always seems to know, with his
posturing and easy anecdotage, and the wholly controlled and
calculated swagger of the jotting on the back of *Don Juan*.

> O would to God that I were so much clay
> As I am blood, bone, marrow, passion, feeling,
> Having got drunk exceedingly today
> So that I seem to stand upon the ceiling,

These lines mime a loss of control and a hungover truculence,
and yet every so often he forgets himself genuinely in a way
there is no mistaking, as in the lines written when he heard
his wife was ill. The chagrined pity of its opening seems to
try, and fail to be, all self-pity, until a kind of hangdog solic-
itude turns to and takes refuge in the relieved virulence of satiric declamation. There is even an unexpectedly startled and
self-disconcerted note in the famous lines: "How little know
we what we are, how less / What we may be." Hardy is in this
kind of way the most vulnerable of all great poets, as witness
the end of "After a Journey," where the poet revisits the sea-
haunts where he had first fallen in love with a wife long estranged and now dead.

> Trust me, I mind not, though Life lours,
> The bringing me here; nay, bring me here again!
>   I am just the same as when
> Our days were a joy and our paths through flowers.

"I am just the same as when . . .": the reassurance he gives
and needs to give has all the eager clumsiness of life: we can
hear the relief of saying it, a relief all the greater because it
can't be true.

I labor this incongruous mixed bag of examples because
they all seem to me to contain something naive and direct that
has vanished or is vanishing from the performance of good poetry. In them we seem to meet the poet when he doesn't expect it; like Sartre's voyeur he is looking at something else so
intently that he is unaware of the reader behind him. And can
it be that Berryman's preoccupation—for it appears to be
that—with establishing the poet's existence in all its hopeless
contingency ("I renounce not even ragged glances, small
teeth, nothing") is both an attempt at what earlier poets—
and bad poets today—do without meaning to, and a recognition that only a formalization of such directness is possible to
him? We can see it in the cunning control of that same poem,
"The Heroes," which slides casually into the subject à propos
of Pound, a "feline" figure ("zeroing in on feelings, / hovering
up to them, putting his tongue in their ear"); then goes on to
distinguish this from the "imperial sway" exercised by Eliot,
Joyce and Yeats; rises to the celebration of heroism already
quoted; and in the last verse shows us where the first six came
from.

These gathering reflexions, against young women,
against seven courses in my final term,
I couldn't sculpt into my helpless verse yet.
I wrote mostly about death.

The ideas are referred to a pre-poetic stage in the poet, when
they were tumbling in the dark together with feelings about
girls and resentment against classes. That self could not have
written the poem, but it had the ideas, and is coincident with
the self that is now sculpting the poetry effectively—perhaps
more than coincident, because its topic was the inclusive and
unsculpturable one of death. Imperial sway can only be exercised over the words that make up the self.

The last line does not nudge us; it simply looms up—a perspective on the dark contingency of the self that heroes don't
have, for they can be sculptured into verse. The self that
can't remains pervasively present, disembodied above the

poem like a Cheshire cat. There is no question of making or remaking that self in Yeatsian style, nor of making legendary figures out of the poet's entourage, as both Yeats and Lowell in their different ways have done. Professor Neff, who gave Berryman a C out of malice at Columbia, in the next poem, "Crisis," is paid the subtle compliment of a rapid, unimpartial write-off; there is no attempt to enshrine him in some immortal rogues' gallery, and Mark Van Doren in the poem is also and simply a real person, as in conversation. The poet's mother and father appear in an equally unspectacular way (constrast again with Lowell), figures briefly revealed by night, unless the night, or pre-dawn, time of most pieces, like the seeming traces of drink or drugs, is another convention for conveying the continuity and actuality of the self.

The self can appear in that dark past as in grand guignol, surrounded by ghosts indistinguishable from itself (129: "riots for Henry the unstructured dead") or it can be transposed into a hauntingly meticulous *doppelgänger,* as in 242.

> About that "me." After a lecture once
> came up a lady asking to see me. "Of course.
> When would you like to?"
> Well, *now,* she said.

After a precise, casual, brittle account of the quotidian campus scene—the poet with lunch date, the lady looking distraught—comes the pay-off.

> So I rose from the desk & closed it and turning back
> found her in tears apologizing—"No,
> go right ahead," I assur-
> ed her, here's a handkerchief. Cry." She did. I did.
>   When she got
> control, I said "What's the matter—if you want to talk?"
> "Nothing. Nothing's the matter." So.
> I am her.

Naturally: she could be nobody else. Only through Berryman can the poem move us, but it does move. The hopelessness, the stasis, is completely authentic. Not so, I think, those poems in *Love & Fame* about the others in the mental hospital, Jill and Eddie Jane and Tyson and Jo. For all their "understanding" "The Hell Poem" and "*I* know" have something insecure about them, as if threatened by the presence of other people. The poet was not threatened of course—we feel his openness, his interest—but the poem is caught between its equation with contingency and the fact that, as form, its contingency can only be "me."

The Berryman *pruzhina*, or spring, snaps as the real presence of these others pulls it too far apart. For the young Berryman, as he tells us in "Two Organs," the longing was to write "big fat fresh original & characteristic poems."

> My longing, yes, was a woman's
> She can't know can she *what kind* of a baby
> she's going with all the will in the world to produce?
> I suffered trouble over this.

"I couldn't sleep at night, I attribute my life-long insomnia / to my uterine struggles." Nothing is more graphic in Berryman than the sickness and struggle of finding oneself about to become a poet, lumbered with an unknown fetus that when it arrives will be oneself. We may note that this is the exact opposite, in this mirror world, of true childbirth, which produces *another person*. Still, the pains are real enough, and so is the comedy. Indeed the black comedy of Beckett again comes to mind, a theater of one. "By virtue of the aesthetic form," generalizes Marcuse, the "play" creates its own atmosphere of "seriousness" which is *not* that of the given reality, but rather its "negation." That kind of portentousness is here in a way, and the theory of the "living theater" has certain affinities with Berryman's drive—if I am right about it—to coincide poet as man with poem as thing.

Berryman's fascination with becoming himself as a poet has—given his genius—an almost equal fascination for us, but it has a drawback too. We can contemplate it but not share it—it is not really a part of the universally identifiable human experience, the experience in Byron or in Gray's "Elegy," to which, as Dr. Johnson observed, every bosom returns an echo. What we have instead is extreme singularity, the Berrymanness of Berryman, which we and the poet stare at together: that he absorbs us as much as he absorbs himself is no mean feat. We want indeed to know "of what heroic stuff was warlock Henry made"—the American hero whose tale

can be only of himself and who is (unlike Wordsworth) bored
by it.

> Life, friends, is boring. We must not say so.
> After all, the sky flashes, the great sea yearns,
> we ourselves flash and yearn,
> and moreover my mother told me as a boy
> (repeatingly) "Ever to confess you're bored
> means you have no
>
> Inner Resources." I conclude now I have no
> inner resources, because I am heavy bored.
> Peoples bore me,
> literature bores me, especially great literature,
> Henry bores me.

Delightful! Our bosoms return an echo to *that*, as to the celebration of the same mother in 100, and her "two and seventy
years of chipped indignities," but what principally gets to us is
the performance of birth, the pleasure of finding the fetus so
triumphantly expelled. *"Le chair est triste, hélas, et j'ai lu tous
les livres"*—that sensation, too, for Mallarmé, existed to end
up in a book, and so it is with the perpetual endgame of
Berryman—"after all has been said, and all *has* been
said. . . ."

We do miss a *developing* world. Having found himself on the
page the poet has found hell, or God—it is much the same,
for in either case there is nothing further there. Compare
with the world of Hardy, say, who was not bored but went on
throughout a long calvary continuing to *notice* things outside
himself, able to bring the outside world into his poetry while
leaving it in its natural place. (Marianne Moore and Elizabeth Bishop have done the same.) And among Hardy's preoc-
cupations "the paralyzed fear lest one's not one"—a poet that
is—did not, as far as we can see, figure. But it is the detri-
ment and dynamic of Berryman's book. Hardy had things casi-
er, for he did not in the least mind writing bad relaxed poems,
and this itself helps to keep him in the outer world, the world
of *true* contingency. His is the natural contrast to the place
discovered and developed by our two in some ways equally Anglo-Saxon giants.

> I say the paralyzed fear that one's not one
> is back with us forever.

So it may be. The struggle to become a great poet, to exercise imperial sway, may indeed be increasingly and ruinously hard, obsessing the poet's whole outlook. But they have shown it can be done.

The novelists of our time have not succeeded in creating a new fictional form as they have created a new poetic one— and that seems to me to have real significance. The bonds that enclosed the novelist and compelled him into his form have up till lately been social as well as aesthetic ones. There was much that he could not say "in so many words," and which therefore had to be said by other means—a style had to be found for creating what society could not tolerate the open expression of: such a style as is created, for example, in the opening lines of *Tristram Shandy*. But in a wholly permissive age the formal bonds of poetry remain drawn taut because they depend on sculpting a voice, graving a shape and pattern. The bonds of fiction slacken into unrecognizability because the pressures of society itself, not of mere craft, which used to enforce them, have withdrawn. The novel form today has no inevitable response to make to its unchartered freedom; it can only concoct unnecessary ones, resurrected devices like those of Barth, Burroughs, Vonnegut and others, which do not impress us with self-evident authority but act as an encumbrance, get in the way. Like the novelist the poet can say anything now, but he must exercise imperial sway as he does so. If he can, poetry has the edge again, and Lowell and Berryman have honed it to a razor sharpness. Despairing art critics, we learn, have been asking not what art is possible today but *is* art possible. As regards poetry, we have our answer. It is still adding to the stock of available reality while expressing the matter in hand.

∿

Love, Art, and Money

Hayden Carruth

John Berryman's new book of poems is in some respects, as
the advance rumors warned us, a departure from earlier
work; but not, as we come to look at it, much of a departure.
True, Berryman now is writing in propria persona, without
the masks and dramatic voices of his *Dream Songs* and *Homage
to Mistress Bradstreet;* he is writing with candor about his own
explicit autobiography; he is writing in simpler, more accessible language than that of earlier poems. But these are changes
in degree only. They are not real departures, not reversals or
innovations.

The contrast with Robert Lowell is irresistible, partly because the change in Berryman's poetry offers a seeming parallel to Lowell's change twenty years ago from the ornate,
sharply formal poems of *Lord Weary's Castle* to the simpler,
more personal poems of *Life Studies*. Beyond this, the two
poets are the same age, of roughly the same background (eastern private schools, Harvard and Columbia, et cetera), of similar literary origins (the New Criticism, the war, et cetera).
They are even, according to Berryman, close friends.

When I was writing about Lowell a couple years ago I said
that I thought the term *confessional*, which had been applied
to his autobiographical poems by several critics, was unfortu-
nate because it suggested an aim far less than his real intention. What Lowell was doing in those poems, I think, was
exploring his own and his family's life, in extreme seriousness, to see if he could give that body of experience an imaginative organization strong enough, in the face of the
depersonalizing force of a modern collective and tech-

Hayden Carruth, "Love, Art, and Money," *Nation* 211 (November 2, 1970):
437–38.

nomaniacal world, to stand as an integrated structure. A will, a personality, a being. He was trying to create a life: his own.

Perhaps such an effort can never succeed, can never rest in achievement. Being finished would mean an end of creation and of life. The value of the autobiogenetic stance in art consists in the effort and the continuing trial. But the point here is that Berryman's new poems give little evidence of trial. They have no real seriousness or creative force, but only a kind of edgy exhibitionism. They are precisely confessional and nothing more, except when they are something less, that is, brags and rants. On the side of "fame" Berryman writes repeatedly and smugly about the success of his books, about his fattening royalties and increasing fan mail, about his honors and his acquaintanceships with exalted people. On the side of "love," where he is even less prepossessing, he gives us schoolboyish bragging exploits, the sequence of pickups and mistresses for thirty-five years, while his three wives get half a line and his children scarcely more, though he says somewhere that children are one of the three "points" of life. The other two, he adds, are "high art" and "money in the bank."

It is all full of self-contradiction, special pleading, vagueness. What emerges is not a personality, not an integrated being, but only a muddlement of crude desires. Toward the end there is some attempt at greater seriousness. The last poem in the book, which is also the longest, is a religious poem, forthright in its devotional feeling and in some passages almost moving, until in the midst of it we are informed, in a tone half blustery and half sneering, that the poet's conversion occurred "three weeks ago day before yesterday." He seems to be saying, "If you believe this you'll believe anything." In a saint or mystic we might accept that, though not without a strain; we might, under certain conditions, even celebrate it. But in this boasting, equivocating secularist? What does he take us for?

Some readers may say that these matters of substance have no importance esthetically and should not concern the critic, whose job is to examine not the experience but how the experience is turned into poetry. I do not agree. A critic has a moral as well as an esthetic obligation, and certainly a journalist-reviewer, as distinct from a critic, has a duty to report the substance of books which he has seen before they are available to the public. Other readers may say—a more cogent objection—that the substance of Berryman's poems is exactly the hang-up between faith and skepticism, self-reliance and self-doubt, hope and despair, which we all know; it is the experience of vacillation, experience with a negative value, the modern experience par excellence, and there is no reason why it should not be made into good poetry. Here I do agree. Who wouldn't, with so many splendid examples—Theodore Roethke, for one—before us? But Berryman has not done it. His experience remains raw and unstructured and far from good poetry.

Which brings us to the crux of the matter, the poetry itself, the language and verbal style. Repeatedly Berryman congratulates himself for his ear and his sense of metric; once he even congratulates God. He is delighted with his "gift." But where is it? What is it? His ability to wrench syntax out of every convention while remaining, though barely, within the bounds of a possible grammar? He is famous for this, of course. But it has nothing whatever to do with metric, it has damned little to do with poetry in general, and I confess I see nothing else in his work. I always thought his earlier poems, with their surface jumpiness, had no metric at all, or scarcely any; they move, not with the basic consistent cadence of essential poetry, but only with their own meretricious push and thrust of hyperbolic and unexpected phrasing. They move, stiltlike, on Berryman's peculiar rhetoric. Now in the new poems, where the language is simpler, I see my feelings confirmed, for with the rhetoric toned down the lack of meter is more than ever obvious. Here are a few lines, random but characteristic (from "The Heroes"):

> They had to come on like revolutionaries,
> enemies throughout to accident & chance,
> relentless travellers, long used to failure
>
> in tasks that but for them would sit like hanging judges
> on faithless & by no means up to it Man.

This is a good deal easier to read than the earlier heavy contortions, and I suppose we should be grateful for that. We would be if it weren't so flat. These lines are limp. They have no meter at all, nothing to sustain the modified but still deviant syntax. The norm of English pentameter, which in theory lies behind the poems, has become putative only, and hence is no help to the poet, and his ear has invented nothing to replace it. Here are a few lines from another poem with complex syntax, bearing about the same relationship to poetic convention.

> Sometimes since you don't love me any more
>> I cannot find an animal spirit
>> to move my feet,
>> or one quits and leaves me in the street
> among the buses and the traffic's roar
>
> as if I were deep in thought, but I am not
>> —until the animal spirit that preserves
>> me still alive
>> takes care of where I am and slowly drives
> my feet their way across the street.

These lines are nothing exceptional perhaps. But am I wrong, doesn't the meter here do its work, both by keeping syntax in order and by making it move? Doesn't it give these lines liveliness and even a minor elegance? I think so. But unfortunately for Berryman (and many of the rest of us), they are by Paul Goodman.

As for diction, we have on one hand Berryman's well-known colloquial cuteness, out-Audening Auden, as in the "faithless & by no means up to it Man," or elsewhere the pitiful death of Peter Warlock who had just "knocked himself off"; and on the other his deliberate archaisms, inversions, the use of fusty words like "moot" and "plaint." Archness, what we used to call sophomorism: in parts of *The Dream Songs* he almost brought it to a pitch intense enough to make an honest effect. But the more I think about those poems, and then about these new slighter ones, the more I think that that effect too was meretricious, a product of verbal *bizarrerie*. Finally there are Berryman's rhymes. They have alway been uninteresting, sometimes awful, and they have not improved. The worst poem in the new book, "The Minnesota 8 and the Letter-Writers," is also the only closely rhymed poem.

In reviewing one of Berryman's earlier books I tried to trace a development in his contorted syntax from his first poems to

The Dream Songs. I knew I didn't like his style, and had never liked it, and out of diffidence or a desire to avert my bias I leaned backward to find some innate necessity or naturalness in it. But now he has confessed, in a poem called "Olympus," his source, quoting it entire: "The art of poetry is amply distinguished from the manufacture of verse by the animating presence in the poetry of a fresh idiom: language so twisted and posed in a form that it not only expresses the matter in hand but adds to the stock of available reality." That is a well-known sentence, or at least it once was, written by R. P. Blackmur and published in *Poetry* in 1935. It stood alone, intended as a wonderful critical *aperçu,* and it suffers the faults of most such attempted distillations, sententiousness and incompleteness; but it hit Berryman hard. "I was never altogether the same man after *that,*" he writes, and goes on to say how "eagerly" he sought out Blackmur's other writings. No doubt the essays on Yeats, Eliot, and the early Wallace Stevens particularly impressed him. But where are naturalness and necessity now? This seems a case where one of the New Critics actually achieved what they all patently wanted, not only the control of taste with respect to poetry already written but the control of poetry still to come. Yet must "fresh idiom" mean "twisted and posed"? And does language ever add to "available reality"? We know the danger of that old fatuity; and doubly dangerous it was for Berryman, I think, because it led him, in its arrogance and his own, to infer, by transversion or contraction or mere muleheadedness, that *poetry* as well as verse might be *manufactured* if only one could invent a fresh idiom in language twisted and posed. This is an oversimplification, more would need to be said in any comprehensive discussion of Berryman's work, but it is still very close to the heart of the matter. And the proof, I believe, lies on every page of his books.

The time has come, surely, to say that Berryman's poetry is usually interesting and sometimes witty but almost never moving, and that in spite of its scope and magnitude it lacks the importance that has been ascribed to it in recent years by many critics, editors, and readers. The "fame" that so much delights Berryman is inflated. When we consider other poets of his generation who have worked in the same general poetic convention—I say nothing of those in other conventions—we see that they have been making poetry while Berryman has been making language twisted and posed: I mean those already noted here, Lowell, Roethke, and Goodman, as well as such others as Cunningham, Schwartz, Jarrell, and Elizabeth Bishop, and even those of smaller ambition, like Richard Wilbur and Anthony Hecht, who have produced individual poems finer in poetic integrity and formal congruency than anything in the works of Berryman. One says these things the more willingly about him, though about another one might keep silent, because his own self-advertising, especially in his new book, has become so vain and outrageous.

≤

"Lost Souls
in Ill-Attended Wards"

BERRYMAN'S "ELEVEN ADDRESSES
TO THE LORD"

PAUL MARIANI

Dante, Blake, Pascal, Baudelaire, Hopkins, Eliot: these, and
Emily Dickinson and—at moments—Roethke . . . and
Berryman. Figures in our post-Augustinian pantheon, and in
the West, who have touched with their words the mudflats of
the human condition and have reported back to us the sense
of having been in their turn touched by the fiery or chilling
finger of God. Consider this cluster of works in that short
space occupying Berryman's own post–Dream Songs world:
Love & Fame (1970), Delusions, Etc. (1972), Recovery (1973),
and Henry's Fate (1977). When Berryman leapt up, over, and
down from that bridge seven years ago, swerving slantwise towards the frozen Mississippi, only the first of these volumes
had yet been born. But we, coming after, and picking up the
pieces as best we can, can begin to piece together from the
scattered limbs of Osiris a pattern—a terrifying pattern—
which includes in its grid an oasis of spiritual recovery before
that battered self suffered its further disintegrations.

Much has already been made of Berryman's alcoholism.
This is of course inevitable, since Berryman himself made so
much of it, whether in The Dream Songs themselves or in
Love & Fame or in his unfinished novel, Recovery, that thinly
disguised fiction about a schizoid figure named Alan Severance (a name which one witty alcoholic character translates

Reprinted from Greg Kuzma, ed., A Book of Rereadings (Best Cellar Press,
1979), pp. 8–21.

this way: " 'Alan' is harmony, right? Celtic, I believe. Your last name is wide open. Tearer-apart of people, disrupter."). Berryman was an admitted alcoholic, but it is his struggle against that condition which seems to me to mark the anxiety of the hell-trapped condition of modern man as much as any condition. It is this self-conscious, self-emptying struggle which in fact informs the movement of Berryman's best book, *Love & Fame,* to inform, indeed, nearly all of the late poetry. My quarrel—such as it is—is with those critics who would try to explain away these poems as evasive techniques, lexical excrement, language distorted, lost control of, either by the delusions attendant upon alcoholism or by the recovery from that disease. Whatever truth there may have been in Berryman's belief that alcohol was necessary to spur the spirit on, to keep the muse in motion (a belief shared by other writers like Hart Crane, Malcolm Lowry, F. Scott Fitzgerald, Eugene O'Neill, Hemingway, Faulkner), this much seems true: in struggling to come at the roots of his own spiritual malaise, in wrestling with those terrifying demons ensnared in the pickerel grass of the subconscious, Berryman has managed to speak with extraordinary force about the human condition in which we all—willy nilly—share. To the point here is the longest of the five quotations which preface the *Delusions* volume: "And indeed if Eugene Irtenev was mentally deranged everyone is in the same case; the most mentally deranged people are certainly those who see in others indications of insanity they do not notice in themselves." And Eliot points the finger at every reader of *The Waste Land,* echoing his own dark encounter with Baudelaire: "You! hypocrite lecteur!— mon semblable—mon frère!" Exactly.

Reading *Recovery,* we are imaginatively transposed to the alcoholic's ward, where we can watch with apparent impunity the complex, devious moves and countermoves people will make to explain or defend their own self-delusions. What we soon realize, however, is that we have really been given an opportunity not so much to view *them*—as though we were London wags of two centuries ago taking a leisurely Sunday afternoon stroll through Bethlehem (Bedlam) hospital, who, having paid our entrance fee, are invited now to employ our riding crops to poke at or strike the more repulsive or unrecalcitrant idiots under our gaze—as to view ourselves, to see that, though sober, many of our actions and impulses, once scrutinized at their murky wellsprings, are anything *but* sane. The drunk reeling against the wall or vomiting over your rug or passing out in some tenement hall somewhere is simply more in the foreground of attention than most of us allow ourselves to be. For I have it on sufficient evidence—as even Jimmy Carter would admit—that our own thoughts and impulses and strong desires are as irrational and as dionysian as the alcoholic's in his insistent frenzy. But then good psychoanalysts, writers, and confessors have known all that for some time.

Berryman had an enormous ego, as his poetry and criticism alone will show. He could be—and was—rude, insulting, dismissive, haughty, bullying, and his dopplegängers in *Recovery* admit to all these . . . and more. But there is in the poetry, in among the verbal evasions and aggressions, a vulnerability, an ability on Berryman's part to laugh at all his ego-flaunting peacock struts. And it is with this eye of self-assessment, this relatively calm eye at the middle of this Lear-like moving storm that dominated Berryman's life, that I would like to turn my attention. And so to the fourth section, the marvellous close, of *Love & Fame.*

A word about the form of these "Eleven Addresses to the Lord." Here, as throughout the entire book, Berryman's characteristic formal signature is the quatrain, a form he also used almost entirely in his follow-up volume, *Delusions,* and which makes its presence felt in *Henry's Fate.* The form as Berryman uses it is amazingly—almost giddily—supple, the lines flexible, proselike, able to contract or expand at need. They can implode in on themselves, condensing to the "inimitable contriver" of the second line of the first address, or explode outwards, expanding into the professional qualifications of a line (from the same poem) like "and I believe as fixedly in the Resurrection-appearances to Peter & to Paul," followed by the clipped parataxis of "as I believe I sit in this blue chair." The addresses themselves range in length from the first (and longest), which is 28 lines, to the seventh, which is only 8. The average length (and six fall into this category) is 16 lines—a paradigm of four fours. What makes cousins of all eleven is that each is, in fact, a direct address to the Lord: a prayer of thanksgiving, praise, confession, or petition. It is form, then, form imposing structure, discipline, tradition, order.

But what is most remarkable about these poems is the *mode* of address, the lexical encounter with the Other, which draws on and releases a magnificent spectrum of linguistic strategies. And unlike many of the language games Berryman uses in *The Dream Songs* in order to conceal or evade or dance about, here in this group of poems there is at heart a serious attempt to encounter, to join frightened self with that Other Self. Berryman's linguistic range is extraordinary, it can swing all the way from the use of special languages—the parlance, for example, of the radio astronomer or the biblical exegete or of the encounter session—to the lingo of blackface, showboat, babytalk. He is as well a brilliant manipulator of syntactic distortion, capable of wrenching the idiom until it yields its virtue, a manipulation which calls to mind, for me, the straining Hopkins of the terrible sonnets. Consider, for a moment, what Berryman can do with the language of astrophysics, exegesis and encounter—mixed in with the traditional mode of the Old Testament hymn, as in the opening quatrain of "Lauds," which initiates the "Opus Dei" sequence of *Delusions, Etc.*:

> Let us rejoice on our cots, for His nocturnal miracles
> antique outside the Local Group & within it
> & within our hearts in it, and for quotidian miracles
> parsecs-off yielding to the Hale reflector.

Nothing in the Psalms will quite prepare us for that (though Auden—an early favorite of Berryman's, and in another key—might). At the other end of the lexical spectrum, Berryman is capable of doing a reputable imitation of the rhythms of jazz, the New Orleans strut, and blackface, all locked into the shattered frame of *Lycidas,* as in the 18th Dream Song, called "A Strut for Roethke," itself a pastoral elegy, lamenting the loss for all man, all nature, of the brother singer:

> Westward, hit a low note, for a roarer lost
> across the Sound but north from Bremerton,
> hit a way down note.
> And never cadenza again of flowers, or cost.
> Him who could really do that cleared his throat
> & staggered on.

But in the "Eleven Addresses" Berryman shies away from both poles, choosing something closer to a middle register. A middle register, that is, for post–*Homage to Mistress Bradstreet* Berryman. For the ensemble of voices which we identify with the speaker of that poem and with *The Dream Songs,* whom we know familiarly as Henry and Mr. Bones, here becomes Berryman, even to the extent of infiltrating that other persona of Berryman's, Alan Severance. "A poet's first personal pronoun is nearly always ambiguous": thus Berryman himself, speaking of the problem of the self-defined and idiosyncratic "I" which informs Whitman's "Song of Myself." Quoting Whitman's own solution to the poetic I—"the trunk and centre whence the answer was to radiate . . . must be an identical soul and body, a personality—which personality, after many considerings and ponderings I deliberately settled should be myself—indeed could not be any other"—Berryman declares that Whitman's voice is a voice "for himself and others: for others as *himself*—this is the intention clearly (an underlying exhibitionism and narcissism we take for granted)." And Berryman's gloss on the nature of the valve in Whitman's line, "Only the lull I like, the hum of your valved voice," is to the point here. It is a safety valve Whitman is speaking of, Berryman says, suggesting for him the sense of outlet, of the poet as

> a mere channel, but with its own ferocious difficulties, [which] fills with experience [until] a valve opens; he speaks them. I am obliged to remark that I prefer this theory of poetry to those that have ruled the critical quarterlies since I was an undergraduate [at Columbia in the '30s]. . . . It is as humble as, and identical with, Keats's view of the poet as having no existence, but being "forever in, for, and filling" other things.

It is that idea of the "I"—as a constricted channel (constricted by all those things that make this "I" its idiosyncratic, specifically defined self) pouring out those things which have filled up the reservoir of the soul—it is *that* sense of "I" which Berryman employs consistently throughout his mature poetry. When he sings, therefore, it is with the range of voices we have come to identify with Henry. That voice has become as

unmistakably Berryman's as Whitman's voice in "Song of Myself" has become Whitman's. Despite Berryman's disclaimer
at the beginning of *His Toy, His Dream, His Rest* that the
Dream Songs are "essentially about an imaginary character
(not the poet, not me) named Henry, a white American in early middle age sometimes in blackface, who has suffered an irreversible loss and talks about himself sometimes in the first
person, sometimes in the third, sometimes even in the second . . . ," it is this complex, painfully self-conscious voice
which Berryman found himself using whenever he would let
that valve fly open. (A look at Berryman's pre-*Bradstreet* poems
should convince any lingering doubters.) The poetic "I"
which we find in most English and American long poems of
an autobiographical cast since *The Prelude* is not, of course,
the voice the poet would ordinarily use in asking the waitress
for a second cup of coffee or in lecturing on the New Testament to a group of undergraduates, and it would be shot down
at once in a heavy group encounter session. But it does become, with time and practice, the "acquired" voice of the poet
in the act of making a poem.

Given this framework, then, we can speak of the muted,
humble, even serenely accepting voice of the "I" of the "Elev-
en Addresses," which I take to be as close to the poet as any
voice can be said to be the poet's own, fairly synonymous at
least with that five percent or so of the total mind he, like any
person, uses when he feels he must articulate his feelings,
even if it means releasing such impulses in the form of a poem
or a prayer. And one of Berryman's most marked successes in
these poems is the way he manages to play a specific, idiosyncratic, seriocomic voice against the traditional, rather rigid
framework of praise and petition associated with the shaping
of a prayer. What this mix produces is a compound of sentiments which are relatively straightforward, honest in their
doubts, quibbles, qualifications, even (yes) weirdly eloquent
in their striving to avoid what we might normally consider
eloquence.

Consider the strategy of the opening address as in some
sense representative of all eleven. Each of this poem's seven
quatrains is not only end-stopped; it is a semantically self-
contained unit. (The only possible exception here—the only
place where there is a slight running-over of sense—is at the

juncture between the fifth and sixth stanzas, where the normal period terminus gives way to the more fluid comma.) The opening quatrain is an exercise in onomastics, a calling on the Lord, who is identified in turn as "Master of beauty," as "craftsman of the snowflake," as "inimitable contriver," and—more expansively—as "endower of Earth so gorgeous & different from the boring Moon." Such a convocation of epithets is close in spirit to the beginning of Hopkins's *Wreck of the Deutschland* (and it is Hopkins who will be indirectly summoned at the close of the tenth address to give his gloss on the real nature of fame). Here, then, are the opening lines to Hopkins's great ode, where the Lord is addressed percussively in these terms:

> Thou mastering me
> God! giver of breath and bread;
> World's strand, sway of the sea;
> Lord of living and dead.

But even closer to Berryman's sentiments are these lines from Hopkins's sonnet in honor of St. Alphonsus Rodriguez (1888), where God is named as the one who

> hews mountain and continent,
> Earth, all, out; who, with trickling increment,
> Veins violets and tall trees makes more and more.

Having evoked, then, the Arch Creator with such gorgeous phrases (three of which, incidentally, are self-reflexive and could apply on a smaller scale to the poet as maker himself), Berryman thanks that Creator "for such as it is my gift." That qualifier is of course all-important, for, as any serious reader of this poet would know, that gift, all-important as it has been in Berryman's scheme of things, has been anything *but* an unmixed blessing.

The second quatrain by contrast is childlike, the good boy reporting his progress to his father. The poet has spent the better part of two days making up "a morning prayer to you / containing with precision everything that most matters." An interesting framing device, this, as the poet stands back in the midst of *this* prayer to comment in passing on that other prayer, an example of microcosmic contrivance, which has lit-

tle, finally, in common with the acts of the "inimitable contriver" he is addressing.

The third quatrain is built around a parataxis, a Hebraic
doubling, each completed sentence taking over half the
quatrain's allotted space: "You have come . . . You have allowed. . . ." These lines form the second thank offering,
thanking an apparently loving God for having rescued him not
once but "again & again," even while He has apparently "allowed" the poet's brilliant friends (Delmore Schwartz? Randall Jarrell?) to destroy themselves. The first thank offering
indirectly comments on fame, then, as the second comments
on the love of the book's title. But those thank offerings are
hesitant, qualified, and those qualifiers begin now to overrun
the surface of the poem. If Berryman has been saved, if he
still finds himself in his mid-fifties functioning, he has also
been "severely damaged." But what is worth noticing here is
the tone, which is one neither of hysteria nor even of resentment; instead, it teeters on a tightrope somewhere between
comedy and pathos, or better, humility.

"Made a decision to turn over our will and our lives over to
the care of God *as we understood Him*," the third of *Alcoholics
Anonymous's Twelve Steps* reads (the italics are mine). It is
with the nature of the relationship between the poet and the
immense Lord which he has been bold enough to address that
Berryman's fourth quatrain is preoccupied. With all respect
for his Addressee, Berrymann finds himself suddenly in the
awkward position of addressing the frankly unknowable, conscious that love for what is unknown is, finally, impossible:
God is "Unknowable, as I am unknown to my guinea pigs."
The only emotions he can feel confident exist in him as he addresses his Lord, then, are, first, *gratitude* for benefits received and duly acknowledged, and then *awe* before this
rescuer. It is these two emotions, in fact, which dominate the
first address; it will take several more addresses before Berryman can admit that what he feels most deeply is in fact love.

If the fourth quatrain faces Berryman's doubts about God's
personal involvement with something as apparently trivial as
man (Berryman by his own admission never had any problems
positing a Deistic watchmaker off somewhere in the em-
pyrean), the fifth and sixth quatrains take up the all-important issue for Berryman of a related question: the possibility

of continued life after death. Neither science nor philosophy
would seem to support such a notion, the poet readily admits,
but, steeped in the tradition of New Testament exegesis, he is
also ready to "believe as fixedly in the Resurrection-appearances to Peter & Paul / as I believe I sit in this blue
chair." (Which is fair enough, unless one questions whether
one is indeed sitting in a blue chair. And just what constitutes
the act of sitting? And what is blue? And what a chair?) This
act of apparent affirmation sets up dissonances not only in the
reader, for Berryman follows this conditional clause with another qualifier, namely, that these appearances "may have
been a special case / to establish their initiatory faith." If the
first stanza opened with a crescendo of unqualified assertions,
the sixth stanza has shifted us to the niggling brackets of the
detached theologian, counting probabilities. With that, however, the last quatrain begins to round again on the poem's initiatory stance.

"Whatever your end may be," Berryman petitions, "accept
my amazement," thus underscoring at once both his confessed *awe* before the Lord and wedging in at the same time
the ambivalent resonances of that word "end." Which end?
God's End? He who has traditionally been thought of as eternal, both alpha *and* omega? Or end as purpose? But God's end
in and for Himself, or for Berryman? The embarrassment and
self-consciousness which the poet feels in addressing the radically unknowable even carries over into the seriocomic petition of his beseeching the Lord that he may remain vigilant to
His promptings, in language which echoes the Psalmist's
watchman waiting for the dawn but which at the same time
lugs into the poem's foreground the picture image of a British
guard at Whitehall, standing "until death forever at attention."

So, even as the poet prays for constant vigilance, part of
him sees that what he is asking for is, at least for himself, at
best improbable. After making his request, a request which a
fellow alcoholic, incidentally, would tell Berryman in Group
was a highfalutin' unrealistic Contract, Berryman ends his
poem by half-asking, half-cajoling the Lord into giving him
assistance again, as He has many times in the past. With this
much quieter petition, the poem rounds on the same epithet
with which it began, with one final qualifier—this one an

onomastic tribute to the Lord who somehow sees more deeply into Berryman than even Berryman's qualifiers will admit— as now he addresses the Lord as "Master of insight & beauty." Having attended to alpha, our exegesis would be incomplete, asymmetrical, ateleological, without some consideration of omega. The eleventh address is one of the shortest and certainly one of the most poignant of Berryman's addresses, as though, approaching the volume's terminus in silence (the inescapable condition of all books), the poet were forced by the gradual stripping away of his linguistic strategies to say what is in his mangled heart, and to utter it as devoid of verbal coy or decoy as possible. The last poem recapitulates the conclusion of the first, but with an important difference, for it is about Berryman's willingness, after all, to stand at some kind of attention—or at least to remain, as best he can, attentive.

There are three quatrains here, the first two centering on two early Christian martyrs, examples culled no doubt from Berryman's long and careful reading in the Church fathers. (Has he not already informed us in "The Search" that he began "the historical study of the Gospel / indebted above all to Guignebert / & Goguel & McNeile / & Bultmann even & later Archbishop Carrington"?) The first example is of the young Germanicus, who, cowboy-fashion, "leapt upon the wild lion in Smyrna" to the crowd's wild applause, "wishing to pass quickly from a lawless life" (Berryman's own deepest wish— and placed in a classic situation: dying before an admiring group there in an amphitheater). The second example is of the octogenarian Polycarp, faced with the "choice" of death by burning unless he renounced his Lord, asking now with a certain inestimable grace how he could be expected to renounce the One who had done him no harm in all those years. Placing his own condition against these two paradigms of witness by martyrdom, Berryman petitions in wrenched syntax the same Lord whom they served that he too may be permitted to offer his own comic, inadequate (yes, qualified), but nonetheless authentic witness:

> Make too me acceptable at the end of time
> in my degree, which Thou wilt award.
> Cancer, senility, mania,
> I pray I may be ready with my witness.

Composition of place, two exempla, an embarrassed petition barely wrenched from the poet, but uttered nonetheless.

Finally, something should be said about this sequence as conclusion, as an honest deflation of the speaker's ego, commenting on the progress of the poet's fortunes with love and fame. Throughout this volume of poems, Berryman's twin themes have been the speaker's preoccupation with those two conditions. This double theme is present from the opening poem, "Her & It," to the close of the book. "Her," incidentally, is a lost love, a girl he was once in love with—and for that matter may *still* be in love with—who probably "now has seven lousy children," and "it" is a questionable fame: "my publishers / very friendly in New York & London / forward me elephant cheques." In fact, *Love & Fame* is a study in the transformation of those two all-encompassing, all-engrossing abstractions. Consider one pole of these intertwined, twinning terms in the closing stanzas of "Drunks," a reminiscence from the poet's undergraduate days, when he was at a New Year's Eve party at his mentor's home— "crawling with celebrities"—where his friend, H,

> . . . got stuck in an upstairs bedroom
> with the blonde young new wife of a famous critic
> a wheel at one of the book clubs
>
> who turned out to have nothing on under her gown
> sprawled out half-drunk across her hostess's bed
> moaning "Put it in! Put it in!"
> H was terrified.
> I passed out & was put in that same bed.

So much for the erotics of the New York publishing world, for one measure of love and fame. For Berryman's own sense of the proper perspective in dealing with these themes, however, we will have to place that wild scene against the tenth of the addresses, the poem which I take to be the key, if you will, to reading the title in its most corrective light, devoid of delusion. It is here that Berryman confesses, finally—and despite his earlier qualifiers—that he has indeed fallen "back in love with you, Father," and asks that his Lord may "Come on me again" (and the sexual pun is surely inescapable) "as twice you came to Azarias & Misael." Love.

And as for fame:

> Oil all my turbulence as at Thy dictation
> I sweat out my wayward works.
> Father Hopkins said the only true literary critic is Christ.
> Let me lie down exhausted, content with that.

It is Berryman's prayer that he may come to see that Christ's judgment on the artist's work may be accepted as sufficient. "Fame," Hopkins had written to his friend Canon Dixon, in 1878,

> Fame whether won or lost is a thing which lies in the award of a random, reckless, incompetent, and unjust judge, the public, the multitude. The only just judge, the only just literary critic, is Christ, who prizes, is proud of, and admires, more than any man, more than the receiver himself can, the gifts of his own making.

If Hopkins—whose magnificent corpus of poems remained in manuscript for thirty years after his death—found the standard he articulated here absolute, precise, exact, and exacting, Berryman must have found it—finally—impossible to follow in more than wish:

> Will I ever write properly, with passion & exactness,
> of the damned strange demeanours of my flagrant heart?
> & be by anyone anywhere undertaken?

That passage seems to capture as well as anything Berryman's anxieties about his craft and his name. If he cannot really follow Hopkins's heroic standards, though, at least he sees them as a distant possibility, a way of getting out from under the debilitating effect of fame as the critics and reviewers only can dispense it.

With the "Opus Dei" sequence—which follows the eleven addresses, if one places *Love & Fame* before *Delusions, Etc.*, where it comes chronologically—the voice is much more qualified and uncertain, noticeably more hesitant and even schizoid. (Which, for example, is the real delusion: to accept the sorry self as one finds it, with all its manias, incessant hungers, egogratifications, etc., or to try to radically alter that self by capitulating to an onomastic pegboard Other that may not, in fact, after all even exist?) Still, the "Eleven Addresses to the Lord" did constitute a kind of oasis for the at-wit's-end

Berryman, did provide a space where the poet could address his God, could, in the very lay of his syllables, find some relief from the feverish heat of poor self grating against itself. For having achieved this with such consummate verbal skill at a cost to the self which only the poet could have measured, for this—among other things—Berryman deserves our affection and—though it is too late to matter much to him, now—our praise.

John Berryman

THE POETICS OF MARTYRDOM

MICHAEL HEFFERNAN

*All the troubles of the time may enter the soul of a man and be mastered by
creative innocence—that is the miracle of poetry. And they may enter the
soul of a man and be mastered by the innocence of the heart—that is the
miracle of sainthood.*

JACQUES MARITAIN

*flame may his glory in that other place
for he was fond of fame, devoted to it,
and every first-rate soul
has sacrifices which it puts in play,
I hope he's sitting with his peers: sit, sit,
& recover & be whole.*

Dream Song 157

In his *Harvard Advocate* interview of 1968 John Berryman was
asked about an "ulterior structure to *The Dream Songs*," and
he answered:

> . . . there is none. *Il n'y en a pas!* There's not a trace of it.
> Some of the Songs are in alphabetical order; but, mostly, they

Michael Heffernan, "John Berryman: The Poetics of Martyrdom," *American
Poetry Review* (March/April 1984): 7–13.

just belong to areas of hope and fear that Henry is going
through at a given time. That's how I worked them out. *

That may have the ring of a last word, so that the close reader
attempting to expose the structure of *The Dream Songs*, like
comparable treatments of the sonnets of Shakespeare, should
quietly give up trying, perhaps after posting on his office door
that lovely crack out of Berryman's poem on Blackmur
("Olympus," from *Love & Fame*): "To be a *critic*, ah, / how
deeper & more scientific."

Meantime the critic of *The Dream Songs* might ask a multi-
tude of questions: Do *The Dream Songs* cohere mainly as poetry or as autobiography? Is Henry simply a version of Berryman, perhaps a photocopy? (Berryman denied this countless
times, but does that matter?) Are they a bona fide long poem
or a scattering of fragments shored against ruin? Do *The
Dream Songs* mirror The Age or merely the pathetic case history of a blighted genius hagridden by alcohol and the curse of
his father's suicide, predestined to his own self-destruction
before he could see sixty? Is it possible for any poet, gifted and
learned as Berryman so variously was, to attempt, achieve,
and survive the making of a personal epic in an age as frac-
tured and schizoid as the present? In short, did the making of
The Dream Songs destroy their maker?

Possibly I am setting these questions forth mainly to grab
some hand-hold on work that endlessly baffles and amazes.
Adrienne Rich precluded a number of inquiries with a single
statement that could scatter whole legions of exegetes: "*The
Dream Songs* aren't literature, they are poetry; and poetry is
real life"†—a view one might dismiss out of hand if Berryman
himself had not supported it, indirectly, by his enthusiastic
endorsement of Whitman's late argument as to his intentions
in *Leaves of Grass:* "to put *a Person,* a human being (myself, in
the latter part of the Nineteenth Century, in America) freely,
fully and truly on record."‡ So poetry for Berryman *was* "real

---

* *Harvard Advocate* 103, no. 1 (spring 1969): 5.

† "Living with Henry," *Harvard Advocate* 103, no. 1 (spring 1969): 10.

‡ See Berryman's 1957 essay "Song of Myself: Intention and Substance,"
The Freedom of the Poet (New York: Farrar, Straus and Giroux, 1976), p. 230.

life," and the consequences of Rich's conclusion might be taken in full: "In a sense *The Dream Songs* want more than a linear reading. And in this, too, they are beyond literature."* And, necessarily, beyond criticism, at least of the literary variety.

Questions of order, unity, wholeness, nonetheless, keep begging to be dealt with, and with them the larger problem of the long poem in the twentieth century. Jacques Maritain has written a remarkable essay on "The Three Epiphanies of Creative Intuition," with an insightful passage on the "luck" of Dante: how he was lucky not only in the "innocence of his heart" and "the firmness of his religious faith" but in the perfect accident of his having come to life in an age pervaded by philosophical and theological stability:

> I am thinking, here, of the heritage of culture received by Dante, and of the articulate universe of beliefs and values in which his thought dwelt. Dante wrestled with his time, which forced into exile the poet threatened with death. But as concerns the spiritual quality of the cultural heritage he was blessed by his time. Then the human mind was imbued with a sense of being, and nature appeared all the more real and consistent as it was perfected by grace. Being still turned toward wisdom, still permeated with rationality and mystery both of which descended from the Uncreate Word, still softened by the blood of the Incarnate Word, the universe of the late thirteenth century, with its ontological hierarchies mirrored in the hierarchies of intellectual disciplines, ensured to the intelligence and emotion of a poet, despite all the evil fevers, discords, crimes, and vices of the time, a state of integration and vitality that the modern man has lost.†

Despite their disparate containments of every sort of criminal and moral squalor, as well as the limits of imaginable sanctity, the cantos of the *Commedia* are rounded like a sphere through the unity of thirteenth-century Catholicism. Berryman's work may appear an exact twentieth-century antithesis: the work of an artist torn to pieces by personal loss of faith, di-

---

* "Living with Henry," p. 10.

† *Creative Intuition in Art and Poetry* (New York: Pantheon Books, 1953), p. 318.

rectly consequent upon his father's self-slaughter, not to mention the less immediate but certainly as painful climate of life in a century of colossal warfare, rampant social unrest, and innumerable varieties of spiritual distress so general and endemic that one of its most widely read philosophers could announce, in the summary opening sentence of his most popular treatise: "There is but one truly serious philosophical problem, and that is suicide."

I want to suggest that *The Dream Songs* represent, through their cumulative portrayal of Henry's "plights & gripes," an open paradigm of grief and loss, fragmentation and spiritual collapse, that their author, as he worked through and beyond them, was obliged to transcend both as person and as poet. The totality of Berryman's spiritual program, his project of redemption, is not contained within the deliberately non-ulterior "structure" of the songs. Berryman wrote, in his last two books, a number of widely unappreciated poems that need to be studied side by side with *The Dream Songs* in order to put the poet of *The Dream Songs* in his own right perspective. Henry, as Berryman seems to have intended him, resides finally neither under our bootsoles nor somewhere off the edge of some planet on the table. By the end of the songs Henry is left where Berryman wanted him—alive and feeling, yet caught forever in his nest of hope and fear, his problems ultimately unresolved. Berryman himself admitted in his conversation with Richard Kostelanetz, that his lack of "solution" made *The Dream Songs*, as Henry's story, a virtual failure;* and, answering the *Advocate* students on the question of Henry "as the hero of a poem," he replied:

> Well, he's very brave, Henry, in that he keeps on living after other people have dropped dead. But he's a hopeless coward with regard to his actual death. That never comes out in the poem, but he is afraid of death. †

This problem of personal mortality connected for Berryman, as a long-term apostate longing to believe, with a far more terrifying problem in eschatology: the reality of Hell as a

---

* *Massachusetts Review* 11, no. 2 (spring 1970): 346.

† *Harvard Advocate* 103, no. 1 (spring 1969): 6.

state of everlasting damnation. Berryman's thinking on the subject, informed in large degree by his reading of Origen's *De Principiis*, extended back a number of years before his well-documented conversion, his rediscovery, in May 1970, of a personal God "interested in the individual life in the ordinary way."* Early in *The Dream Songs*, in Song 56, Berryman imagines Origen's Hell at the moment of *apocatastasis*, a time "known to God alone" when "the goodness of God through Christ will restore his entire creation to one end" and God will be "all in all," with even the demons brought into a state of virtue, if they desire it:†

> Hell is empty. O that has come to pass
> which the cut Alexandrian foresaw,
> and Hell lies empty.
> Lightning fell silent where the Devil knelt
> and over the whole grave space hath settled awe
> in a full death of guilt.

Henry is clearly dreaming or wishful-thinking, and the rest of the song moves toward irresolution and ambiguity as Henry, having imagined himself as a deer trapped by hunters closing on him with clubs, poses two virtual opposites in the vision of Hell emptied "in a full death of guilt" and the terrifying prospect of dying into a speechless silence like an animal. Berryman, for the moment, is testing out, from different angles, an idea which, some years later, he came to accept as a necessary article of his renewed faith, with its vision of a "God of rescue" devoted in the end to restoring His Creation. Berryman's need to absorb this as a personal and an artistic principle can be placed in a fuller context by an examination of a development in the later *Dream Songs*.

A moment of clarity happens in Song 324, "An Elegy for W.C.W., the lovely man." William Carlos Williams here appears as Henry's veritable antithesis:

> Henry in Ireland to Bill underground:
> Rest well, who worked so hard, who made a good sound

---

* See John Haffenden's essay, "Drink as Disease: John Berryman," *Partisan Review* 44, no. 4 (1977): 576.

† Origen, *On First Principles*, trans. G. W. Butterworth (New York: Harper & Row, 1966), pp. 52–88.

constantly, for so many years:
your high-jinks delighted the continents & our ears:
you had so many girls your life was a triumph
and you loved your one wife.

At dawn you rose & wrote—the books poured forth—
you delivered infinite babies, in one great birth—
and your generosity
to juniors made you deeply loved, deeply:
if envy was a Henry trademark, he would envy you,
especially the being through.

Too many journeys lie for him ahead,
too many galleys & page-proofs to be read,
he would like to lie down
in your sweet silence, to whom was not denied
the mysterious late excellence which is the crown
of our trials & our last bride.

This homage to Williams may seem unusual at first, coming
from a poet whose earliest masters were Yeats and Auden.
James E. Miller has noticed the "metamorphosis" that took
shape in Berryman's work during the late fifties, roughly con-
temporaneous with the publication of Ginsberg's *Howl* and its
earliest impact, though Miller pinpoints Berryman's relatively
late discovery of Walt Whitman as the turning point in his
growth from the impersonal, highly derivative mold of his
first poems. * It is certainly tempting to identify Whitman
and his mid-century followers, among them Ginsberg and
Williams, as generally responsible for Berryman's shift away
from the tight stanzas of *The Dispossessed* and *Homage to Mistress Bradstreet* to the open stanzas of *The Dream Songs*, and
Berryman himself emphasized his debt to Whitman in his
Paris Review interview with Peter Stitt. † The problem of influence, direct or indirect, can be difficult to resolve. The
rugged "personality" of Whitman in "Song of Myself" is final-

---

* See the first chapter of *The American Quest for a Supreme Fiction: Whitman's Legacy in the Personal Epic* (Chicago: University of Chicago Press,
1979).

† "I think the model in *The Dream Songs* was . . . 'Song of Myself'—a very
long poem, about sixty pages. It also has a hero, a personality, himself. Henry
is accused of being me and I am accused of being Henry and I deny it and
nobody believes me. Various things entered into it, but that is where I started." *Paris Review* 53 (winter 1972): 90–91.

ly not Henry's; neither does "W.C.W., the lovely man," provide Berryman with much more than an invidious contrast to the lives of Henry and his friends. Williams represents for Henry, and for Berryman, a figure of grace and accomplishment, a completed master able in his old age to "crown" his labors in the craft with the brilliantly plain-spoken measures of "Asphodel, That Greeny Flower" and to renew his own imaginative vitalities with the further illuminations of the Unicorn Tapestries. Reviewing *Paterson Five* in 1959, Berryman wrote: "The gaiety of this old man is adorable."*

Counterpointing the celebration of Williams in Song 324 is a disquieting sense of Henry's spiritual exhaustion: the elegy for Williams occurs as a bright surprise amid a large cluster of songs full of bitterness, desolation, and a more than usual air of hopelessness. Henry addresses Williams from a

> land of ruined abbeys,
> discredited Saints & brainless senators,
> roofless castles, enemies of Joyce & Swift,
> enemies of Synge,
> enemies of Yeats & O'Casey
>
> *(Song 321)*

Several songs earlier (309) Ireland has appeared a place of "fallen leaves and litter." Henry goes shopping and comes home with a book on the Easter Rising in which all of his "old heroes . . . spring back into action, fatuous campaigners/ dewey with phantastic hope." The last stanza concludes:

> Phantastic hope rules Henry's war as well,
> all these enterprises are doomed, all human pleas
> are headed for the night.
> Wait the lime-pits for all originators,
> wounded propped up to be executed,
> afterward known as martyrs.

Enhancing this perception of the failure of political movements toward national renewal is Henry's awareness of Ireland's religious heritage, both Christian and pre-Christian,

---

* *The Freedom of the Poet*, p. 314.

equally "phantastic" for a country "full of con-men / as well
as the lovely good" (Song 313):

> Saints throng these shores, & ancient practices
> continue in the dolmens, ruined castles
> are standard.
> The whole place is ghostly: no wonder Yeats believed in fairies
> & personal survival. A trim suburban villa
> also is haunted, by me.
> Heaven made this place, also, assisted by men,
> great men & weird. I see their shades move past
> in full daylight.
> The holy saints make the trees' tops shiver,
> in the all-enclosing wind. And will love last
> further than tonight?

In the midst of the evidence of the blessed dead, Henry feels
only "need need need" (Song 311); and, in Song 314:

> Penniless, ill, abroad, Henry lay skew
> to Henry's American fate, which was to be well,
> have money in the bank
> & be at home. He can't think what to do
> under this cluster of misfortune & hell. . . .

Set as it is ten songs later, the elegy for Williams details the
pure achievement of one American poet whose "fate . . . was
to be well, / have money in the bank / & be at home." Williams is also the accomplished person Henry would like to be,
both as poet and lover. The placing of Berryman's homage to
Williams in this section of generally dispirited songs sheds
light on the nature of Henry's "hunger":

> Hunger was constitutional with him,
> women, cigarettes, liquor, need need need
> until he went to pieces.
> The pieces sat up & wrote.
>
> (*Song 311*)

Henry admires in Williams more than his life of "triumph,"
more than his love of one woman and his "being through."
Unlike Yeats, whose "majestic Shade" (Song 312) fills Berryman with nearly speechless awe, Williams is Henry's more

accessible idea of the poet who kept his life together, loved his "one wife" (despite his "many girls"), and finally produced, in his last years, poems that reveal a harmony of life and art. As of Song 324, Henry feels remote from such perfection: "Too many journeys lie for him ahead, / too many galleys & page-proofs to be read."

Forty songs later, on the verge of the final developments of *The Dream Songs*, Henry's tone approaches self-elegy as he explains what we can make of (and take from) "These Songs" now all but behind us:

> Chilled in this Irish pub I wish my loves
> well, well to strangers, well to all his friends,
> seven or so in number,
> I forgive my enemies, especially two,
> races his heart, at so much magnanimity,
> can it at all be true?
>
> —Mr Bones, you on a trip outside yourself.
> Has you seen a medicine man? You sound will-like,
> a testament & such.
> Is you going?—Oh, I suffer from a strike
> & a strike & three balls: I stand up for much,
> Wordsworth & that sort of thing.
>
> The pitcher dreamed. He threw a hazy curve,
> I took it in my stride & out I struck,
> lonesome Henry.
> These Songs are not meant to be understood, you understand.
> They are only meant to terrify & comfort.
> Lilac was found in his hand.
>
> (*Song 366*)

The echo of Whitman in that last line seems obvious. Less obvious, and probably not intentional at all on Berryman's part, though certainly interesting to consider, is a parallel with the opening of Book III of Williams's "Asphodel, That Greeny Flower":

> What power has love but forgiveness?
>   In other words
>   by its intervention

what has been done
    can be undone.
        What good is it otherwise?
Because of this
    I have invoked the flower
        in that
frail as it is
    after winter's harshness
        it comes again
to delect us.
    Asphodel, the ancients believed,
        in hell's despite
was such a flower.

Berryman's appreciation of the older poet's "mysterious late excellence" implies a response to Williams's final resolutions in terms of a poetry of love. Berryman's own post–*Dream Songs* development toward *Love & Fame* and *Delusions, Etc.* involved him in a series of love poems as important as any in his canon. These are the poems of his late-found and, I think, arguably genuine love for the Father he discovered in his last years to replace the earthly father who had abandoned him.

The loss accounted for in *The Dream Songs* is the traumatic loss both of the parent and of the vision, in an ultimate Father, of the object of true belief. Complicating his later poetry of conversion is a crucial difficulty, carried over from the songs: if I myself am Hell, in the sense of Lowell's Miltonic line from "Skunk Hour," then how do I avoid Hell even though, in the end, I find my way toward acceptance of a "God of rescue"? In "Eleven Addresses to the Lord," the sequence at the end of *Love & Fame*, Berryman begins to work out a resolution, at first tentative and speculative:

May be the Devil after all exists.
. . . .
Man is ruining the pleasant earth & man.
What at last, my Lord, will you allow?
Postpone till after my children's deaths your doom
if it be thy ineffable, inevitable will.
                        ("Eleven Addresses," 2)

Gradually his assertions become surprisingly more confident, and confidential, addressing God as a friend, the way Hopkins did in "Thou Art Indeed Just, Lord," but without the irony:

> Holy, & holy. The damned are said to say
> "We never thought we would come into this place."
> I'm fairly clear, my Friend, there's no such place
> ordained for inappropriate & evil man.
>
> Surely they fall dull, & forget. We too,
> the more or less just, I feel fall asleep
> dreamless forever while the worlds hurl out.
> Rest may be your ultimate gift.
>
> *("Eleven Addresses," 5)*

As lines like these reveal, Berryman had begun to implicate more thoroughly than ever into this work the writings of the early Christian Fathers, and especially those of Origen and, with special complexity, the martyrologist of St. Polycarp.

Two of the critics who have worked most closely with Berryman's late poems seem curiously indisposed to a precise exposition of the religious poems and their implications. While Peter Stitt describes the growth "in power and technical mastery" of "Eleven Addresses to the Lord" over the earlier poems in *Love & Fame,* he gives us hardly any actual detail from these important poems, transitional as they are to the crucial "Opus Dei" pieces in *Delusions, Etc.,* about which he has somewhat more to say, concluding that the word *if* in the clause "If He for me as I feel for my daughter" ("Compline") lends the poem and the book both a sense of doubt and "an underlying ironic dimension." Stitt chooses to ignore the rest of "Compline," with its important argument about Hell. *

Similarly, Ernest Stefanik has devoted considerable space to the religious element in Berryman's late work but, like Stitt, he elects to omit from discussion some of the more troubled passages. Writing in the pages of the Catholic journal *Renascence,* Stefanik argues that "*Love & Fame* is not simply a collection of lyrics assembled under a common title . . . but a narrative that presents a self-portrait of the poet beginning his religious quest, his encounter with God and, concomitantly, with self. . . . Through his suffering and courage both

---

* "Berryman's Last Poems," *Concerning Poetry* 6, no. 1 (spring 1973): 9.

as a ragged hero and as a foolish victim, he elicits and enlists the reader's sympathies as he reconstructs his past, confronts the unknowable in a meaningless world, and finally adopts a posture of Christian acceptance."* Stefanik's reading of *Love & Fame* is generally fair and useful, but he fails to grasp one of the most difficult statements in all of Berryman, the last sentence of the last poem of the book's final sequence, the "Eleven Addresses." Stefanik's problem is a tendency to traditionalize the nature of Berryman's "posture of Christian acceptance." Quoting only the last stanza of the brief #11, he writes: "Berryman is now able to accept the mutability of the world and the inevitability of God's will; and the final effect of the sequence unalterably moves toward an affirmation of the poet's being and a reversal of failure, concluding with a gesture of surrender to God's will."†

The "gesture of surrender" at the end of #11 needs to be placed not only in the context of the poem in its entirety but in the light of the evidence supplied by an examination of the poem's sources. Here is the poem:

> Germanicus leapt upon the wild lion in Smyrna,
> wishing to pass quickly from a lawless life.
> The crowd shook the stadium.
> The proconsul marvelled.
>
> "Eighty & six years have I been his servant,
> and he has done me no harm.
> How can I blaspheme my King who saved me?"
> Polycarp, John's pupil, facing the fire.
>
> Make too me acceptable at the end of time
> in my degree, which then Thou wilt award.
> Cancer, senility, mania,
> I pray I may be ready with my witness.

A relatively brief pursuit of references will reveal the text from which virtually everything in the first two stanzas came to hand: Kirsopp Lake's translation of "The Martyrdom of St. Polycarp, Bishop of Smyrna" in *The Apostolic Fathers*, vol. II,

---

* "A Cursing Glory: John Berryman's *Love & Fame*," *Renascence* 25, no. 3 (spring 1973): 115.

† Ibid., p. 126.

from the Loeb Classical Library. Polycarp suffered martyrdom about the year 155 during the proconsulship of Statius Quadratus, at Smyrna. According to the martyrology, "the most noble Germanicus" was martyred before him:

> and he fought gloriously with the wild beasts. For when the Pro-Consul wished to persuade him and bade him have pity on his youth, he violently dragged the beast towards himself, wishing to be released more quickly from their unrighteous and lawless life. So after this all the crowd, wondering at the nobility of the God-loving and God-fearing people of the Christians, cried out: "Away with the Atheists [i.e., the Christians]; let Polycarp be searched for."

Polycarp's hiding-place is searched out and he is brought, eventually, into the arena, where he is met by "a great uproar." Having tried to persuade Germanicus to "have pity on his youth," the Pro-Consul bids the aged Polycarp to "respect his age," to no avail; so

> when the Pro-Consul pressed him and said: "Take the oath [of allegiance to Caesar] and I let you go, revile Christ," Polycarp said: "For eighty and six years have I been his servant, and he has done me no wrong, and how can I blaspheme my King who saved me?"

Polycarp is bound to the stake and burned "for an oblation, a whole burnt offering made ready and acceptable to God."*
    Berryman's borrowings from this text are remarkable for a number of reasons. They represent, for one, a considerable departure from his usual practice, especially in the second stanza, which is drawn virtually word for word from the Lake translation. The most interesting use of "The Martyrdom of St. Polycarp," however, is the precise association which Berryman brings to the word *witness* at the end of the poem (and the volume), a complex and disturbing meaning underscored by the translator's note at the beginning of the Loeb Library version, referring to the significance of Polycarp's martyrdom in terms of an etymology that Berryman would

---

* Harvard University Press, 1st printing 1913, pp. 317, 325, 331. All other extant translations differ significantly from Kirsopp Lake's.

have been likely to take into account: "It is not clear whether *martyrion* ought to be translated 'martyrdom' or 'witness': there is an untranslatable play on the words."* It is surely this play on words that Berryman intended for the end of *Love & Fame*. "I pray I may be ready with my witness" (emphasizing *my* to associate more directly with Germanicus and Polycarp) involves a readiness to leap upon the wild lion or face the fire, to abandon the self in martyrdom whether from cancer, senility or, more problematically, mania. It was the last of these that Berryman suffered, praying to be made "acceptable at the end of time / in my degree." The eleventh of the "Eleven Addresses to the Lord" can be taken as a kind of palimpsest which itself embodies a metaphor of Berryman's struggle in the cross-winds of faith and self-destruction.

Berryman is at his prayers throughout *Delusions, Etc.* In the opening sequence, "Opus Dei," based on the canonical hours, he prays especially

> not to be lost from You—
> if I could hear of a middle ground, I'd opt:
>
> a decent if minute salvation, sort of, on some fringe.
> I am afraid, afraid. Brothers, who if
> you are afraid are my brothers—veterans of fear—
> pray with me now in the hour of our living.
>
> *("Nones")*

Later, in the powerful "Compline," Berryman turns again to Origen to verify his own version of the End of Time:

> If He for me as I feel for my daughter,
> being His son, I'll sweat no more tonight
> but happy hymn & sleep. I have got it made,
> and so have all we of contrition, for
>
> if He loves me He must love everybody
> and Origen was right & Hell is empty
> or will be at apocatastasis.
> Sinners, sin on. We'll suffer now & later
>
> but not forever, dear friends and brothers!

---

* Lake translation, p. 313.

Berryman seems to have maintained this conviction through to the end of *Delusions, Etc.* "The Facts & Issues," written the summer before his death, carries Berryman's view of God and hellfire beyond theodicy. It is not a well-made poem but rather an extended burst of loose free verse in which Berryman speaks once for all unmistakably in his own voice and person about the life he was beginning to find unbearable. Perhaps Adrienne Rich would be right about this one: it is beyond literature, beyond criticism, showing us finally how far Berryman had extended himself beyond his own capacity to stay in one piece:

> I really believe He's here all over this room
> in a motor hotel in Wallace Stevens' town.
> I admit it's weird; and *could*—or could it?—not be so;
> but frankly I don't think there's a molecular chance of that.
> It doesn't seem hypothesis. Thank heavens
> millions agree with me, or mostly do,
> and have done ages of our human time,
> among whom were & still are some very sharp cookies.
> I don't exactly feel missionary about it,
> though it's *very* true I wonder if I should.
> I regard the boys who don't buy this as deluded.
> Of course they regard me no doubt as deluded.
> Okay with me! And not the hell with them
> at *all*—no!—I feel *dubious* on Hell—
> it's here, all right, but elsewhere, after? Screw that,
> I feel pretty sure that evil simply ends
> *for the doer* (having wiped him out,
> by the way, usually) where good goes on,
> or good *may* drop dead too: I don't think so:
> I can't say I have hopes in that department
> myself, I lack ambition just just there,
> I know that Presence says it's mild, and it's mild,
> but being what I am I wouldn't care
> to dare go nearer. Happy to be here
> and to have been here, with such lovely ones
> so infinitely better, but to me
> even in their suffering infinitely kind
> & blessing. I am a greedy man, of course,
> but I wouldn't want that kind of luck continued,—

or even *increased* (for Christ's sake), & *forever?*
Let me be clear about this. It is plain to me
Christ underwent man & treachery & socks
& lashes, thirst, exhaustion, the bit, for *my* pathetic &
    disgusting vices,
to make this filthy fact of particular, long-after,
faraway, five-foot-ten & moribund
human being happy. Well, he has!
I am so happy I could scream!
It's *enough!* I can't BEAR ANY MORE.
Let this be it. I've *had* it. I can't wait.

The railing of the Washington Avenue Bridge was half a year
away. William Meredith, who was with Berryman in Connecticut at the time of the poem's composition, has com-
mented that "The Facts & Issues" "ends with the baffling
spectacle of a man fending off torrents of a grace that has become unbearable. It is a heroic response to that crisis, as I
think his death was too."* These last words bear a burden of
proof that is truly outside the range of common criticism, but
they state the case with startling offhandedness and plau-
sibility. Berryman came to view himself, in his poetry,
through Henry and beyond, as the hero of a work that had
gradually, and terribly, become one with the life of its maker.
"Happy to be here / and to have been here," and at peace with
the idea of a God who would save even Satan, Berryman leapt
upon his own wild lion and drew his life and his poem together into a triumph of self over circumstance. Suicide became for him a kind of martyrdom at the hands of forces
darker and more ambiguous than the ones that stood Polycarp
in the fire. As he wrote of the heroes of the Easter Rising:

    Wait the lime-pits for all originators,
    wounded propped up to be executed,
    afterward known as martyrs.

Risky as it may seem to suggest this, it is not impossible to
think the same for the originator of Henry and his Songs.

---

* "In Loving Memory of the Late Author of *The Dream Songs*," reprinted
in Richard J. Kelly's *John Berryman: A Checklist* (Scarecrow Press, 1972),
p. xix.

After I completed this essay in 1980, Eileen Simpson published her memoir, *Poets in Their Youth* (New York: Random
House, 1982). Her "Afterword" (ch. 10) provides much useful
detail from Berryman's last days. I agree, in spirit, with her
final argument that "it was the poetry that kept [Berryman]
alive," though largely in the sense that it was through his poetry that Berryman enabled himself to believe in an ongoing
life for the soul despite bodily decrepitude and the imminent
arrival of "his subtle foe." I do not believe, however, that
Berryman killed himself, as Simpson suggests, because his
muse had deserted him. On the contrary, Berryman had
achieved, in his last poems, a synthesis through which the
prospect of death, "ambiguous ahead," had positively become
an accessible point of egress from "the wide hell in the world"
("King David Dances"—the final poem in *Delusions, Etc.*).
Poetry became his consecrated ground.

Bibliography

I. Works by Berryman

Books

Berryman, John. *Berryman's Sonnets.* New York: Farrar, Straus & Giroux, 1967.

———. *Delusions, Etc.* New York: Farrar, Straus & Giroux, 1972.

———. *The Dispossessed.* New York: William Sloane, Inc., 1948.

———. *The Dream Songs.* New York: Farrar, Straus & Giroux, 1969.

———. *The Freedom of the Poet.* New York: Farrar, Straus & Giroux, 1976.

———. *Henry's Fate & Other Poems, 1967–1972.* New York: Farrar, Straus & Giroux, 1977.

———. *His Thought Made Pockets & The Plane Buckt.* Pawlet, Vermont: Claude Fredericks, 1958.

———. *His Toy, His Dream, His Rest.* New York: Farrar, Straus & Giroux, 1968.

———. *Homage to Mistress Bradstreet.* New York: Farrar, Straus & Giroux, 1956.

———. *Love & Fame.* New York: Farrar, Straus & Giroux, 1970.

———. *Poems.* Norfolk, Conn.: New Directions, 1942.

———. *Recovery.* New York: Farrar, Straus & Giroux, 1973.

———. *Short Poems.* New York: Farrar, Straus & Giroux, 1967.

———. *Stephen Crane: A Critical Biography.* New York: Meridian Books, 1962.

Berryman, John, Mary Barnard, Randall Jarrell, W. R. Moses, and George Marion O'Donnell. *Five Young American Poets.* Norfolk, Conn.: New Directions, 1940.

Berryman, John, Ralph Ross, and Allen Tate. *The Arts of Reading.* New York: Thomas Y. Crowell, 1960.

Uncollected Prose

Berryman, John. "Auden's Prose." Review of *The Dyer's Hand,* by W. H. Auden. *New York Review of Books,* 29 Aug. 1963, 19.

———. "British Poet in America." Review of *The Age of Anxiety,* by W. H. Auden. *Commentary* 5 (1948): 282–84.

———. "Coleridge Chronicle." Review of *Samuel Taylor Coleridge:*

A Biographical Study, by E. K. Chambers. *Nation,* 17 June 1939, 760.

———. "Days of Crisis in the Great Experiment." Review of *The New Men,* by C. P. Snow. *New York Times Book Review,* 9 Jan. 1955, 4–5.

———. "Epics from Outer Space and Wales." Review of *Aniara: A Review of Men in Time and Space,* by Harry Martinson. *New York Times Book Review,* 21 July 1963, 4–5.

———. "The Long Way to MacDiarmid." Review of *Selected Poems,* by Hugh MacDiarmid, and six other books. *Poetry,* Apr. 1982, 52–61.

———. "Matter and Manner." Review of *Poetry and the Age,* by Randall Jarrell. *New Republic* 2 (Nov. 1953): 27–28.

———. "Metaphysical or So." Review of *The Well-Wrought Urn,* by Cleanth Brooks. *Nation,* 28 June 1947, 775–76.

———. "More Directions." Review of *New Directions 1940,* ed. James Laughlin. *Kenyon Review* 3 (1941): 386–88.

———. "Mr. Moult and the Poets." Review of *The Best Poems of 1943,* ed. Thomas Moult. *New York Times Book Review,* 14 Jan. 1945, 16.

———. "Native Verse." Review of *Lee in the Mountains and Other Poems,* by Donald Davidson. *New York Herald Tribune Book Review,* 8 Jan. 1939, 12.

———. "Neither Here Nor There." Review of *A Piece of Lettuce: Personal Essays on Books, Beliefs, American Places and Growing Up in a Strange Country,* by George P. Elliott. *New York Times Book Review,* 31 May 1964, 3, 14.

———. "Nightingale of the Mire." Review of *Tristan Corbiere Poems,* trans. Walter McElroy. *New York Herald Tribune Book Review,* 12 Oct. 1947, 3.

———. "A Philosophical Poet." Review of *The Collected Poems,* by Laura Riding. *New York Herald Tribune Books,* 11 Dec. 1938.

———. "Poetolatry." Review of *The Personal Heresy: A Controversy,* by E. M. W. Tillyard and C. S. Lewis. *New York Herald Tribune,* 1 Oct. 1939, 18.

———. "Provincial." Review of *The Last of the Provincials: The American Novel, 1915–1925,* by Maxwell Geismar. *Partisan Review* 15 (1948): 379–81.

———. "A Scholarly History." Review of *A Critical Study of English Poetry,* by Herbert J. Grierson and J. C. Smith. *Nation,* 21 Dec. 1946, 733–34.

———. "Shakespeare's Text." Review of *The Editorial Problem in Shakespeare: A Survey of the Foundations of the Text,* by W. W. Greg. *Nation,* 29 Aug. 1943, 218–19.

_____. "Spender: The Poet as Critic." Review of *The Making of a Poem*, by Stephen Spender. *New Republic*, 29 June 1963, 19–20.

_____. "The State of American Writing, 1948: A Symposium." *Partisan Review* 15 (1948): 855–94.

_____. "Three and a Half Years at Columbia." In *University on the Heights*. Ed. Wesley First. New York: Doubleday and Co., 1969, pp. 51–60.

_____. "Types of Pedantry." Review of *Smith: A Sylvan Interlude*, by Branch Cabell, and two other novels. *Nation*, 27 Nov. 1935, 630.

_____. "Young Poets Dead." Review of *Poems*, by Samuel Greenberg, and *The Collected Poems*, by Sidney Keyes. *Sewanee Review* 55 (1947): 504–14.

II. Reference Works

Arpin, Gary Q. *John Berryman: A Reference Guide*. Boston: G. K. Hall, 1976.

Kelly, Richard J. *John Berryman: A Checklist*. Metuchen, N.J.: Scarecrow Press, 1972.

Stefanik, Ernest C., Jr. *John Berryman: A Descriptive Bibliography*. Pittsburgh: University of Pittsburgh Press, 1974.

III. Works by Others

Books

Arpin, Gary Q. *The Poetry of John Berryman*. Port Washington, N.Y.: Kennikat Press, 1978.

Connaroe, Joel. *An Introduction to the Poetry of John Berryman*. New York: Columbia University Press, 1977.

Haffenden, John. *John Berryman: A Critical Commentary*. New York: New York University Press, 1980.

_____. *The Life of John Berryman*. London: Routledge & Kegan Paul, 1982.

Linebarger, J. M. *John Berryman*. New York: Twayne, 1974.

Martz, William. *John Berryman*. Minneapolis: University of Minnesota Press, 1969.

Simpson, Eileen. *The Maze*. New York: Simon and Schuster, 1975.

_____. *Poets in Their Youth*. New York: Random House, 1982.

Articles and Reviews

Alvarez, A. "Berryman's Nunc Dimittis." Review of *His Toy, His Dream, His Rest*. *Observer* (London), 4 May 1969, 30.

————. "I Don't Think I Will Sing Any More." Review of *Delusions, Etc. New York Times Book Review*, 25 June 1969, 1, 12, 14.

Browne, Michael Dennis. "Henry Fermenting: Debts to the Dream Songs." *Ohio Review* 15, no. 2 (1974): 75–87.

Galassi, Jonathan. "Sorrows and Passions of His Majesty the Ego." *Poetry Nation*, no. 2 (1974): 117–24.

Haffenden, John. "Drink as Disease." *Partisan Review* 44 (1977): 565–83.

————. "Paris and a Play." *John Berryman Studies* 2, no. 2 (1976): 66–70.

————. "A Year on the East Coast: John Berryman, 1962–63." *Twentieth Century Literature* 22, no. 2 (1976): 129–45.

Howard, Jane. "Whiskey and Ink, Whiskey and Ink." *Life*, 21 July 1967, 67–76.

Hyde, Lewis. "Alcohol & Poetry: John Berryman and the Booze Talking." *American Poetry Review*, July/Aug. 1975, 7–12.

Jackson, Bruce. "Berryman's Chaplinesque." Review of *77 Dream Songs. Minnesota Review* 5, no. 1 (1965): 90–94.

Lowell, Robert. "The Poetry of John Berryman." Review of *77 Dream Songs. New York Review of Books*, 28 May 1964, 2–3.

Mazzocco, Robert. "Harlequin in Hell." Review of *Berryman's Sonnets. New York Review of Books*, 29 June 1967, 12–16.

Mendelson, Edward. "How To Read Berryman's Dream Songs." *American Poetry Since 1960—Some Critical Perspectives*. Ed. Robert B. Shaw. Chester Springs, Pa.: Dufour Eds., 1974.

Ricks, Christopher. "Recent American Poetry." Review of *His Toy, His Dream, His Rest. Massachusetts Review* 11 (spring 1970): 313–38.

Simpson, Louis. "On Berryman's *Recovery*." Review of *Recovery. Ohio Review* 15, no. 2 (1974): 112–14.

Thompson, John. "Last Treatment." *New York Review of Books*, 9 Aug. 1973, 3–6.

Index

Agee, James, 47, 48, 49
Aiken, Conrad, 115, 133
Alvarez, A., 21, 133, 167
Anna Karenina (Tolstoy), 35
Aragon, Louis, 24
Auden, W. H., 15, 16, 20, 93, 94, 200, 201, 222; influence on Berryman's writing, 5, 23–24; stylized meaningfulness in his poetry, 203–4, 205
Augustine, St., 23, 41

Baldwin, James, 179
Barth, John, 212
Bayley, John: *The Romantic Survival*, 203
Beckett, Samuel, 193, 210
Bell, Marvin, 86
Bellow, Saul, 44, 76, 143, 146; *The Adventures of Augie March*, 24, 28, 34–35, 74, 143–44
Benn, Gottfried, 156
Berryhill, Michael, 141
Berryman, Jill Angel (Martha Little; mother), 4–5, 52, 53, 54–55, 57–64
Berryman, John: alcoholism, 53–54, 78–79, 83, 219–20; alienation of, 150–51; childhood, 3–4, 54; conversation, 74–75; craftsmanship, concern with, 113; crisis, perspective on, 86–87; epilepsy, 63, 64–65; fainting spells, 62–63, 64; father's suicide, 55–57, 59–60; forms of behavior preferred by, 83–85; friends' attitudes toward, 67–68; in group therapy, 35–36, 40, 77; health, disregard for, 63–64; hell, belief in, 235–36; insom-

nia, 56; institutionalization of, 76–78; job interviews, 49–50; jobless in New York, 47–51, 65–66; as liberator of other poets, 137–38; mother, relationship with, 53, 54–55, 59–64; name for himself, 57; photographs of, xv; poetry as real life, 233–34; prenuptial party, 51–53; psychological instability, 66; readings given by, 78, 82; religious beliefs, 41–42, 149–50; religious conversion, 39–41; reputation among poets, xvii–xviii; resolution, reform and relapse, cycle of, 79; reviews, attitude toward, 19–20; as scholar, 21–22; suicide, 247–48; suicide considered by, 51, 62; as teacher, 4, 15, 22–23, 77; tombstone inscription, preference for, 83; university student, 4, 5; writing process, 13–14, 15
Berryman, John, writings of: accuracy of form, 84; "confessional" poetry, 21, 213–14; fear as subject of, 91–96; first, 4–5; *Five Young American Poets*, 113; humanity of, 140, 147; "I" (self) created in, 192–212, 223–24; as language twisted and posed, 217–18; obscurity and private allusion, 95; as pastiche of other contemporaries, 136; as poetry of pain, 144; prosody in, 83–84; as psychotechnical literary feat, 142–43; religious aspects, 41–42, 232–48; science-fiction novel, 5; as search for individual and spiritual haven, 144–147. *See also specific works*

253

Berryman, John Angus (step-
father), 59–60, 61n
Berryman, Kate (third wife), 81, 82
Berryman's Sonnets, 41, 147, 200–
201; Sonnet 6, 107; Sonnet 10,
105; Sonnet 12, 107, 108; Sonnet
21, 102; Sonnet 25, 104; Sonnet
27, 103–4; Sonnet 31, 106; Sonnet 33, 106; Sonnet 36, 102; Sonnet 40, 102; Sonnet 45, 106;
Sonnet 46, 107; Sonnet 47, 99;
Sonnet 50, 107; Sonnet 53, 107;
Sonnet 55, 99; Sonnet 57, 106;
Sonnet 58, 107; Sonnet 66, 103;
Sonnet 72, 105; Sonnet 75, 97;
Sonnet 76, 106; Sonnet 79, 109;
Sonnet 87, 99; Sonnet 98, 106;
Sonnet 100, 103; Sonnet 107,
108; Sonnet 109, 99; Sonnet 115,
98; The Dream Songs, relation to,
108–9; Hopkins's influence on,
103; humor of, 107–8; introducto-
ry poem, 98–100; as least in-
teresting of Berryman's poems,
97–98; literary influences, 102–
3; as moral drama, 105–7; Pe-
trarchan form, 101–2; plot, 105;
revision of sonnets, 9–10; sea or
sea-peril image, 104–5; as self-
contained experiences, 103–4
Bishop, Elizabeth, 16, 193, 211
Bishop, John Peale, 25
Blackmur, R. P., 80, 143, 194, 217
Blake, William, 30
Bly, Robert, 11
Bogan, Louise, 16
Bradstreet, Anne, 110–11, 124,
163. See also Homage to Mistress
Bradstreet
Bread Loaf School of English, 81–82
Bridges, Robert, 20
Brodsky, Joseph, 184
Brown, Norman O., 168
Browne, Michael Dennis, 86
Bryant's Minstrels, 173
Bunting, Basil, 16
Burroughs, William, 168, 192, 212
Byron, George Gordon, Lord, 192,

196; Don Juan, 141, 207

Cage, John, 181
Campbell, Bhain, 48–49, 63, 64
Camus, Albert, 144, 235
Carruth, Hayden, xvii
Chambers, Whittaker, 49
Chatterton, Thomas, 20
Chaucer, Geoffrey, 9
Christy's Band of Original Virginia
Minstrels, 173
Coleridge, Samuel Taylor, 194, 195
Conrad, Joseph, 19, 93
Corvo, Baron, 163
Crane, Hart, 26, 110, 220
Crane, Stephen, 7, 21, 178–79
Crook, Arthur, 38

Dana, Richard Henry, 111
Dante, 234
Delusions, Etc. (Berryman), 43, 72,
221; "Compline," 245; "The Facts
& Issues," 87, 150, 246–47;
"Henry's Understanding," 73;
"He Resigns," 84; "King David
Dances," 248; "Lauds," 222;
"Nones," 245; "Opus Dei" se-
quence, 222, 242, 245–47; pre-
fatory quotations, 220; "Scholars
at the Orchid Pavilion," 12–13,
42–43, 83–84
Dewey, John, xv
Diamond, Stanley, 182
Dickey, James, xvii
Dickinson, Emily, 10
The Dispossessed (Berryman), 24, 91;
"At Chinese Checkers," 136;
"Boston Common," 136; "Canto
Amor," 83, 84; "Desire Is a World
by Night," 200; "Narcissus Mov-
ing," 24; The Nervous Songs, 12;
"Night and the City," 25; "1 Sep-
tember 1939," 200; "A Point of
Age," 92; "Rock-Study with Wan-
derer," 95–96; "World-Telegram,"
200
Dodsworth, Martin, 139
Donne, John, 200, 201

The Dream Songs (Berryman), xviii–
xix, 127–28, 130–32; Song 1,
175, 189; Song 2, 172, 175; Song
3, 175; Song 7, 149; Song 9, 149;
Song 16, 156–57; Song 18, 222;
Song 22, 180; Song 23, 85, 161;
Song 28, 157; Song 29, 157, 189–
90; Song 38, 155; Song 40, 176;
Song 42, 106; Song 48, 155; Song
56, 236; Song 66, 137; Song 75,
187–88; Song 76, 181, 186–87;
Song 86, 146; Song 90, 146; Song
97, 205; Song 108, 83; Song 124,
142; Song 129, 209; Song 133,
158; Song 141, 158; Song 143,
155; Song 145, xx; Song 147, 22;
Song 148, 158; Song 157, 232;
Song 171, 162; Song 219, 158;
Song 242, 142, 209; Song 261, 85;
Song 264, 147; Song 285, 162;
Song 293, 158, 160; Song 305,
158; Song 309, 238; Song 310,
148, 155; Song 311, 158–59, 239;
Song 312, 239; Song 313, 239;
Song 314, 239; Song 321, 164,
238; Song 324, 236–38, 239–40;
Song 354, 152; Song 366, 196,
240; Song 370, 158; Song 385,
164–65; arithmetic notation, system of, 171; as Berryman's long
poem, 152; Berryman's own experience portrayed in, 155–57; Berryman's reading of, 82; blues
rhythms, 174–76; Christian message, 137; "couvade" in, 141–42;
creation of a world, 31, critic's
questions about, 233; death and
birth as subjects of, 86, 146; "destination" of, 181; diction, 186–91;
discarded songs, 9, 32; discipline
of dramatic character, 157–58,
162–63; *Don Juan* and, 141; as
the egotistical sublime, 158, 163–
64; epigraphs, 169–71; gap between the two volumes, 6; "God of
rescue" principle, 236–41;
Graves's theory on the origins of
poetry and, 183–84; Henry's

friend, 8; "I" (self) created in,
192–98, 210–11; ideas transmit-
ted and concealed simultaneously,
176; interlocutor role for Berryman, 171–72; *Lamentations*
and, 169, 170, 171, 177; meaning
and external sense banished in
the manner of dreams, 175–77;
minstrelsy, role of, 8, 171–77,
180–81, 182–84; model for, 29,
30–31; negative opinions on, 133–
38, 168–69; Negro dialect, 9,
129–30; obscurity of, 134; as one
poem, 5–6; as open paradigm of
grief and loss, 235–36; passion
and perception, relation between,
164–66; pleasantly suggestive
quality, 134–35, 137; plot, 7, 131,
157; poverty of thought and feeling, 136–37; prose disclaimers,
100; prosody, 83; *pruzhina*
("sprung" interior), 197–98; as
ritual dream, 181–83; as search
for individual and spiritual haven,
145–46; self-as-subject, 141–43;
serial significance, 196–97;
Shakespeare's influence, 22;
Shiva, role of, 182–83; single
voice of the later songs, 163; solution to, 184–85; *Sonnets*, relation
to, 108–9; stanzaic structure, 12;
Stephen Crane and, 177–81, 183–
84; syntax, 159–60; talking verse,
192; as theodicy, 31, 140–41; ulterior structure, 6, 29–31, 157–
59, 232–33; Victorian diction,
186–91; voices in, 153–54, 155,
163; writing of, 82. *See also*
Henry
Dunn, Douglas, xv

Eliot, T. S., xvii, 5, 25, 138, 163,
165, 189, 220; Berryman's at-
titude toward, 24–25; *The Waste
Land,* 29, 220
Ellison, Ralph, 9
Emerson, Ralph Waldo, 130
Extremist poets, 70, 151

Faulkner, William, 27, 220
Fearing, Kenneth, 205
Fiedler, Leslie, 176
Finkelstein, Sidney, 144
Fitzgerald, F. Scott, 220
Fitzgerald, Robert, 115
The Freedom of the Poet (Berryman), xvi
Freud, Sigmund, 30, 179
Frost, Robert, 20–21, 23, 87, 155; meetings with Berryman, 81

Genet, Jean, xv
Germanicus, 244
Ginsberg, Allen, 15–16, 185, 237
Giroux, Robert, 52
Gluck, Louise, 86
Godard, Jean-Luc, 128
Goddard College symposium, 82–83, 85–86
Goethe, Johann Wolfgang von, 5, 148
Goldensen, Barry, 86
Goodman, Paul, 216
Gordon, Caroline, 67
Grace, Teddy, 8
Graves, Robert, 183

Haggin, Bernard, 68
Hamann, Johann Georg, 17
Hardy, Thomas, xvii, 207–8, 211
Haydon, Benjamin, 35
Hecht, Anthony, 218
Hegel, G. W. F., 30, 180
Hemingway, Ernest, 192, 220
Henry, 128–29, 235; Berryman, relation to, xviii–xix, 7, 142–43, 153; Berryman's intentions regarding, 140; "birth" in suicide of Berryman's father, xix–xxi; Crane's writings and, 178–81; as disguise for Berryman, 160–62; as hero of a poem, 7; as "Mr. Bones," 8; origin of his name, 7, 32
Henry's Fate (Berryman), 221
Hewitt, Geof, 86
His Toy, His Dream, His Rest (Berryman). See *The Dream Songs*

Hitler, Adolf, 91
Hodgson, Ralph, 165
Hofman, Michael, xvii
Hölderlin, Friedrich, 114
Holmes, Oliver Wendell, 111
Homage to Mistress Bradstreet (Berryman), xvii, 23, 24, 163, 199–200, 201; ambitiousness of, 110; *Augie March* and, 143–44; Bradstreet's poems worked into, 124; as "crisis poem," 86; critical acclaim for, 115–16, 133; dense and involuted style, 113–15; diction, 118–19; "fable" of the poet and his subject, 119–22; failure of, 112–16, 125–26, 136; historical justification for, 110–11; Hopkins's influence on, 24, 114–15, 117, 119; metrical plan, 30; model for, 29; notes to, 125; opening verses, 133–34; as psychotechnical literary feat, 142; puritanism of, 122–23; rhythm of, 118; sources of, 10; stanzaic structure, 12, 115, 117–18; structure-content conflict, 112–13; summary of, 111–12; voices of, 154–55; Winthrop episode, 123; writing of, 33–36
Hopkins, Gerard Manley, 6, 20, 23, 102, 242; "Eleven Addresses to the Lord," influence on, 225, 230, 242; *Homage to Mistress Bradstreet*, influence on, 24, 114–15, 117, 119; *Sonnets,* influence on, 103; "The Wreck of the Deutschland," 24, 103, 117, 225
Housman, A. E., 22
Hughes, Ted, 186
Humphrey, Hubert, 12
Hutchinson, Anne, 125

"The Imaginary Jew" (Berryman), 9, 154

James, Henry, 158, 178, 198
Jarrell, Randall, 26, 68–69, 70, 142, 167

Johnson, Lyndon B., 152
Johnson, Samuel, 6
Jones, LeRoi, 173–74
Jonson, Ben, xvi
Joseph, Lawrence, xvii
Joyce, James, 165, 181

Kafka, Franz, 148–49, 155
Keats, John, 5–6, 163, 207
Kees, Weldon, 70
Kennedy, John F., 11
Kermode, Frank, 21, 133
Kerr, Bob, 55
Kierkegaard, Søren, 17
Kinnell, Galway, 86, 189
Kostelanetz, Richard, 140

Lamb, Charles, 177
Lamentations (book of the Bible),
    169, 170, 171, 177
Lawrence, D. H., 15
Leadbetter, Huddie "Leadbelly," 177
Lévi-Strauss, Claude, 184
Lindsay, Vachel, 26
Love & Fame (Berryman), xix, xvii,
    72, 143, 209–10, 220; Cambridge
    days described in, 84, 199; as
    comment on Berryman's past,
    202–3; criticism by Berryman's
    friends, 38–39; diction, 216; dou-
    ble theme, 229; "Drunks," 229;
    "Ecce Homo," 42n; "Eleven Ad-
    dresses to the Lord," 150, 221–
    31, 241–45; "Formal Elegy," 11;
    "The Hell Poem," 209–10; "Her
    & It," 229; "The Heroes," 206,
    208, 215–16; "I Know," 209–10;
    as long poem, 36; "The Martyr-
    dom of St. Polycarp," 243–45;
    meter, 215–16; "The Minnesota 8
    and the Letter-Writers," 216; as
    narrative of religious quest, 242–
    43; negative review of, 213–18;
    "Olympus," 217; poems deleted by
    Berryman, 78; religious subject
    matter, 39; rhymes, 216; "Shirley
    & Auden," 38; "Surprise Me," 78;

talking verse, 192; "Two Organs,"
    204, 210; writing of, 37–38
Lowell, Robert, 24, 28, 115, 133,
    151, 167, 168, 186, 241; Ber-
    ryman's assessment of, 15, 28;
    confessional poems, 213–14; on
    The Dream Songs, 172, 176; "I"
    (self) created in his poetry, 192,
    193, 195, 198–99, 201, 202, 203,
    204, 206, 209, 212; Life Studies,
    198, 213; Lord Weary's Castle, 24,
    28, 69, 215; narrative poetry by,
    10
Lowry, Malcolm, 220
Luther, Martin, 185

McCarthy, Eugene, 11
McCarthy, Mary, 194
Madame Bovary (Flaubert), 35
Mailer, Norman, 179, 192
Mallarmé, Stéphane, 211
Marcuse, Herbert 210
Maritain, Jacques, 232, 234
Marlowe, Christopher, xvi
Marvell, Andrew, 163
Marx, Groucho, 205
Mauriac, Claude, 144
Melone, Deborah, 87
Mendelson, Edward, 139
Meredith, George, 102, 196
Meredith, William, 178, 247
Merwin, W. S., 23
Miller, Henry, 192
Miller, James E., 237
Milton, John, 38
Minneapolis, 75–76
Minnesota Review, 41
Minstrelsy, 8, 171–77, 180–81,
    182–84
Moby-Dick (Melville), 15
Moore, Marianne, 16, 180, 211
Muir, Edwin, 16
Muni, Paul, 155

Narrative poems, 10
Nelson, Paul, 86
New York Review of Books, 168
Nixon, Richard M., 12

O'Hara, Frank, 188
"Old Pee Dee" (song), 175–76
Olson, Charles, 185
O'Neill, Eugene, 220
Origen, 236

Pascal, Blaise, 41
Personality, poetry as expression of, xvi–xvii, 5–6
Persona theory, 161–62
Phillips, Wendell, 111
Plath, Sylvia, 26, 70, 196
Poe, Edgar Allan, 30
Poems (Berryman), 91; "The Dangerous Year," 91–92
Polycarp, St., 243–44
Pound, Ezra, 15, 162, 189, 193, 194; Berryman's meeting with, 69; as liberator of other poets, 137–38; persona theory, 161–62
The Prisoner of Shark Island (film), 155
Pushkin, Aleksandr: Evgeny Onegin, 196, 197, 203

Quarles, Francis, 125–26

Ramsey, Frederic, 177
Recovery (Berryman), 146, 219–21
Rice, Thomas Dartmouth "Daddy," 172–73
Rich, Adrienne, xvii, 233, 246
Ricks, Christopher, 31, 140–41
Rilke, Rainer Maria, 24, 194, 202
Rimbaud, Arthur, 20
Rockefeller, Nelson, 11
Roethke, Theodore, 26, 28, 160, 167, 176, 215
Rosenthal, M. L., 201
Ross, Ralph, 75

Santayana, George, 163
Sapir, Edward, 119
Sartre, Jean-Paul, 208
Saturday Review, 39
The Scarlet Letter (Hawthorne), 15, 35

Schreiner, Olive, 170; Dreams, 169–70, 176, 178
Schwartz, Delmore, 19, 22, 26, 47, 67–68, 167; In Dreams Begin Responsibilities, 28, 31
Scott, Mrs. Frank A., 82
77 Dream Songs (Berryman). See The Dream Songs
Sexton, Anne, 205
Shakespeare, William, xvi, xix, 22, 38
Shapiro, Karl, 167
Shelley, Percy Bysshe, 11
Simic, Charles, 86
Simpson, Eileen, 248
Smith, Bessie, 8
Smith, John Allyn (father), 54, 55, 58, 66; suicide, 55–57, 58, 60
Smith, Stevie, 149
Snodgrass, William, 23
Solkonikoff, Vladimir, 52–53
Sonnets, 12
Sophocles, 13
Spender, Stephen, 94, 206
Spenser, Edmund, 200
Spivey, Victoria, 8
Stafford, Jean, 67
Stanley, Henry, 178
Stefanik, Ernest, 242–43
Stephen Crane (Berryman), 177–81, 183–84
Stevens, Wallace, 158, 193, 194
Stitt, Peter, 242

Tate, Allen, 133, 135
Tate, James, 86
Teasdale, Sara, 26
Tennyson, Alfred, Lord, 141
Tertz, Abram, 169–70
Thomas, Dylan, 25–26, 136, 199
Thoreau, Henry David, 193
Tocqueville, Alexis de, 15
Toynbee, Philip, 176

Valéry, Paul, 143, 194, 202
Van Doren, Mark, 5, 39, 57, 58, 209
Vietnam War, 11

Virginia Minstrels, 173
Vonnegut, Kurt, 212

Waller, Edmund, 162
Warren, Robert Penn, 25
Webster, Jean, 56, 58
Webster, John, 118
Whitman, Charles, 14
Whitman, Walt, 30, 158, 159, 161,
    194, 223, 233, 237, 240; "Song of
    Myself," 29, 30–31, 153, 223
Wilbur, Richard, 38, 218
Williams, William Carlos, 10–11,
    193, 236–38, 239–41
Wilson, Edmund, 38–39, 78, 115–
    16, 133, 203

Winters, Yvor, 16
Winthrop, Henry, 123
Winthrop, John, 122–23
Wittke, Carl, 169
Wolfe, Thomas, 27, 202
Wordsworth, William, 158, 163,
    193, 194
Wright, James, 188

Yeats, William Butler, 119, 161,
    201, 203, 209, 239; Berryman's
    meeting with, 26–27; influence
    on Berryman's writing, 5, 12, 23–
    24, 195

Zimmer, Heinrich, 182